ROVING COMMISSIONS 34

ROYAL CRUISING CLUB
JOURNAL 1993

Edited by TREVOR WILKINSON

Editorial Acknowledgement:

Firstly, I would like to thank all our contributors (including those whose articles have not been included due to a finite limit on space) for their time and skill in presenting material and, where necessary, for putting up with the needs of heavy editing.

Secondly, to put on record my gratitude to Anne Hammick and Sarah Gleadell for all they have done over the past five years; their skill and patience made the task an enjoyable one. And, finally (which it really is, since this is my last year as Editor), I owe a great debt to Bill Smith for his unstinting help with the design and the charts, and to Jan Oliver for all her unseen but invaluable help.

ISBN 0 901916 13 7

Typeset, Printed and Bound by
The Charlesworth Group, Huddersfield 0484 517077

Contents

III

CLEAN DECKS IN THE SUNSHINE

Have you been to the new Club rooms yet? Those who have are lyrical in their praise: the decor is attractive, the chairs are comfortable and the library seems to have taken on a new lease of life — the lighting is brighter and the books have somehow become more accessible. Among them are some gems, one being the *Journal* for 1911. Printed on hand-made paper and beautifully bound, the library copy is from a set which once belonged to Walter Edwin Ledger, a bibliophile (proud owner of a wonderful collection of Oscar Wilde books) and something of an eccentric. Apparently, he would come up to London from his Wimbledon home dressed as 'an old-fashioned Jack Tar, wearing a blue and white sailor's collar and bell-bottomed trousers'. Pasted into the front of the 1911 volume, to which Ledger had contributed a cruise, is an enthralling letter from Arthur Ransome extolling the virtues of his highly readable account:

> There are no two opinions to be held about your log. It is about as solid, square, delicate and delightful a bit of writing as I have ever read. We poor brutes who write for a living and write too much can never [match] that freshness, that feeling of clean decks in the sunshine that you seem to capture without the slightest effort. And you bind the whole thing together so well — poetry, music and the price of eggs.

While for the fortunate few like Ledger it appeared to be all as effortless as a breeze on a summer sea, such was not the case for everyone. Admiral Goldsmith — a man renowned for the bravura length of his logs — reminded his friends that 'writing a log for the Journal was *no joke!*' Even Willy Ker was threatened with a sense of humour failure this year while writing up *Assent*'s cruise: 'I've been *sweating blood!*' came a heartfelt cry from misty Somerset, but with what superb results. Clearly sailing affords an infinitely greater pleasure than writing something for the Journal — ask any of this year's contributors — for a lot of extra effort goes into the preparation of even the shortest account. So we should be profoundly grateful to all who burn the midnight oil on our behalf.

As with each of the past one hundred and some years, it seems highly

likely that 1993 too will go down as an exceptional year. Two or three members are a step nearer the completion of their circumnavigations; one, Hugh Merewether, gives us a charming account of *Blue Idyl*'s passage through the archipelagoes of East Asia, most of the time singlehanded. Hugh Clay took the opportunity to circumnavigate Tierra del Fuego on his way home from Tasmania to the Beaulieu Meet, while Willy Ker sailed to Siberia, using the Beagle Channel as a sort of short cut. Impressive though these longer voyages are, the cruises nearer home are no less remarkable. Who can resist Winkie Nixon's unquenchable enthusiasm for the Faeroes? And Johnny Bourne's tale of a cruise down channel in an open boat without an engine has the timeless quality of earlier days. Then there is James Burdett's chilling story of a storm in the Bay of Biscay; new readers should be sitting comfortably before they begin this one.

This is my last effort as Hon Editor. I have enjoyed every minute of it — well, almost every minute. The only downside is a growing tendency among members to go for the killer length — *l'art d'ennuyer est celui de tout dire* — which I attribute to the hypnotic power of their word-processors. People too easily get carried away. So what's the answer? Some very kind person — a description which immediately makes me think of Libby Heiney — some kind person told me how a really *pukka* editor would go about shortening the long ones: simply tell the computer to delete *every third word*. Quite remarkably, it doesn't even appear to alter the meaning.

On the title page of *Change and Decay* Sir Arthur Underhill quotes from a contemporary issue of *Punch*, echoing down the years one of the more compelling reasons for publishing a Journal. It is more than a record of weighing anchor at 0915 or of noting in the log that the wind was Force 3; like memory itself, and at a more personal level, it can 'shed the light of former years around us', a sort of scrap book of people and places:

I want to recall my shipmates and the look of their faces
Folk I liked or didn't afloat and ashore;
And the loveliness of ships and the queerness of foreign places
I want to think about them after I see them no more.

Aldeburgh   TREVOR WILKINSON
January 1994

UP FROM UNDER

by Hugh Clay

(The cruise for which the RCC Challenge Cup was awarded.)
Tasmania may be a great place to keep a boat (wonderful, uncrowded and varied cruising, and cheap too). But it's a long way away when you are living and working in UK. Something had to give, and in September 1992 I resigned my job and flew out to Tasmania to bring *Aratapu* home.

Preparations

I bought *Aratapu* when I was working in Australia in 1988, and fell in love with her during an extended cruise round New Zealand (1990 *Journal*). She is a 38ft 'Koonya' designed in 1959 by Alan Payne (designer of the *Gretel* 12 metres) and built in multi-chine steel by David Benson in Sydney in 1970. He cruised her extensively (including to Ireland and back in 1979–80), so she's built very strong and simple. With long keel and heavy displacement (12 tonnes on 28ft LWL), she's not the best performer to windward, but otherwise she's easily driven, wonderfully surefooted and reassuring in a blow — I can't think of a better boat for tackling the Southern Ocean shorthanded.

I had produced an Outline Plan (probably overambitious) for *Aratapu*'s Homeward Voyage and circulated it to all my friends. To my surprise I had volunteers for most legs, and filled gaps with two RCC cadets. I wanted to spend time in the Chilean channels and in Labrador, with a swift passage through the low latitudes, broken by a few interesting stopovers. My revised and equally overambitious plan was tutted over by various wiser and more experienced members, who were soon proved right when I left Australia a month late.

Aratapu had been laid up ashore for 2½ years, except for a brisk three week gallop round Tasmania at Christmas 1991. I expected a busy month fitting out, but it took a full two months, and would have taken far longer without

the help of Ross Ingamells and Mandy Beecroft (veterans of the New Zealand cruise), and of Mandy's family. The new diesel tank was to blame: I had measured to the millimetre the space behind the engine for a new 55 gallon tank, but I didn't measure the hatch. Once we'd cut out the cockpit floor to get the tank in I found I could get at two other jobs I'd always meant to do. We moved the rudder from the back of the keel to a small vertical skeg (this has transformed her handling at low speeds) and replaced the cockpit floor in stainless with drains forward, as the old aft drains used to fill up the cockpit at speed. With skilled welders on hand we also added a piece to the front of the keel to give it more bite to windward. The wonders of a steel boat! The refit grew like topsy, and included new mast, furling gear and sails, new galley and diesel heater, and so much new gear that we needed to go to sea to stop me spending any more money.

Mandy, the only person foolish enough to volunteer to cross the Southern Ocean with me, stayed in Launceston to say her farewells, while Ross agreed to stay on for the shakedown passage to Hobart. We were seen off on 27 November by the Pococks (*Blackjack* RCC) who had sailed in by chance the previous day and quietly set to helping us to get away. A variety of conditions on the Tasmanian east coast showed everything important working but lots of little things to sort out. Mandy now joined with most of the provisions, while Ross flew home to his farm. Constitution Dock in Hobart is a central and convenient place for final preparations but everyone is too friendly to get any work done. So in desperation we cleared Customs on 4 December and spent a full four days at the mouth of the Derwent River, stowing ship and completing the jobs list, including painting the decks.

Tasman Sea

The rolling hills round the D'Entrecasteaux Channel were looking lovely on the sunny evening of 8 December as we motored out to sea. The wind filled in as we cleared the land and I looked forward to a Tasman crossing to match our seven days in 1989. Instead a large high gave frustratingly slow progress for 72 hours before the normal procession of fronts resumed. The first front didn't quite produce a gale, but tested our sealegs. Another day's calm was enough to chafe through the main halyard (badly led on the new mast), but a full gale from the north-west soon had us running under staysail alone. We had our first solid water down below when a big sea caught her stern and broached her to port pulling off one of the vane gear blocks. The starboard dorade vent (by the mast) was underwater long enough to shoot a big jet of water onto the saloon bunk. As the engine controls were also leaking water from the cockpit onto my quarter berth life was distinctly unfunny for a while. The breeze backed south-west, blew itself out and left us wallowing for a day, with a little seal for company. The next front caught us approaching the Auckland Islands, uninhabited islands 250 miles south of New Zealand. The squally north-westerly gale raised a nasty steep breaking

sea as the depths reduced from 3500 metres to 150 metres in 50 miles. A couple of waves broke straight over the stern but *Aratapu* shrugged them off good temperedly. Dawn on 17 December revealed the bleak ironbound west coast of the Aucklands, with dolphins frolicking around us in even more spectacularly nasty seas. The vane gear couldn't cope (one block was destroyed by the strain) and after the second broach I had to hand-steer. Once in the lee of the islands ferocious squalls and calm patches reduced progress, so I started the motor only to have it cough and die after two minutes. It was a long and frustrating beat up Carnley Harbour, the spacious inlet between the impressive wooded mountains on Auckland and Adams Islands.

The engine problem was quickly diagnosed: the fuel filler cap (which I had loosened during deck painting in Hobart) had filled the tank with four buckets of seawater. While remedying this we also attacked leaks round windows and forehatch, re-rove the main halyard, replaced blocks on the vane gear, plus all the other irritations revealed by the first thrash after a big refit. The Aucklands are a nature reserve (Adams Island is a unique habitat undisturbed by man or rats) so we couldn't land, but enjoyed the company of seals and birds. We were surprised to see a small cruise ship, *Pacific Ruby*, full of bird watchers, under the command of Gerry Clark, 1986 Tilman Medal winner for his incredible sub-Antarctic circumnavigation researching birds in the 28ft *Totorore*. There was no time to pick Gerry's brains, but he kindly relayed a message to my parents through Wellington Radio.

Southern Ocean

I didn't believe the satnav when it told me to steer 150° to Cape Horn, but it didn't take long to work out that this Great Circle course (from 50°S via 66°S to 55°S at Cape Horn) involved rather too much icebreaking. But when I saw the rhumb line course was 660 miles further (at 4500 miles), I plumped for a compromise, aiming for 57°S 110°W (4160 miles). This is much what Gerry Clark in *Totorore* and Rick Thomas in *Northanger* did (though one of the crew we met in Launceston reckoned they should have gone further south). The imponderable is icebergs: *Totorore* and *Northanger* saw none, and David Lewis in *Icebird* well south of the Antarctic Convergence doesn't mention any in the Southern Ocean. But with the extreme iceberg limit well north of 50°S, we'd need to keep a good watch.

We left the Aucklands on 21 December, a bit apprehensive about the passage ahead. We had a few easy days with fair winds of Force 4–6, which was a good thing as I felt distinctly below par. The wind died on Christmas Day (seen in by Mandy at 0100: 'I'm not sure Yalumba winery meant their cardboard Shiraz to be drunk with licorice Twisties'). Mandy's mother had sent us off with lots of goodies parcels (occupying most of a bunk) which ensured a good Christmas dinner. Unfortunately her other gift, a substantial peat bog (mushrooms for the cultivation of) never recovered from its salt

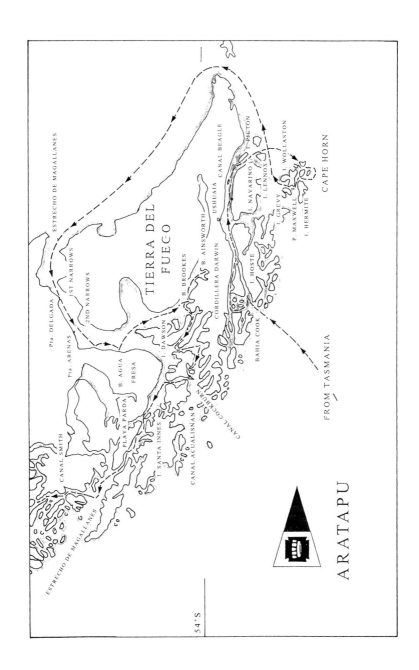

ARATAPU

water soaking approaching the Aucklands and had to be ditched. We crossed the Date Line late on Christmas Day, so enjoyed a second Christmas Day, but we had run out of presents. A shortlived northerly gale on 26–27 December gave way to three days of north-easterlies, a most unwelcome harbinger of the weather pattern for the rest of the passage. At 2155 on 29 December we heard the dismasted *British Steel II* calling Chatham Islands Radio on 2182, and soon after heard Aberdeen Coastguard announcing a forecast for the North Sea fishing fleet — at 53°S 165°W, we couldn't have been much further away! On this and all subsequent occasions, our ancient SSB (once described as 'like something out of the Science Museum') failed to make contact.

Life aboard was fine, as the log records: 'eating, eating, always eating', 'Hugh's had breakfast in bed *again*!', 'working up an obstacle course to use excess energy: from galley to loo round heater without touching chimney pipe or floor', 'feels b. cold in wind, but maybe it's because I've had a wash'. Our watch system (three-on, three-off at night, and four and four during the day) worked well and we got plenty of sleep. We got the Sony shortwave receiver working and became avid World Service listeners, but even I drew the limit at the football results on Saturdays. New Year's Day dawned calm and garish, with a swell rolling from the west, but the wind filled in from east-north-east and we sagged further south on port tack. By 4 January we were still on the wind, but on starboard for a change, and at last closer to Cape Horn (2530 miles Great Circle) than Hobart. As we were twenty-four sailing days from Hobart it was disappointing progress (especially against my overoptimistic plan of 1000 miles a week). It was now I finally admitted to myself we hadn't a hope of making the planned detour from Chile to the Antarctic Peninsula.

The next week was very hard work. We must have been close to the Antarctic Convergence at 57°S 147°W with many more birds around and much colder. We had the heater on and discovered hotwater bottles for cold feet and damp sleeping bags. Relief when the wind finally veered south was shortlived. It picked up to a gusty southerly Force 7–9 and blew a gale for six days as the barometer edged slowly down to 985 and back up to 1005. Iceberg danger was also at a maximum, and on 9 January we spotted our first berg at 57°S 128°W, a big tabular berg making the huge seas look puny. We were already keeping a good look-out, but we increased our radar checks to every half-hour, hoping we'd only find bergy bits close to bergs which showed up on radar. Everything was a struggle: soup ended up on the cabin floor, reefing the main became acrobatic when a bight of luff between two slides got caught round a mast step, and waking each other at change of watch became difficult as we were both very tired. Mandy claims I slept right through one of my watches. The seas had little vice in them, but after six days of south-westerly 8–9 they were dauntingly large and there was plenty of water on deck. Pilot whales surfing through the seas looked small. The storm cover over the companionway kept us dry below, even when a big cross sea hit the sprayhood broadside and bent its frame. Just after this I wrote in the log 'I'm not enough of a fatalist to sail down here. Will this gale ever end?' and almost immediately it started to drop. Within twelve hours we were rattling and rolling in a zephyr, with the occasional half-hour puff to test our sailhandling.

I now killed the motor for the second time. *Aratapu*'s exhaust comes out of the counter, and as I can't get to the skin fitting at sea I have a valve on the back of the motor to stop water backing up the exhaust into the engine. Before firing up the engine I *should* drain the exhaust system aft of the valve, and this in my impatience I failed to do (after all I'd never yet found much water to drain). But this time as soon as I opened the valve I filled up the engine with water. We had plenty of calm weather to try repairs, to no avail. I couldn't shift the injectors, so we just flushed water out of the sump with warmed oil and hoped for the best. At least the Ampair towed generator kept the batteries charged for running instruments and proper lights at night. Progress was lamentable and frustrating for three days, with runs of 50, 16 and 46 miles, but we were both glad of one night's uninterrupted sleep. Mandy complained of sunburn! The pilot charts show 0 percent of calm for this area and very few easterlies, so I found difficulty in explaining the weather pattern and still do. I thought at the time we were too far south, with depressions passing north of us. But yachts we met later who were further north also found a high percentage of calms and easterlies, and one claimed a cyclone hitting Easter Island had upset normal weather patterns. When the wind returned it was north-easterly Force 4 and veering, so we had two uncomfortable days on port, then two hard thrashing days on starboard before it freed a little. This beat took us to our furthest south (58°45'S 105°W) and out of the iceberg zone, less than 1000 miles from Cape Horn.

The Southern Ocean had one last throw, a sudden strong westerly gale. This arrived so suddenly that we still had up the double-reefed main when it started blowing, and Mandy was getting me up to help reef when the self-steering was overpowered and she gybed. As always we had a preventer rigged, but the strain broke the cast stainless becket on the preventer block, while the compression on the boom broke the gooseneck, bending a neat right-angle into the stainless plate between the vertical and horizontal pivots. Overnight it blew very hard from a pitch black sky, and at dawn the seas were mesmerising. One big sea caught us, broke the elastic on the storm cover, and funnelled down the hatchway over Mandy and her bunk, but luckily not her mattress or sleeping bag, which were airing in the cabin. I am ashamed to say I felt too tired to spend my off-watch helping clear up. But by evening we were slopping about again in a light westerly, ventilating and washing ourselves and the boat.

Now (25 January) less than 300 miles from the Horn, I was keen to get in to shelter before the next depression. So we changed course for Bahia Cook at the west end of Beagle Channel, 170 miles away. We were both getting impatient. We talked of calm anchorages, and about fresh meat (me) and icecream and salad (Mandy) even though we still had a few Australian tomatoes left after seven weeks. So 'Land Ho' on 27 January, with the glaciers and snowy mountains of Tierra del Fuego on the bow, was a big thrill. As we approached, the tentative northerly died completely and gave me an interesting night beating in zephyrs under trysail and genoa between the rocky shores of Bahia Cook. At dawn a Chilean Navy tug appeared from nowhere to examine our papers. Yachts are apparently forbidden from the whole Bahia Cook area, so they towed us (at 10 knots or so) back to the main shipping route at Timbales, where Mandy enjoyed a day's slow sailing among albatross, admiring her first glaciers on the Cordillera Darwin. When the same tug returned in the evening they offered us a tow to Puerto Williams, 80 miles away. As we had survived the morning's tow we braced their tow rope to two foredeck and two midship cleats and sat back for a sleigh ride. *Aratapu* sat down at the stern, raising a huge noisy breaking stern wave that washed over the stern and ran forward to the scuppers. She was easy enough to steer despite much rudder shuddering and we made breakneck progress past spectacular scenery through a calm starlit night. Dropped by the tug off Puerto Williams, we short-tacked with some difficulty under the trysail and genoa up the narrow river to the naval wreck *Micalvi*, which is as close as you get to a marina in Tierra del Fuego.

Hugh riding out a gale at Puerto Maxwell near Cape Horn

Chile

We soon learnt the major drawback of cruising in Chile — the Navy bureau-cracy. Particularly near Cape Horn, they have had to rescue too many incompetent / unlucky yachtsmen, and with our broken boom and engine, the Port Captain obviously thought we were another. But his minions were very helpful: the gooseneck plate was straightened enough to use (and strengthened in Punta Arenas). And a very friendly engineer (who had learnt about Listers when running the generators on an Antarctic base) mended the engine by the simple expedient of removing the injectors and turning over the starter-motor until all the water in the cylinders was on the cabin roof. Amazingly it ran immediately and has continued to do so. Before leaving we needed a *zarpé* or permission to navigate Chilean waters, and here we ran into difficulties. Many interesting places are out of bounds, only major shipping routes are open to foreign vessels, and the Port Captain was applying the rules strictly. Eventually we decided to 'do' the Horn, then head for Punta Arenas via the Atlantic and Magellan Straits, hoping for a more flexible attitude there. Meanwhile we enjoyed life ashore and did some very basic shopping (though we avoided Puerto Williams vegetables as our Australian onions, potatoes, cabbages and apples were in much better condition). We chatted to a French father and son just in from Tahiti, and briefly to three French charter boats loading up French TV crews to cover the Globe Challenge race passing Cape Horn. And best of all we enjoyed a Christmas parcel of cake and letters left by the Ormerods and Willy Ker when *Assent* passed through a month earlier. What a pity we'd left Australia too late to meet up for the Inaugural RCC Tierra del Fuego Meet.

We had a good run east out of the Beagle Channel past the rolling hills of the Harberton estancia (still owned by the Bridges family of *Uttermost Part of the Earth*) and spent the night at Isla Lennox (one of the islands disputed by Chile and Argentina). We woke to a south-westerly gale in the morning and stayed put, enjoying a slothful day of Scrabble. Woken early on 7 February by an unusual north-easterly blowing into the anchorage, we set sail for the Wollaston Islands and Cape Horn. Passing through the narrow Paso Mar del Sur at 1300 we caught our first sight of Hornos Island, with the fanged rocks of Isla Deceit to port. The weather was beautifully sunny as we turned west to beat round the Horn, with great views of the rocky pyramid Cape. We didn't escape unscathed: the weather deteriorated fast as we beat across Bahia San Fransisco to a sheltered anchorage at Puerto Maxwell. It was blowing south-westerly Force 9 by the time we had two anchors down, and we had a worrying night with regular screaming squalls. A passing cruise ship reported to Hornos Radio that it was Force 11, but we think they were trying to impress their passengers. There was a lull after twenty-four hours but it soon veered west and started screaming again. The next day we managed to row ashore for a scramble with impressive views of torn cloud, misty mountains and white sea. It finally blew itself out on the third night, and we motored north through the Wollaston Group in a flat calm surrounded by seals, shags and albatross, past the exposed anchorage where Hal Roth came to grief. We were now racing against time to meet crew in Punta Arenas on 14 February. So we headed east, quietly reaching to Lemaire Strait, with the moon painting a magical picture of the mountains to north and west. Popped like a cork out of the Strait (12 knots over the ground with the tide), then slogged miserably to windward for $2\frac{1}{2}$ days all the way up the east coast of Tierra del Fuego, into a foul head sea which made us both seasick (my first bout of the cruise). We were very relieved to reach the low sandy east entrance to the Magellan Straits, and report first to the Argentinian radio station at Cape Virgines, then to the Chileans at Punta Dungeness 5 miles away. The barometer was dropping fast as we sailed through a myriad of oilrigs up the Straits. As we approached the First Narrows 40 miles in we were almost blown back out by a sudden gale, but managed to fight our way into the partial shelter of Punta Delgada. We had a grandstand view of the wicked seas kicked up in the morning by a westerly gale over a 5 knot tide. The gale dropped in the evening and we caught the tide at 0145 through the First and Second Narrows, escorted much of the way by beautiful black and white Commersons dolphins. As we approached Punta Arenas next morning the daily gale blew up and we had another fight to get in. Punta Arenas is an awful place for a yacht, but we anchored off and went alongside the overcrowded and unsheltered pier only when we had to (once hitting the shoal Tilman hit in front of an admiring crowd).

Here we were joined by Robin Cowan and Ian Annetts, friends from university days, and by Peter Ingram (RCC cadet). Robin and Pete are both used to skippering, but Ian has done very little sailing. They were all peeling from a day spent lying in the sun on the hills above the town keeping a sleepy lookout for us. With five pairs of hands we did a quick two days' shopping and repairs, even if the boat seemed very crowded for a while. I spent most of the time negotiating with the Navy for a *zarpé* which allowed us to go where I wanted. After various faxes to Valparaiso we eventually got our *zarpé* on the evening of 17 February and had a short evening sail to Bahia Agua Fresca, full of relief at escaping bureaucracy and civilisation. From here on we'd be on our own.

The Magellan Straits themselves are broad, exposed and not particularly scenic, so I planned to detour south to the north side of Tierra del Fuego and sail through the islands westwards. We had a fast run 60 miles south to Bahia Brooks, our last good fair wind sail till the north end of the channels a month later. After a night at the entrance we motored 20 miles down to the head of the Bahia Brooks, with every corner showing up better views of glaciers and mountains, though cloud covered the tops. The basin at the head is surrounded by 6000 foot mountains of the Cordillera Darwin, with a 7500 foot peak three miles from the head. As soon as we put the dinghy in the water for pictures of *Aratapu* under sail all the mountains started

Aratapu *smoking along in a williwaw in Brookes Bay*

producing squalls, so the pictures were rather more impressively hectic than I intended as she smoked along between the ice floes. We found an idyllic shallow anchorage in a side fjord and climbed a bare rock hillside for views of the fjord and glaciers. The next morning was glassy calm and cloudless, revealing snowy peaks and razor sharp reflections. We just had to have another look at the basin at the head, where Pete posed the boat (looking tiny) in front of the glaciers while the rest of us climbed an island to record it on film. We acquired an ice floe to keep the meat fresh (we were eating well since Punta Arenas), and motored out of Bahia Brooks and south to the next glacier at Bahia Ainsworth (Ainsworth was Master of HMS *Adventure*, drowned during the 1827 survey with HMS *Beagle*). Here we couldn't get anywhere close as the glacier is receding, and a strong flow through the sediment bank was pushing ice floes past us at 4–5 knots. We spent the night close to local *centolla* (spider crab) fishermen, a hardy band who dive in the freezing water using an ancient brass diving helmet supplied with air from a hose and hand pump on the fishing boat. We exchanged beer for scallops and fish.

We were lucky to have our best weather — dry, settled and mostly sunny — for the most spectacular cruising in Chile, but it was also windless so we had to motor everywhere. We headed up Canal Gabriel (toasting my uncle Gabriel en route) to spend the night by a small reversing falls where Robin came to grief trying to ride the falls in the rubber dinghy. We emerged into Canal Magdalena at Punta Anxious, inhabited by an unanxious colony of fur seals, with turkey vultures on sentry duty behind, waiting for scraps. As we turned the corner, the twin corniced peaks of Mount Sarmiento (7330ft) cleared of cloud, a superb sight. Soon after we spotted a humpback whale with calf, which we followed as they dived regularly, unsure where they would next surface. We and the whale were surprised when it surfaced just by the stern, and it hastily dived under the boat. My picture of this shows nothing but a huge expanse of black shiny back, speckled with barnacles. We spent that night below a thundering waterfall close to a glacier in Seno Chico, and did some more ice-shunting in the morning to get close up to the glacier snout, which gave the nesting shags a fright every time it shed a photogenic chunk with a thunderous roar.

With regret we left the coast of Tierra del Fuego and crossed Cockburn Channel in search of 'a snug harbour [where] a well-worn trail led to a large deposit of refuse, evidence that the natives had worked there for centuries and to this day are to be seen the rounded masses of iron pyrites from which, with great labour, both Yaghan and Alacaloof obtained their supplies' (Bridges: *Uttermost Part of the Earth*). The native Indians prized pyrites for lighting fires, though they normally kept fire alight in moss in the bottom of their canoes. As we beat up Mercury Sound in light drizzle one could see the importance of fire to the Indians who navigated these waters nearly naked until early this century. We found a snug little harbour, but no sign of Indian remains or pyrites. One of the pleasures of cruising hereabouts is the incomplete surveys, and we enjoyed conning our way through an unmarked channel

Near miss with a Humpback in Canal Magdalena

(minimum depth 2m) north of Isla Diego, then through Canal Acualisnan to the Magellan Straits. This channel was unknown 'until Acualisnan told us it was not in fact one island but split in two parts by a channel ... with Acualisnan as pilot we followed this channel's devious windings and the Admiralty charts now perpetuate his name' (Bridges). There are still no soundings on any of the charts or any directions. We found a strong foul tide and had a struggle edging through the narrows (minimum depth 9 metres) at 7 knots, with swirls pushing us back at times and seals jumping at speed as they overtook us. We found an unmarked cove off Seno Pedro for a quiet night before braving the Straits. The shore party, Robin and Mandy, distinguished themselves by capturing a delicious *centolla* from thigh-deep water using only an oar and bare hands, though Mandy claimed the crab gave up at the sight of Robin's boxer shorts.

Paradoxically, more has been written about sailing in the channels than most places, with Slocum, Tilman, David Lewis, Davenport, Hal Roth and Gerry Clark all writing in some detail. I'd marked the anchorages referred to by each of them on the chart, and the next stage of our route had page references littered over it, reflecting the struggles most people have to make ground west into the prevailing winds. We were lucky, with calm overcast drizzly weather which made it easy to spot the blow of our second pair of humpbacks in Paso Froward. We motored most of the day, up Paso Ingles, past Fortescue Bay and Charles Island (where Slocum repelled Indians with a Martini-Henry rifle and tin-tacks), past Mussel Cove, named by Cavendish in 1587 'because there were great store of them', to anchor for the night in Caleta White. Though I say anchor, in fact we usually put one or two lines ashore with an anchor astern, or occasionally just lay to two anchors. With a cut away forefoot it was easy to put the pulpit over the rocks to drop one of the ship's acrobats (Pete or Robin) ashore with a warp, then reverse out to drop the anchor offshore. Our routine became more polished, and light work with lots of willing hands. We detoured to Bahia Ventisquero (Glacier Bay), seduced by Davenport's 1951 description, and while the glacier was nothing to compare with others we'd seen, we had a good walk/scramble, and got vertigo taking pictures of the boat from the top of the cliffs. We spent the night in Tilman's anchorage at Playa Parda, a bit gloomy with a narrow pass 'within a few yards of a wall of rock as smooth and straight as a dockside' leading to 'the inner anchorage, a most beautiful cirque of rock'. I think *Aratapu*'s crew will remember it more for the memorable wash in a glacier stream next morning. Only the skipper was foolish enough to submerge, though Robin ('I'll only stay warm if my feet stay warm") made an interesting picture in two pairs of ski socks, gumboots and nothing else.

Another day's beating took us to Caleta Sylvia (one of Lewis' anchorages), within striking distance of Isla Tamar and the turning point for Canal Smyth and the channels north. It was a calm overcast day as we motored round the corner, radioing in very broken Spanish to Navy radio operators at Bahia Felix and Isla Fairway, our last contact with officialdom for a fortnight (though our *zarpé* contained the impossible condition that we should report in every day). We started sailing as wind and sun reappeared in the evening, with beautiful light over the glaciers of the Cordillera Sarmiento. Soon afterwards a large shoal of dolphins started jumping all round us, almost as if celebrating the return of good weather. We spent the night and watered ship in Bahia Isthmus, and walked up the local hill (on a mossy surface described by Ian as 'shag-pile') for superb views over the rocks in Canal Smyth which we'd negotiated the day before, and inland over the channels to Puerto Natales, where 14 knot tides run in the pass through the mountains. Leaving late, it was almost dark when we found an unmarked anchorage in islands in Paso Cubillo, and predictably we got a warp round the prop for the first time. Mandy volunteered for hypothermia and cleared it quickly, but the coffee and malt took rather longer to warm her up afterwards. Gloomy drizzle didn't lift in two days' beating up Canal Sarmiento, so I can't enthuse as others do about this area. Nor did the crew enthuse about Ian's cooking when he added a tin of condensed milk (mistaken for tinned cream) to a fish sauce. But I do remember the two anchorages, both unsurveyed with total protection behind interesting rocky entrances, and the huge vulture swooping ominously over us on a shore jaunt. From here on impenetrable foliage made walks ashore almost impossible.

The most scenic view is up Aratapu's *mast; Calvo inlet, in front of Tilman's glacier*

The name Peel Inlet has a resonance to all Tilman readers, and I was keen to see the glacier Tilman climbed to cross the Patagonian Icecap. As we turned the corner the cloud cleared temporarily to give great views of pinnacles and the rounded bulk of the icecap behind. We first explored Peel Inlet itself, which has receded even further than when Tilman was there and now has a nice sheltered anchorage behind islets two miles behind the glacier front as charted in 1963. The noisy fur seals on the islets woke us in the morning. Tilman decided against climbing this glacier, and went instead to Calvo Inlet, 20 miles north. Yet again we were lucky with the weather, which cleared as we threaded our way between floes into Calvo Inlet, until thick ice stopped us opposite Tilman's glacier. We went alongside a substantial floe with a clean side and banged pegs into the ice to moor up. Tea was taken on the floe, and much film was shot of *Aratapu*'s unusual mooring, with Tilman's glacier behind and other rather more spectacular glaciers pushing through 6000 foot mountains further up the inlet, with the icecap rising to 9000 feet above everything. After an idyllic day we had a disturbed night in a rather exposed anchorage (first anchor watch since Cape Horn), and woke in the morning to filthy westerly weather, with cloud obscuring the mountains almost to sea level. We found ferocious williwaws roaring down the valleys, one of which got her moving under staysail alone at $8\frac{1}{2}$ knots in flat water so it must have been considerably more than 50 knots. It was less squally as we left Peel Inlet, but blew up rapidly. We stopped in islands in Bahia Pitt, and only moved 5 miles in the morning to an even more sheltered anchorage on Isla Chatham (both unsurveyed as we were off the main shipping route here). With the heater fired up there was little to do except play fiercely competitive games of cards and wait for the gale to blow itself out.

It was a double-dip depression, so it was three days before we were under way again (10 March), beating and motoring northwards. It is an unfortunate fact that the wind generally blows down the channels, and we made far better progress motoring in a flat calm than beating when the wind blew. I didn't envy Tilman trying to get out to sea without an engine, particularly sailing at night through the islands without radar. It is churlish to say that one forested mountain looks much the same as another in a rainstorm, but with hindsight we should have gone out to sea from here and spent our time exploring the Chiloé and Puerto Montt area. Instead we rushed on through the channels, motoring most of the way. It was getting colder, with snow below 1000 feet most mornings and water (at 10°C) often warmer than air temperatures (below freezing overnight). We stopped briefly for fuel at Puerto Eden, the only settlement for hundreds of miles, where lovely green humming birds flitted around ramshackle corrugated iron shacks. After passing the English Narrows (not very narrow but a fair run of tide), we went west up Canal Fallos (German surveys on this part of the coast for some reason). We had a good run (our first fair wind for weeks) out to sea to look at bird rocks off Isla Byron, where we could just identify a few rockhopper penguins

Ice floe tea party: l to r, Mandy Beecroft, Hugh Clay, Ian Annetts, Robin Cowan, Pete Ingram

and chicks on the top of the island. Gerry Clark discovered this colony breeding far north of their previous known range and sent his crew ashore in the swell to climb a precarious rock bridge and rugby tackle a penguin for detailed study! With mares tails in the sky, I was loath to head on across the infamous Golfo de Penas, despite the fair wind. I was also keen to see Isla Byron (named after Midshipman Byron, grandfather of the poet), where HMS *Wager* was wrecked in 1741 after losing touch with Anson's fleet in a storm off the Horn. In a classic story of mismanagement and bravery, the crew mutinied and took the boats south through the channels and Magellan Straits, then north to Brazil, while the officers were rescued by Indians and taken north by canoe to the Spanish colony on Chiloé. We spent the night in Bahia Speedwell, named after *Wager*'s longboat, where the beach was attractive enough to tempt me into an ill-advised swim.

As the expected gale hadn't materialised, we put to sea escorted by dolphins and had a quick reach across Golfo de Penas, but met north-north-east Force 8–9 as soon as we poked our nose round Cape Raper. With the barometer dropping fast, we ran back round the Tres Montes peninsula overnight, and spent most of the morning beating back to an anchorage. As Ian had a plane to catch we left in the evening at the first sign of a break in the weather. We spent a day beating north against the current, making little progress into a foul steep sea, and only when it backed north-west did we start making good northing. Overnight we had dolphins playing round us, like phosphorescent torpedoes between the breaking crests. It blew up again as we bore off into Canal Darwin and the shelter of the channels. Once inside the wind dropped right away, so we motored overnight up Seno Aysen to Puerto Chacabuco, where Ian jumped ship just in time to catch his plane. This caused problems with the Port Captain, who wasn't used to yachts and decamping crew members: a phone call to HQ almost caused navy search parties to chase Ian to the airport, until they realised he had 'the captain's (i.e. my) permission' to leave. It took a whole day to sort things out with the Navy, but at least we had our first baths and a good meal at the hotel to celebrate Robin's birthday — there are compensations in civilisation.

From Puerto Chacabuco we were in less rugged country, and enjoyed the contrast, with hot sulphur baths at the head of Canal Puyuguapi, horses for Mandy to talk to behind Isla Refugio, and lovely farming / fishing communities on Chiloé where every other building seemed to be a church. The scenery was different, lusher at the shoreline, with impressive snow-topped volcanoes on the horizon. Still the wind blew from the north or not at all, and we had one hectic sail across to Chiloé, where we lost and recovered an oar in a Force 7, then had a fraught landfall. It was just after dusk, in heavy rain (the rain dripping off the tri-light to port looked like wine), and we were reaching too fast for a gap the chart showed (wrongly) as $1\frac{1}{2}$ miles wide but which measured 0.7 miles on the radar. In fact we were fine and, as I wrote in the log, 'if you hadn't got the gizmos, you probably wouldn't have worried'. Of our few anchorages on Chiloé I particularly remember Isla Apiao, where trading boats, still working under sail, were anchored in the bay with us, where simple subsistence farms ran down to the beach and wading birds crowded the shore. As we approached Puerto Montt in a flat calm we started to see pelicans, surely the most inelegant of feeders, bellyflopping into the water. After an obscene amount of motoring we were reduced to adding paraffin to the diesel tank and moving the fuel feed onto the tank drain to get the dregs out of the tank.

Puerto Montt is civilisation, and the markets and supermarkets have everything you might want to buy (except for Vegemite, my breakfast fare). As a result we went mad on shopping and I'm still eating through the results. We were sorry when Pete decided to go off to see more of South America by land. We celebrated his departure in a splendid local restaurant, but I made the mistake of ordering sea urchins, which had a smell and aftertaste more disgusting than anything I have ever tried before. We eventually cleared out (luckily the Immigration Officer was amused when Mandy couldn't find her passport; it was April Fools' Day) and spent most of a day at anchor stowing our excess of provisions.

Our last anchorage on mainland Chile was at Abtao, which I liked from the moment we saw the farmer harness up his cow to tow his dinghy up the beach. With the snowy volcanoes of Hornopiren, Osorno and Calbuco standing up clear on the horizon, and the yellow fishing boats and rust red houses of Abtao intensely coloured in the evening light, the scene is one of my strongest memories of the cruise. Ashore Mandy was adopted by a litter of piglets who followed her up and down the beach, while their mother seemed content to act as a perch for a hawk. From our anchorage we had a clear view of the sun setting over Canal Chacao, the narrow strait between Chiloé and the mainland, with the tide ripping through. We caught the tide out in the morning, and cut over the shallows into Bahia Maullin to stay with the northerly tide, past lots of fishermen diving for clams. The smoke from fires on Chiloé smudged the horizon as we picked up the first of the South East Trades to take us offshore.

Chile to Galapagos

I was sorry to leave Chile, particularly as we hadn't seen enough of the less rugged waters round Chiloé, but time was marching on and my cruise plan had us half way to Galapagos by now. We quickly settled into seagoing routine, enjoying some sailing for a change – and what sailing! The Trades blew a steady south-easterly Force 4–6 and with two big genoas set on the Profurl we could always keep her almost overcanvassed. We peeled off layers of clothing and re-acclimatised to life in the cockpit as she thundered north, 150 miles a day most of the week out to Robinson Crusoe Island. The island is a spectacular landfall, with moon-like mountains on the south side contrasting with luxuriant vegetation on the north side, sheltered from the Trades. Pretty open whalers work close to the rocks lobstering. The open roadstead off the settlement at Bahia Cumberland is swellbound, and the only decent anchorage is full of moorings for the lobster boats. Ashore there were green and red firecrown hummingbirds flitting around a pleasant sleepy village, which survives on lobster fishing and a small amount of tourism. Relics from First War naval ships look a bit incongruous, but presumably come from the German cruiser *Dresden*, sunk in the bay by HMS *Glasgow* in 1915. She was sole survivor of the German Pacific fleet after the 1914 Battle of the Falklands and hid until March 1915 in the Chilean channels (supplied by sympathisers in Punta Arenas, one of whom David Lewis met). It was good to see *Assent*'s name in the Port Captain's book, a month ahead of us. We climbed to Alexander Selkirk's lookout (1800 feet), with spectacular views over the moonscape mountains to the south, and found the 1868 plaque (put up by HMS *Topaze*) to commemorate Selkirk's rescue in 1709 after four years and four months on the island. As we left we motored into Bahia del Oeste, where you can clearly see Selkirk's cave, but there was too much swell to land.

From Robinson Crusoe Aratapu *went north to the Galapagos, a distance sailed of 2834 miles; then after a further 976 miles she transitted the Panama and into the Caribbean. Cutting a dash through the low latitudes* Aratapu *continued her journey through the Windward Passage to the Bahamas and thence round Hatteras to New York. We rejoin Hugh and Mandy in Maine in early July.*

As we sailed through the fog across the Gulf of Maine I warned Mandy we'd probably be in fog from now until we left Labrador, but we sailed out of it as we approached Monhegan Island and had a week of perfect sunny, hot and windless weather in Penobscot Bay: 'it's amazing; 80°! It's never that hot in Maine'. Offshore there were minke whales and seals, and inshore there were schooners on the horizon all the time. I thought we were very smart beating up a gut on Vinalhaven to anchor ahead of a schooner, but we were soon upstaged by a larger schooner beating in past us without fuss. We spent a wonderful evening with Ed and Ottsie Kendrick (RCC) at their summer house on Deer Isle and I enjoyed some live music for a change at a superb recital by the Vermeer Quartet in the newly restored Rockport Opera House. On 9 July we were lucky enough to coincide with the Great Schooner Race, a splendid spectacle. The schooners were all at anchor in Fox Islands Thorofare, while the skippers started ashore and raced out in their dinghies. I particularly admired *American Eagle*, a Grand Banks fishing schooner, and *Bowdoin*, built by the US Navy for Arctic work. Unfortunately the race itself was a fiasco, a drifting match eventually abandoned because of thunderstorm danger.

The thundery weather lasted just long enough to produce a classic Maine sunset, with wooded islands floating in light mist as the sun sank through a rosy blanket of cloud. We called in at the Wooden Boat School, 'a kid's camp for adults' as the instructor said, who was teaching total novices to produce a cold moulded canoe in a week. My only disappointment in Maine was the much-hyped Mount Desert Island, but at least we got good pictures of

Mandy and Ed Kendrick (RCC) at Deer Isle, Maine

Aratapu under sail in Somes Sound. We cleared out of the USA at Bar Harbour and ran under spinnaker across a foggy Bay of Fundy, then motored up the Nova Scotia coast through the backmarkers in the Marblehead to Halifax Race.

Nova Scotia to Strait of Belle Isle

As soon as we cleared into Lunenburg, Nova Scotia, we saw the first signs of the total ban on cod-fishing that has devastated communities all along the Canadian east coast. The unthinkable has happened and the most prolific fishery in the world is fished out. Despite the mothballed trawlers and fish plants, Lunenburg has more hope than most and is turning its famous fishing past (as *Bluenose*'s home port) into tourist dollars with an excellent fisheries museum. *Bluenose II* was daysailing out of Halifax and looking splendid as we sailed in, but Scott Sandford, a former *Bluenose* crew who looked after us royally in Halifax, told us she's got serious rot problems. We were in Halifax to buy the few Labrador charts I hadn't borrowed (in fact, thanks to the generosity of RCC members and others, the only charts I had to buy for the whole cruise). Scott joined us for a wonderful reach down the coast to Sheet Harbour Passage, 6 knots plus the whole day in smooth water. It was difficult to sail straight past so much wonderful cruising country, but we had to get a move on if we were to see any of Labrador before the Atlantic crossing. We had another blowy reach to Little Dover Run and muddled our way close in round Cape Canso on a rather inadequate chart, then into St Peters Canal and the Bras d'Or Lakes. We heard a good deal of VHF chatter from a CCA Cruise in Company, but didn't see them. The Alexander Graham Bell museum was still open when we got to Baddeck at 8pm (a pleasant contrast to 10–4 hours of US museums) and well worth a visit.

Despite a south-westerly Force 9 forecast, we put to sea (20 July), rerigging the storm cover and putting the trysail on its track. We were off the Newfoundland coast before it blew up, and then barely to gale force, so we ran steadily through the fog and rain, watchkeeping by radar below. The mountains round Bonne Bay looked attractive but we sailed on to a tiny anchorage at Port au Choix (22 July). We had a cold beat to Forteau Bay on the Labrador side of the Strait, which had us searching out warm boots and gloves again. As we reached Forteau we saw a big group of humpbacks all round, about twenty in all in groups of two or three, none very close but a splendid and heartening sight all the same. 25 miles on was Red Bay, which I'd visited on *Assent*'s 1986 cruise when they were still excavating. Now an excellent visitor centre gives you a good picture of the Basque settlement that was 'World Whaling Capital 1550–1600' and the whaling ship they excavated and reburied in the silt of the Bay. We had a bumpy ride back across the Strait of Belle Isle when it blew up very suddenly to north-north-east Force 7 as we approached Cape Bauld. We ducked into Quirpon (pronounced Carpoon) and using a rough sketch by *Heptarchy*'s crew (1984

Journal), we found our way through the narrow 'tickle' behind the Cape, missing the rock in mid-channel at the narrowest point. The sky cleared as we ran south to St Anthony, which must be the perfect natural harbour, where we found *Belvedere* (John Bockstoce, RCC) on her way home to Maine from Scotland via Iceland. We hired a car to pick up Phil Hare and Nicky Hart from the airport, and then paid homage to the Vikings at L'Anse Meadows and to Sir Wilfred Grenfell (*in 1892 he was the first member of the RCC to sail the Atlantic* — *Ed*) at Grenfell House, the museum celebrating his work in establishing health services for the remote communities 'down north' in Labrador. St Anthony is not a good place for provisioning, but we stocked up with enough basics to last us three weeks in Labrador and across the Atlantic. A quick sail to Griguet in the evening gave us another chance to talk to fishermen about the end of the cod fishery. In a place where fish means cod and fishing is the only industry, what else can they do but spend their welfare benefit on beer and outboard fuel zooming round their old fishing grounds?

Down North in Labrador

Having Phil and Nicky aboard was a breath of fresh air. They were keen and enthusiastic about all the things we were getting blasé about, and again made me glad I had committed to regular crew changes despite the hassles involved in meeting up. Nicky cheerfully succumbed to seasickness and Phil retired to his bunk with a bucket as we crossed the Strait again in a rising gale, passing close to the weathered bulk of Belle Isle. We spent the night at Battle Harbour, which has been a fishing station since the 18th century, and at its heyday in the 1850s a huge operation with a thousand permanent and up to ten thousand transient Newfoundland fishermen. The buildings are now being restored by a team led by Tom Paddon, who showed us round and invited us home to show us old photographs of the station. Mandy and Nicky enjoyed playing with his dog, a retriever called 'Cluett' after the Banks schooner that Tom's father and grandfather used for summer visits when they were doctors at the Grenfell Mission HQ at Northwest River. After a wet and windy night we called briefly at Mary Harbour, where we moored up at the only busy plant we saw in Canada, processing crab caught 180 fathoms down 80 miles out to sea. We met up again with the Grenfell dentist, a South African we'd met in St Anthony who had bought a small fishing boat (but no dinghy) and was notorious for swimming out to her mooring in icy water, under the concerned gaze of the nurses at the Mission. Here too we had our first serious brush with the infamous Labrador insects, but nothing compared to that night's anchorage at Port Charlotte (as in Chile, 'Ports' and 'Harbours' in Labrador are just natural protected inlets, usually uninhabited). There Phil jumped off the pulpit to put a warp ashore, and had to be rescued swiftly while he danced like a dervish but failed to drive off the cloud of insects.

The overcast weather gave way to a bright sun and mares tails as we sailed behind Denbigh and Granby Islands to Duck Harbour, with 'shorts and goosepimples the dress of the day'. Cutting the skipper's hair was Mandy's job for the day, causing much hilarity and a light scattering of hair all over the deck. The forecast blow passed south of us, but brought in fog and a following breeze as we sailed north spotting minke whales near many of the headlands. It is hard to believe that this was the worst fog we found on the coast of Labrador: from now on we had perfect weather, little wind and good visibility (or as the Newfy forecasters said, 'good, except in fogbanks', which we only found well offshore). We sailed into sunshine inside the Island of Ponds (a tricky shallow passage by Porcupine Island), and anchored at Indian Tickle where we had great views from the top of the hill of a minke whale swimming round the boat and of the waterlogged rock and marsh landscape of central Labrador.

If we were to cover the ground we had to use all daylight hours, so we developed a good routine. Phil, a natural early riser, routed me out of bed at 0500 with a cup of tea and we stood watch until the late-rising females emerged at 1000 for an extended brunch, after which the men retired for a midday snooze. This also meant our shore expeditions tended to be before 0500 or after 2000, with the advantage of wonderful light for photographs. From Indian Tickle we had a long day crossing the entrance to Hamilton Inlet, to Smokey Tickle, another lifeless fishing station, just modernised with federal and provincial money and now mothballed. The tricky unmarked

The Barber of Labrador

channel inside Brig Harbour Island had me worried for a while, but in a glassy calm we couldn't do much damage. The temperature continued to rise, and when the wind dropped again we were hot enough to try a (rather brief) swim, despite the icebergs on the horizon. It was even warmer ashore when we scrambled up Webbeck Island in the evening (we needed a second swim when we got back on board). Nicky, a rock climber, logged 'three-star bouldering on sun-warmed granite slabs' and Phil spouted knowledgeably about glacial erosion, but I remember great views over the hills behind Cape Harrison, the big icebergs grounded on the 70 fathom Makkovik bank offshore, and of course looking down on *Aratapu*, bright and beautiful in the evening sun and looking almost toylike in such big country. The views were more ghostly at 0500 with light mist and a full moon, but the morning brought cloud and wind, so we sailed most of the way to Makkovik. Makkovik is friendly, and we were offered coffee and showers by a couple studying salmon: they had failed to find a single tagged salmon this summer (bad news for the fishery) and spent their time studying the shape of a bone in the head which may show whether the salmon originates from North America, Europe or Greenland.

From Makkovik I decided to sail offshore direct to Cape Chidley. Since cruising Labrador on *Assent* in 1986 I'd wanted to go to Cape Chidley, northern end of Labrador and south entrance to Hudson Strait. We headed 70 miles offshore to clear the Nain Bank in daylight, where bergs ground and so bergy bit danger is highest. In fact we had head winds so couldn't get quite far enough out before dark, but with so little sea clutter the radar was reassuringly sensitive, picking up sleeping birds and so (we hoped) bergy bits. We cleared the last berg at midnight, seeing it clearly between fog patches, eerily lit by Northern Lights. We had a very cold thirty-six hours on the wind, with foggy breeze cutting through endless layers of clothes, and a worrying episode when the radar (totally reliable up to now) went loopy and started showing targets on the beam which were actually dead ahead. Luckily we could see enough of passing bergs to work this out. We motored the rest of the way, with superb 70 mile views of the Torngat Mountains as we closed the coast again. The surveys of the area are incomplete, marking only a single recommended track, with lots of blank space and dotted lines round large areas offshore marked 'numerous uncharted ledges'. We picked up the Argo Islands and followed the track into Bowdoin Harbour, named after the schooner we had seen in Maine, which presumably carried out the 1943 US survey on which the chart is based. With clear skies, brooding mountains and snow down to sea level, we needed the heater fired up as soon as it got dark, and a nip of malt to warm the inner man.

In such a busy and enjoyable three weeks it's hard to believe now that my most vivid memories of Labrador were all crammed into one day, 8 August, when we circumnavigated Killinek Island. We were ashore at sunrise for great views of the mountains circling Bowdoin Harbour, with rock and snow reflections in the water only disturbed by a lazy seal. Leaving at 0630 we paid our respects to Cape Chidley (our chosen Cape Chidley, as the two charts disagree on it's exact position), a fine upstanding lump with white-veined 1000 foot cliffs dropping sheer into the sea, and then passed through McGregor Strait inside the Chidley Islands. Here we started to pick up the fair tide (up to 7 knots at springs), and among the eddies, a mass of seals ducking and diving all round us, and huge numbers of fulmars flying in all directions and resting in flocks on the water. We took a brief detour into Blandford Harbour, an unsurveyed inlet on the north coast with a narrow channel through to Ungava Bay, but even I baulked at running that gauntlet when I saw how much tide was flowing through. Instead we rounded the cliffs north of Bush Island and started south down the west coast of Labrador. To the north the Button Islands across Gray Strait were miraging madly, levitating themselves in thin cloud, while to the west the huge, calm expanse of Ungava Bay was only broken by a few distant icebergs and yet more fulmars. As this is one of the foggiest places in the world we were incredibly lucky to have perfect visibility. We stopped for a walk in Munro Harbour, another unsurveyed inlet with just enough room to lie to a stern anchor with the bow over the rocks. All of us swam in sun warmed lakes, while Phil braved the sea again.

We were heading for McLelan Strait (or Grenfell Tickle) which separates Killinek Island from the rest of Labrador. A fine fjord through the mountains on the east side just breaks through Labrador into Ungava Bay through a

Aratapu *in Unmentionable Bay, McLelan Strait*

narrows one cable wide. The tide runs at 7 knots through the Strait (according to the *Arctic Pilot*), though Grenfell reports being 'carried bodily astern' when steaming at 9 knots through the narrows. Like Grenfell we 'shot through' the narrows but not, I hope, 'an impotent plaything on the heaving bosom of the resistless waters'. The rest of the crew were up the mast for a better view and got a bit of a shock when I did a 360° turn in the narrows to check the tide (6 knots on the first of the ebb). The eddying on both banks was impressive, and I am glad there were no bergs around to jostle through with us. In the calm beyond the narrows I felt we had really got away from it all, until Nicky pointed out the jet trails above us in a cloudless sky, and a jet every five minutes thereafter on the transatlantic flight path.

At the east end of the strait I was intrigued by a bay shown on the chart with a narrow gut leading to a nice basin among the hills. As we approached, Mandy and Phil on the pulpit were adamant it was too shallow, but with a little tide against us to give a controlled cop-out if required I pushed gently into and through the gut with a minimum depth of 3 metres. As soon as we were in the gear lever gave up the ghost (life would have been interesting if it had lasted a few minutes more or less). Phil cobbled a temporary repair, while I managed to get the radar to heal itself using an adjustment that shouldn't have worked! Nicky was feeling miserable with a spectacular reaction to mosquito bites which all our lotions and potions could not help, and which prevented her going ashore for the rest of the cruise. Mandy and I went for a scramble, disturbing a grazing caribou and getting superb views of *Aratapu* in the bay, 'Aratapu's Gut' and back down McLelan Strait. After supper I decided we had better move on to avoid getting caught in the bay in the morning. I thought it was half flood, but in fact it was only an hour after low water. Mandy went off in the dinghy to get photos which proved rather more spectacular than intended. As Nicky's depth readings dropped rapidly from 4 metres to 1 metre we hit the rocks in the middle of the gut, and bucked to a standstill. The flood tide pushed her back and slewed her across the gut (all of 45 feet wide) as she bumped across the rocks, and I throttled up to get her straight again. We sat for three or four minutes on the shallowest point before the tide lifted and we bounded forward with a last bump into deep water. Mandy came back on board with a grin: 'that's one photo you won't be showing the RCC'. We left Unmentionable Bay with some relief, or as the log records, 'even Hugh voiced mild concern afterwards'. It's no excuse, but a steel boat is reassuringly indestructible, at least in calm water at low speed. As we motored south to Clark Harbour there was a bloody sunset streaked with mist over McLelan Strait to end an unforgettable day.

A twenty-one hour day on 9 August saw us motoring the length of the Torngat Mountains in perfect weather. The mountains became bigger and gloomier as we went south, and offshore the rocks and icebergs were miraging spectacularly. When I last saw Cape White Handkerchief it was a patch of rock through a brief clearing in the fog above our heads, as *Assent* groped

"That's one photo you won't be showing the RCC."

into Nachvak Fiord from Greenland in 1986. This time we could see the headland most of the day, and much of the night as the sun set behind it. Off the Cape itself you could clearly see the huge white patch on the cliff, like a white handkerchief dangling from a foppish wrist. After nightfall I was enjoying a peaceful interlude on the loo when mad screams from Mandy had me rushing on deck: it was just the start of an extended and spectacular display of Northern Lights, magically flickering over the Nachvak mountains and across the whole sky. We got into Ramah Bay at 0200 and were ashore at 0630 to walk up the hill for a view of the rather dull bulk of Cirque Mountain (5500ft). Better was Phil's sighting of a huge pair of antlers as we climbed the hill, which soon proved to be attached to a big bull caribou, splendid on the skyline as he looked back at us disdainfully for disturbing him. For the first time in Labrador we were sharing an anchorage with another yacht, full of Quebecois fishermen, the first yacht we'd seen since Mary Harbour. After a cooling swim we had our first sail for days past Saglek Fiord and, under motor again, into Hebron. The Moravian Mission there was abandoned in 1918 after Spanish flu, introduced by the mission ship *Harmony*, killed eighty-six of the hundred people at Hebron within nine days. The buildings have been 'stabilised' as a historic monument and we walked right through the long building and up to the attics, complete with rusty iron mangle. We chatted to two kayakers camping ashore who seemed unconcerned that the fishing boat picking them up was already two days late.

We found a spectacular berg offshore for the obligatory 'my boat sailing past an iceberg' shots, and then headed for the most famous tickle of them all.

Mugford Tickle is hardly the narrow ticklish gut implied by the name, but a ½ mile broad stretch of water through the Kaumajet Mountains. Our first view was in many ways the most impressive, with the Bishops Mitre (3750ft) to the north-west of the Tickle dropping sheer into the sea. The 3000 foot slopes on both sides of the Tickle were a little disappointing until a passing fishing boat gave it some scale. Even better, the *Erin Muriah* stopped to swap fish and caribou meat for tinned milk and beer. We spent the night in Green Island Harbour with clear views back over the mountains luxuriating in a long red sunset. The Arctic char was wonderful, baked simply and served with boiled spuds, and lots of it. A calm foggy passage to Port Manvers followed, and we saw nothing of the mountains till we were through the First Rattle when the bulk of Mount Thoresby cleared of cloud. Supper was delayed by the glass in the oven door exploding while the caribou was roasting, but pot roasted in the pressure cooker it made a memorable farewell meal for Nicky and Phil. We dropped them at the airport in Nain (right next to the anchorage) and came on board to find Nicky had left a nonsense poem in the log: 'the Worm and the Plankton went to sea in a beautiful indigo boat ... they dined on beans with custard and cream which they ate with a whaler's harpoon. And when the weather was nice at the edge of the ice, they swam by the Labrador moon'. (Mandy has a splendid Plankton T-shirt and my crew nickname was Worm when I rowed at Oxford with Phil). We went ashore to the Grenfell Hospital for showers and were shown the old hospital case book from 1930s, with lots of TB, scurvy and neglected children, and the occasional dog bite, gunshot wound and groin bruising from collision of a sledge with an ice hummock. There are also glimpses of village life, with spring cleaning as soon as the ice started cracking in May, and the visit of HMS *Challenger* in July 1932 (she fired rockets at 11pm as a display for the Eskimos). My favourite was the sixty-six year old patient with a septic hand who discharged herself in March 1931 'to put a mountain mouse on the wound': it healed.

We had a weekend before picking up the Atlantic crew which we spent in Kauk Harbour, a natural basin south of Nain. We put *Aratapu* on the mud for a very chilling scrub and antifoul, and then repainted the decks — we always seem to rely on wet paint for non-slip on the first few days of a passage. There were splendid Northern Lights both nights which I tried (and failed) to photograph. We were back to Nain first thing on Monday to meet Jon Marsh, Sarah Richards and Bob Masterton. Sarah was aboard *Assent* in Greenland in 1987 and Jon for the 1984 Three Peaks Race; they now have their own Ohlson 38 and were keen to try an ocean passage. Bob is also experienced and has his own Westerly. As all three are doctors (and Mandy is a nurse), I could forget sailing and concentrate on not falling ill. We had a fast reach out to the edge of the islands and a last anchorage at Queen's Lake Tickle. We topped up with water from a stream black with

My boat sailing past an iceberg ....

mosquitoes, whose bites made Bob's wrist swell alarmingly despite
treatment.

North Atlantic

We left at first light to get across the offshore banks with their grounded
bergs before dark. We had an easy few days for the crew to bed in, and Jon
and Bob, who both enjoy maintenance, attacked the many jobs that had built
up over the months, from the oven door (replaced with sheet metal and loft
insulation) to broken locker doors and corroded navigation lights. We saw
two or three big bergs (a first for Jon and Bob), a school of pilot whales
and good Northern lights. The wind filled in to a solid southerly Force 6,
giving us a storming wet reach for two days until it headed us and strengthened to south-east Force 8–9. We kept slogging into it, heading rather closer
to Cape Farewell than I liked, but at least making progress. When it veered
south-west and eased I thought we'd had our fair share of gales and head
winds, but after a day it backed south-east again. Mandy, on being told we
had 990 miles to go, was heard to say, 'I think in thousands, so when it's
less than one, we're nearly there'; if only!

We went right through the middle of the next gale, with south-easterly

Force 9 dropping to southerly Force 6 for just long enough to get me shaking out a reef, then slamming back in at south-westerly Force 8, blowing the crests off the south-east swell and raising a horrible peaky confused sea. That was the last blow, but with a huge high over Ireland the wind swung back south-east and we fetched on eastwards, wondering if we'd end up in the Shetlands instead of Falmouth. As pressure rose the wind dropped, and we had to motor the last three days to the Fastnet. I was woken on 2 September by Mandy reporting black smoke from the exhaust, and lifted the engine casing to find clouds of steam and water up to the bottom of the engine. There was a tense minute of manic pumping before Jon confirmed the level was dropping. Jon and Bob soon had a diagnosis, even though they couldn't explain how it happened. The belt to the raw water pump had broken (so the engine overheated, with black exhaust smoke) and there was also a split in the sea water inlet pipe, which was pumping the bilge full of water. New impeller, belt, change of oil and a new bit of pipe had the motor running again, but I still don't like waking up to find my boat sinking. We could now hear the reassuring brogue of Valencia Radio and called them up to ring home ('what call sign's that? Australia, begod. You've come all the way?') which had the whole of my family trying to guess our ETA Falmouth. In fact we had a nice reach to the Scillies and after a frustrating beat to the Lizard, put the motor on to get into Falmouth before dark. As we approached Black Rock I saw a familiar blue sail, and there was *Eel*, my 17ft open boat, full of frantically waving children — my brother Henry had guessed our ETA right.

Since St Anthony we'd been living on cabbage, potatoes and tinned sweet corn, so you can guess what vegetables were served when I joined my parents for dinner at their hotel. It was good to see them and thank them for holding the fort for me at home throughout a difficult year, while my mother was ill and they were moving house. We stayed four days in Falmouth while the Customs sorted out *Aratapu*'s VAT status and eventually confirmed that I didn't have to pay. It only remained to sail up channel to Beaulieu for an excellent RCC Meet alongside my uncle Gabriel in *Fubbs*. We spent an uncomfortable thirty-six hours galebound after the Meet in the Beaulieu River with four anchors down, more than we had needed anywhere en route. After a leisurely sail down channel, I left *Aratapu* on *Assent*'s mooring on the Tamar and spent my first night ashore since leaving the Tamar in Tasmania $9\frac{1}{2}$ months before.

LAST MANGOES ON KAUAI

by David Lewis

This has been my seventh dismasting. The others took place in more or less exotic places, like the North Atlantic or the Southern Ocean — at sea at any rate. This one was when I was securely tied up in a marina. Oh well! Things go downhill when one gets older!

The eve of Hurricane *Iniki* found us busily collecting fallen mangoes from our favourite roadside trees. We reasoned, correctly, that very soon there would be no more in usable condition.

Next morning, Friday 11 September, increasingly dire radio warnings of the approaching storm had us putting below or lashing and stowing everything movable and tripling and anti-chafing our mooring warps. We moored bow out, stern to the expected east-northeasterly initial blow, in order to keep our mast out of synch with the yachts next door.

"If you have to leave the ship take refuge in the toilet block. It is a solid building", advised a port official. So we duly stowed our Portabote in the women's section ("Probably safer than the men's", said Mimi). This was indeed fortunate. When the solid roof eventually blew off scattering 8 inch diameter ferro-cement beams like matchsticks, the women's section, though roofless, was intact, while its male counterpart was choked waist high with debris.

With generous help from PTS supporters, my wife, anthropologist Dr Mimi George, and I acquired *Gryphon* last year. *Gryphon* is a William Atkins Eric, a scaled-down Colin Archer in the designer's words, 32ft long on deck, double-ended, gaff cutter rigged, ferro-cement hull. She has been provisioned and fitted out for a voyage of exploration back into time — seeking tutelage by the last remaining star path navigators in the Pacific. Our companion, Don Logan, is a veteran of the 1989 kayak crossing of the Bering Strait and of our quite respectable 21 day trip from Port Townsend to Hilo.

Nawaliwili, in 21°57′N 159°21′W, lies near the south-east extremity of the Hawaiian island of Kauai. The small boat harbour is doubly protected by outer and inner breakwaters. The two tiers of slips are mounted on concrete piles, and are not floating. There were upwards of fifty yachts and powerboats in the slips plus a number at moorings or at anchor in the inner and outer harbours or alongside the mangroves in the river.

The following is largely from the log:

1020: bar 1006 mb, light ENE, drizzle, heavy surf over outer breakwater. Report *Iniki* approx 450 miles to south, moving north at 17 mph and speeding up. High water spring tide 1500.

1220: bar 1001, ENE est 40 kts, surge.

1420: bar 982, est 70 kts, limited by driving spray. Ketch ashore.

1530: well over 100 kts. Beneteau 34 in next slip parted its starboard bow warp and mounted our deck, demolishing gallows, stanchions, and bulwarks, all with enormous shocks. We could hear nothing above the thunder of the storm. Mimi futilely tried to secure her, wading through thigh-deep water over the dock, wearing safety harness. The Beneteau next took out a chain plate and smashed our solid 8 inch diameter spruce mast at the deck, broke boom, gaff, and fife rail and at last came free to drift ashore to leeward. Meanwhile, the Columbia 20 on our other side came briefly aboard, was holed on the dock and sank alongside.

1550: bar 965, wind remains ENE, violent pressure effects on ears, force in gusts unbelievable, glimpses of flying debris, trees, masts, whole small craft.

1600: bar 945. LULL. Eye of the storm. Three 50-plus footers are piled up on the dock as well as smaller craft.

1620: bar 964 rising. Hurricane wind from WNW, quickly moving to WSW. Yachts ashore break loose, the Beneteau of ill omen drifting out of the harbour. We suddenly realise that a drifting Freedom is manned. Its dimly seen occupant, Ferdinand Jansen, can be glimpsed juggling three anchors. He still drags, but his dedicated seamanship is rewarded when he comes within reach shortly before 1800 and Mimi and Don, keeping their footing with utmost difficulty, help him secure.

1655: bar 971, WSW, tornadoes passing. Don, who had climbed aboard a sports fisherman to secure its lines, found our skylight (intact) in its cockpit!

1750: bar 981, WSW hurricane force still.

1800: first lull.

1844: bar 991, severe gusts.

1940: bar 1000, wind slackening.

How strong was the wind? Estimates are hard to come by. Most of the island's instruments were destroyed. The crew of the Coast Guard cutter alongside at Nawiliwili were sheltering ashore so could not monitor their instruments. In any case a multihull at anchor a quarter of a mile beyond the inner breakwater became airborne and wrapped itself around the cutter's bridge, which it demolished. The best estimates seem to be a sustained strength of 140 knots with gusts of 160.

There were instances a-plenty of unselfish courage. Mimi and Don helped others at the risk of their own lives. I mostly remained cravenly under cover, being less agile and fearful of being blown into the sea. I have already mentioned Fernando's three-hour ordeal.

Earl Edwards and Jody Gardner aboard their 55ft cutter *Imagine* found their ship swept up on its side onto the dock. A prow coming through the side into the cabin persuaded them to evacuate at the height of the storm. Swimming and wading waist deep in water and carrying the ship's cat, they made it. Then they realised that Paddy Kaliher was still aboard her 30-footer, now crushed beneath a 50ft cabin cruiser. They had started back for her when she crawled out of the wreckage and struggled ashore unaided.

Our overwhelming impression since the blow has been of fellowship. Tim and Colleen Meyer aboard their sports fisherman *Hawaiian 40* had prudently reinforced their mooring lines with ropes and anchor chain round tree boles. They suffered only minor damage because of their foresight and their good luck in being out of the path of airborne visitors. Their galley has been occupied continuously since the storm with cooking Red Cross supplies of fish, meat and vegetables, and their fridge overflowed with cold drinks. Everyone has been welcomed to partake, and the scene in their crowded cockpit at mealtimes made us dub them 'the hospitality boat'.

The instance of yachtsmen's community spirit could be multiplied a hundred-fold. The Coast Guard and civil authorities too, labouring among downed powerlines, blocked roads and wrecked buildings have been magnificent. Not one of the yachties we met has been despondent, whatever their grievous losses. All are cheerfully getting on with the jobs of salvage and repair.

Our own halyards, shrouds, and lifelines have been unreeved or unshackled, coiled, labelled, and stowed. The naked spars await the attention of my oldest friend (we met on a reef in Hahine in 1965), master shipwright Curt Ashford, who is dropping everything to fly over from Oahu to help. We have purchased a section of broken mast to scarf into our own for two six-packs of beer.

The extent of the damage? I have not the slightest idea. Three 50-footers and several smaller yachts are lying atop the dock and neighbouring vessels, an unknown number have sunk. The foreshore on all sides is festooned with craft in various states of disintegration.

The lessons? The overwhelming one is that mooring lines were inadequate and that poorly secured yachts caused 90 percent of the damage to others. People who remained aboard during the hurricane were able substantially to safeguard their own boats and their neighbours. Besides which the (hopefully) once in a lifetime experience of living through a hurricane in your own craft is one not to be missed.

SOUTH TO STANLEY

by Pete Hill

(The cruise for which the Romola Cup was awarded.)

Although we had intended to leave England directly after the Beaulieu Meet, it was not until 26 September that we managed to sail from Falmouth.

A minor overhaul of *Badger*'s motor had turned into a major re-engine job, when the cost of repairs turned out to be more than the eight year old engine was worth. Much agonizing over the options available brought us to buying a 6 hp Seagull, the only cost-effective option. The motor now sits on the starboard quarter and can drive *Badger* at 4 knots in flat calm; an economical cruising speed is $2\frac{1}{2}$ knots. On passage it stows below, safe and dry.

The forecast was for easterly winds, too good an opportunity to miss, so despite Annie being laid up with a heavy cold I rowed ashore to clear Customs and do the last-minute shopping. Although the east wind backed to north-west we made good progress to clear the Channel, until the shipping forecast the following evening. This suggested that the remnants of Hurricane *Charlie*, which had just hammered the Azores, were heading for Biscay and Western Approaches. As we have a policy of never starting a passage on a hurricane warning we turned tail and ran towards Brest. We were reprieved the following morning: Hurricane *Charlie* had decided to go up to Rockall instead, so we continued on our way.

Our plan was to sail to the Algarve, the Canaries and then directly to Montevideo to restock with fresh food. We hoped to be in the Falkland islands for Christmas and cruise around the islands for the rest of the southern summer. The schedule would have been tight had we left as intended; by now it was looking distinctly optimistic.

A spell of winds from south and south-west slowed us down, but then the wind came round to the north and we had four days of splendid runs which brought us to the entrance of Faro. We arrived at the bar just after midnight, when the wind deserted us, so we put the engine on and motored in to anchor inside the entrance.

We spent five days anchored off the island of Culatra, visiting friends. Having studied the channel over the bar at the eastern side of the island we sailed out at high water, bound for La Palma in the Canary islands. We generally had light westerly winds for the passage, which was not a fast one. By now it seemed that our plans were unrealistic and any chance of getting to the Falklands until late in their summer was remote. Why not cruise down the coast of Brazil, sail to Uruguay and Argentina in the spring, and arrive in the Falkland islands early in the following summer? We decided to turn the cruise on its head.

We arrived in Santa Cruz de la Palma on 22 October, ten days after leaving Portugal. The North East Trades had come in with a bang the previous day, in a vicious squall. An uncontrolled gybe while reefing the foresail broke one of the battens and badly tore the sail. We lashed the two good battens on either side of the damaged one together, effectively removing the damaged sail panel, and carried on.

The harbour at Santa Cruz was in the throes of much change. The main breakwater was being extended and a new fishing boat harbour was under construction to the south of the town. These alterations were being brought about due to the world recession and the consequent glut of empty shipping containers. The old fishing boat and yacht harbour was about to be filled in, to be used for the storage of containers. Too late, the local residents woke up to what was happening. We had a ringside seat as protesters tried to halt the dumper lorries filling in the beach. No provision has been made in the new plan to accommodate visiting yachts and it appears that the new fishing harbour is quite small and shallow. Will it be possible to visit Santa Cruz again?

We spent a month in La Palma. Repairing the foresail and batten didn't take long, but we had to wait until a stray parcel arrived. Having changed our plans, we were not tearing our hair out at the delay, but enjoying our stay.

Having never visited El Hierro, we called there before setting off south on 22 November, drifting along in a virtual calm. The breeze filled in from the north-east after midnight and had picked up to a nice Force 4 by dawn. We were off. We followed the directions given in *Ocean Passages for the World*, our route taking us west of the Cape Verde islands with a good trade wind until in their lee, six days later. Here the wind went light and shifted to the south-east, accompanied by thick haze, but by the next morning the wind was back in the east and blowing a fresh Force 5. Once past the Cape Verdes we were heading for a position $3°00'N$ $25°00'W$; there we could turn west and head towards our destination — Fernando do Noronha.

First, however, we had the Doldrums to cross. The width of this belt varies from month to month and from year to year. There is no way of telling what to expect, but they are often 200 to 300 miles wide and can take six weeks to cross. We were not looking forward to them. At 0900 on 4 December the North East Trades left us in a thunder squall; we had entered the Doldrums in $5°00'N$. We had light winds and several showers until, at sunset, another squall gave us a south-easterly breeze. The breeze strengthened

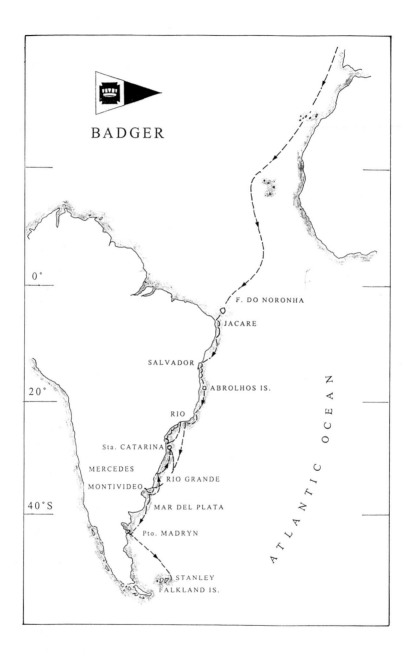

BADGER

F. DO NORONHA
JACARE
SALVADOR
ABROLHOS IS.
RIO
Sta. CATARINA
MERCEDES
MONTIVIDEO
RIO GRANDE
MAR DEL PLATA
Pto. MADRYN
STANLEY
FALKLAND IS.

0°

20°

40°S

ATLANTIC OCEAN

overnight and remained in the south-east. We couldn't believe our luck. We had passed through the Doldrums in only a few hours.

By the next day we had reached 3°00′N 25°00′W and could bear away and ease sheets. It had been hot work getting south. Spray on deck had meant keeping the forward hatches shut so that there wasn't much of a draught below. On 7 December, just after noon, we crossed the Equator. Neptune must have been busy that day as he didn't find time to climb over *Badger*'s bow, so Annie escaped being shaved and feathered. We celebrated with a bottle of champagne, which we had cooled by wrapping it in a damp cloth and leaving it in the wind. An optimist might have called it chilled.

The night before we made our landfall there was a total eclipse of the moon, which was quite a way to end a splendid passage. We picked up the flashing light on Fernando at 0300 and were at anchor off the island by breakfast. It had taken just under eighteen days for the 2300 miles.

Fernando do Noronha is about 200 miles north-east of the eastern tip of South America. The island has been used for a variety of purposes since its discovery in 1500 — in more recent years it has been a prison (the fate of many Brazilian islands), a World War II airbase, a missile tracking station and now a national park. Landing has always been a problem as a continual surf on the beach meant you either had to anchor the dinghy off the line of breakers and swim ashore or take it through the surf, capsize and swim ashore. A recently built breakwater now makes landing much easier. Fernando is a delightful island with many deserted beaches, walks in the national park and plenty of bird life. The drawback, however, is the US $10 a head Park Tax and a $10 a day anchoring fee (first day free). Because of this, we only stayed three days before carrying on for Jacaré on the mainland.

Jacaré is only a tiny village on the Paraíba river, near the port of Cabedelo, but anyone who has visited always warmly recommends it. Brian Stevens cruised into here eighteen years ago and has never left. He now runs a boatyard and is a friend to visiting yachts. We spent three weeks here over Christmas and New Year, along with half a dozen other yachts — quite a crowd for Brazil, as we were later to realise. We were waiting for our Christmas mail, but in the end decided to give it up for lost. Annie went into the Post Office one last time while I cleared out with the Port Captain. She was determined to find the mail and persuaded the ladies to keep on looking after every shake of the head. They eventually found it — it had arrive in Joâo Pessoa the same day as ourselves — a week before Christmas!

There were two yachts at Jacaré that had cruised up from the south and by picking their brains and copying a few Brazilian charts, we had acquired quite a list of places to call at along the coast. Our plan was to visit the smaller towns and villages and to try to avoid the cities, where there is a big crime problem.

Our first stop was Port Orange, 60 miles down the coast, a little way north of Recife. We arrived mid-morning about low water and touched the bottom a few times as we sailed in over the bar, but there was no sea running and we found deeper water closer to the reef. Carrying on past the fort we anchored off the town of Itapissuma, 5 miles further up. After a quick look round, we beat back to anchor off the fort. Fort Orange was built by the Dutch in 1631, when they were trying to gain a hold on the coast. It had gone to rack and ruin, until a time-served convict at the nearby prison (Fort Orange is on the island of Itamaraca) decided to try and restore it. He has been doing a splendid job and the work continues, largely funded from a craft shop which sells many items made by the local prisoners. It is interesting to note that most of the cannons at the fort and in the rest of north-east Brazil have the coat of arms of King George and the Broad Arrow on them. Obviously Britain has been in the arms business for a long time!

An overnight sail brought us to the River Suape, south of Recife, which has a narrow entrance between a rock headland and the end of a drying reef. We entered just after dawn, with a light breeze from astern taking us in slowly against the ebb. Fort Nazaré guards the entrance and it was reassuringly deep as we passed the reef. A bay opened up behind the headland, with several small fishing boats on moorings. However, we were soon in shallow water, which was shoaling quickly, so we turned around and started tacking back. As we failed to find the channel, we carried on past the reef. Here the ebb was causing a few overfalls and *Badger* missed stays. We had left just enough room to wear round and the ebb took us past the reef on the next tack. It was still only 0630, with the day before us.

We carried on south to Ilha Santo Aleixo, a small island that the *Pilot* suggested gave good shelter. As we sailed past the reef on the island's south side a large catamaran came into view anchored in the lee. Once past the reef we tacked up to anchor. A Zodiac zoomed up to us from the catamaran and

The fortified walls of Port Orange

we were warned that there were several coral heads nearby; it then guided us into the best spot. The catamaran looked a 'high-tech' racing machine of about 60 feet. Once anchored, we rowed over to thank our 'pilot'. The catamaran had been built by a French couple from La Trinité, very cheaply, and had been rigged and outfitted with surplus equipment from several Grand Prix racing multihulls whose skippers had been their neighbours. Together with their young son they were working their way around the world, earning a respectable income from beach chartering. After lunch the charter party hoisted the heavy Kevlar mainsail and they whizzed off back to a nearby hotel.

We called at the village of Tamandaré the next day and then sailed overnight to the city of Maceió, 80 miles to the south. All along this stretch of the coast we came across the *jangadas*. These sailing fishing vessels were originally built as balsa rafts, with daggerboard, a notch in the stern for a steering oar and an unstayed leg-o'-mutton sail. The balsa logs are no longer available, but the *jangadas* remain basically the same except that the hulls are now built of plywood or planks. At Maceió we anchored near to the fishing community and each morning several *jangadas* would sail past on their way to a day's fishing offshore, returning just before sunset.

Fifteen miles south of Maceió is Barra São Miguel. We anchored for the night behind the reef at Porto Francés, sailing out at dawn to arrive at São Miguel with the flood. As we approached the vicinity of the reef I climbed up a couple of battens on the foresail and spotted what looked like the entrance. We lowered the sails and started the engine to keep our speed down as we approached the reef, the wind being from astern. Standing on the sail bundle forward I was beginning to have doubts when Annie called that the bottom was shoaling rapidly. We turned round and started to motor off. There was a bit of cavitation in the waves, but then a big one rolled in and swamped the engine. The sails were quickly up and we continued along the reef until we saw the real entrance and anchored off, deciding to have a look at the entrance from the dinghy first. The leadline showed 3 metres in the break in the reef, but the waves were too big to rely on motoring back out and the channel too narrow for tacking. Getting in was no problem, but getting out again might well have been. We hauled the dinghy aboard and set off towards Salvador, 250 miles to the south.

The city of Salvador stands on the east side of Baía de Todos os Santos. This is a large bay with many islands scattered across, the largest being Ilha de Itaparica. We anchored off the hospitable Yacht Club, a safe place to leave your yacht when the wind is in the east, to do our tourist bit in the city. The old part is well worth a visit for its countless baroque churches and charming, dilapidated stucco buildings. Much restoration work was in progress, an uphill struggle with so many deteriorating structures. We then spent a month exploring the bay, which is a fine cruising ground.

At the island of Itaparica there was a small gathering of cruising boats, a rare event in Brazil. As it was *Badger*'s tenth birthday we thought this was a suitable occasion for a party. Two buckets of *cachaça* punch (*cachaça* is a

A jangada *under sail*

wicked firewater sold at giveaway prices) were consumed, but I think that everyone got home safely.

The Rio Paraguaça is a picturesque river and we had heard that it was possible to get up to the town of Cachoeira. The upper part of the river is off the chart, but we thought that we would have a try. The water is not clear, but by using the echo-sounder we found a channel and followed it up. The depth was decreasing, but there appeared to be deep water ahead next to a beach, which, being a Sunday, was crowded. The impression of deep water disappeared — all those people up to their necks in water had been sitting down! We quickly turned around, but too late; we touched bottom and ground to a halt. The true horror of our situation can only be appreciated by those who have experienced a Brazilian beach at the weekend. We were soon surrounded by a score of young men eager to lift *Badger* back to deep water, and by a score of young boys eager to tip the dinghy over. There was no hope of getting off as the tide was ebbing quickly, but the helpers were having too much fun to worry about that or about the large quantities of soft antifouling all over their hands and shoulders. Meanwhile, we had to haul the dinghy on deck to save it, all this accompanied by much shouting and laughing. We fitted *Badger*'s legs and at low water found the best route to the channel and laid out the anchor in that direction. The joys of exploring. We floated off that evening, and crept up the river to anchor off the village of Najé. The next morning we tried to continue, but the channel seemed too tortuous to follow so we retreated.

It was now the middle of February and as we had decided to spend Carnival in Ilhéus it was time to move on. We called in at Morro de Sâo Paulo and explored up the river to Cairu, stopped a couple of days in Itacaré, and arrived in Ilhéus just as Carnival was starting.

Carnival is a big event in Brazil, a gigantic street party with lots of food and beer stalls. The Carnival procession now seems dominated by *Trois Electricos*. Imagine a large removal van, each side of which is covered by loudspeakers, with a stage on the roof for the performance. They play pop music with the volume turned up to the top. To walk past one is a moving experience and they are still loud from over a mile away. The party goes on all night and people recover during the day. This continues for five days!

We left Ilhéus, tacking out of the harbour with a light wind. On the final tack to clear the breakwater the wind gradually died and it looked as though we would not go clear. I put the helm down to go about, but we had lost steerage way. The next puff pushed the bow off and we headed back for the breakwater. There was now no room to wear round. I called Annie up from below while I got the engine ready to run — why I didn't just drop the anchor I'll never know. Annie tried to tack again, but we didn't have enough way on. The engine started first pull and I put it into gear. There was some swell and backwash from the breakwater of loose stones, which was now very close. I revved up, but the propeller came out of the water, the engine raced and, as it immersed again, the force cracked the slide mount and the engine fell off. It stopped as it got dunked, but it was tied on and I pulled it aboard. Annie had the boathook out to fend off and two fishermen clambered down the rocks to help push off. A puff of wind came. *Badger* luffed to it and sailed herself past the end of the breakwater with inches to spare. I could have shaken hands with the two white-faced fishermen. Saved by a stroke of luck usually reserved for tyros. Once clear we anchored to collect our shaken wits and to tidy up the broken engine mount. Annie never commented on my 'seamanship'.

We explored some quiet anchorages as we sailed south, but were finding it very hot. The trade wind was lighter and the sun was nearly overhead; in fact it was too much. Annie wrote in the log:

SOME THOUGHTS FROM ABOARD

Oh! to be in Greenland, now th'Equator's near.
 Chilblains all forgotten, as I sip on lukewarm beer,
Rememb'ring sighting icebergs, dismissing thoughts of fear
 (Of fogs and gales and growlers — mem'ries still too clear).

I long for chilly nights again, when bed seemed such a treat
 Snuggled with my duvet, warm socks on my feet.
Now I toss and turn all night, fling aside the sheet,
 Slapping at mosquitoes, cursing at the heat.

The 20/20 Club abound — its members love it here.
They like the twelve hour night-time, the quite unchanging year.
I say I like more daylight — they think I'm rather queer.
Oh! to be in Greenland, now th'Equator's near.

Instead of spending a further three months in Brazil, we decided to head down to Uruguay to cool off and to come back in the winter. After calling at the Abrolhos Islands, Buzios (where we repaired the engine mount) and Cabo Frio, we went to Rio to clear out. We arrived at dawn on a fine morning, after sailing all night towards the floodlit statue of Christ on Corcovado. The setting of the city is superb, but it has an evil reputation for crime so we only stayed two days before setting sail for Uruguay.

We left on 16 March and had a mixed bag of weather for the first five days, with thunderstorms, calms and Force 5 headwinds, but then it settled down and we had a fair breeze and clear skies for the remainder of the passage. The log notes how pleasantly cool it was at 80°F! We spoke to a yacht, six days out, *Nora* of El Tigre in Argentina. This is a rare event for us, as we assume that yachts call up on VHF but sail on when they get no reply. We spotted *Nora* and headed her way as she did likewise. We exchanged news and as they were going to La Paloma, in Uruguay, we decided to go there ourselves.

We stayed in La Paloma for a day and then sailed along the coast towards Punta del Este. The east wind eased off after sunset, so we went and anchored in a small bay at José Ignacio for the night. A rude awakening just before dawn by a southerly Force 4 sent us on our way from the exposed anchorage and we arrived at Punta del Este by lunchtime. The town has a fairly large yacht harbour, geared up to deal with a flood of Argentinian yachts who call at the fashionable resort in the summer. The season was obviously over and we anchored outside rows of empty mooring buoys. The next morning just before dawn we had to shift berth to the lee of Isla Gorritti, two miles away, as a fresh westerly arrived with a squall. This was to set the pattern for the next five days, because we had to re-anchor seven times to get shelter from a series of *pamperos*. The last one blew at gale force from the south-west and we had five fishing boats for company, while we watched three yachts drag their moorings onto the beach. When we cleared out at the *Prefectura* the next day we asked if this weather was normal and were told that it was — they proved to be correct!

Our next stop was at Puerto del Buceo, near Montevideo. We anchored in the harbour and as the next blow arrived, rowed out two more anchors to try and hold us in the soft mud bottom. We had just sorted ourselves out when the boatman from the Uruguay Yacht Club came over and suggested that we would get more sleep by tying up to a laid-up fishing boat in the lee of the harbour wall. This seemed a sound scheme, so three anchors came in, with mud everywhere, and we motored up to the fishing boat and put a stern anchor out. Here we sat comfortably and waited ten days for a break in the weather so that we could sail further up the River Plate. A fine easterly sent us quickly to the Rio Rosario, 60 miles west of Montevideo. *Nora*'s skipper had recommended it and we felt our way in over the bay into a delightful *pampero*-proof river, one of the Plate's rare natural harbours. We anchored just past a derelict factory, complete with rusting steam tug and barge at the tumbledown dock. It was very peaceful and three weeks went by, painting and varnishing, during a spell of fine but cool weather.

We carried on up the River Plate, sailing against light headwinds and a knot of current. A dawn to dusk sail gave us about 15 miles on our way. One fine, cold morning saw us underway just as the sun rose. I lit the diesel heater and let Annie have a lie-in while the cabin warmed up. Smoke started erupting from the chimney and a look below between tacks showed the heater roaring away, so I switched it off. It continued to roar away, out of control now — the valve had stuck. I turned if off at the tank and woke Annie. Smoke was starting to escape inside the cabin and burning diesel dripped onto the sole. This was serious. The first fire extinguisher failed to operate so I got the other one from the lazarette, but that didn't work either. Annie got out a pot of bicarbonate of soda and tried to sprinkle that on the fire, but it was too lumpy to have much effect. I wrapped our fire blanket around the heater, which at least contained the flames. By now the cabin was

Badger, *a 34ft LOA junk schooner*

dark with acrid smoke and we were getting pretty worried. I went on deck and forced the top off one of the fire extinguishers, then poured the powder down the chimney and, thankfully, the fire went out immediately. While all this had been going on *Badger* continued to sail herself in the light breeze. We opened all the hatches to clear the smoke out and surveyed the damage. The cabin was filthy from the smoke, which had got everywhere, but apart from a little scorched wood and a distorted carburettor there was little real damage. If the fire extinguishers had worked there would have been none at all. They were ten years old but in good condition and the manufacturer had not put on a 'best before' date. I know that it's unlucky to be superstitious, but things happen in threes, so we wondered what the third one would be. Annie spent the next four hours cleaning up. Breakfast was a little late that morning.

We anchored well after dark off the town of Carmelo, and after a look around the following morning carried on north. The next section was quite tricky as the Rio Plata narrows just where it is formed by the junction of the Rio Paraná (which goes up through Argentina to Paraguay) and the Rio Uruguay (which forms the border between Uruguay and Argentina). The current increased to 2 knots and we still had a light wind against us. We were on the point of anchoring at dusk, having made little headway, when the breeze shifted and increased enough to allow us to make some progress.

We carried on up the Rio Uruguay and after we'd passed the narrows at Nueva Palmira the wind freshened. Soon we were making real progress, so decided to carry on as long as the wind held. The Admiralty chart of the Rio Uruguay gives only scanty information, because the channel and buoys frequently shift and pilotage is compulsory for 'all ocean-going vessels, without exception'. We were sailing in the dark, but as one lit buoy came abeam we could just make out the next. The buoys had the advantage that they were marked with the distance from Nueva Palmira, so that by sailing close by and shining a torch on them we could check our progress. Towards dawn, a bend in the river forced us to start tacking and the easing of the wind further slowed us down. By using the echo-sounder we tried to keep just outside the deep water and thereby cheat the current a little. By lunchtime the wind had gone so we anchored, and as it showed no signs of returning eventually motored up to the entrance to the Rio Negro, which branches off east into the heart of Uruguay. The Rio Uruguay is several miles wide at this point, with gentle, rolling hills to the east and low ground on the Argentine side. The Rio Negro is narrower, with much of its banks wooded and interspersed with the pasture of cattle ranches. *Estancias* could be seen on the sides of nearby hills, well above the flood level.

We had heard that local yachts often sail up to Mercedes and although we only had a general map of the Rio Negro we thought that we'd give it a try. Our first stop was at Soriano, a small town in the centre of cattle country. Time seemed to have passed it by since its prosperity a hundred years ago, but it was gratifying to see the odd *gaucho* riding by. We bought a litre of milk in one tiny shop. They expected us to bring our own container, but solved the problem by using a whisky bottle. This hasn't happened to us since we bought a pint of milk in a whisky bottle in Glandore in 1979. Even such a backwater as Soriano has its *Prefectura* and the official seemed quite pleased to see us; he can't have much business at the end of May. On the wall in his office was a chart of the river up to Mercedes. As I was studying it he asked if I would like to take a copy. He then produced tracing paper and a pencil and it was with more confidence that we carried on that afternoon.

It took us three days to sail the 29 miles up to Mercedes. The river meanders a lot so that the wind was not always against us, even if the current was. It was fine sailing, tacking up the narrow river to the next bend and then easing sheets for a brief spell until the following turn. There was always plenty to see on either bank and it made quite a change from coastal sailing. Mercedes was as far as we got, for there we decided to turn back. The town of Fray Bentos was not far away, so we took a bus to visit it — how could we miss going there, the spiritual home of corned beef? It is an economic mystery to us that a tin of corned beef costs nearly twice as much here as in England.

Retracing our steps down the river was a piece of cake. The current was with us and, with rare justice, the wind held, turning what had been a headwind into a fair breeze. We flew down the river and were even bold enough to anchor for lunch. The only drawback of such swift progress was keeping to the, at times, narrow channel — much more difficult than feeling our way along as we tacked up. We arrived at the mouth of the river at sunset, just as the wind eased off and silently glided into the Riacho Yaguan to anchor. Ashore two *gauchos* rode up to a corral and talked quietly as they unsaddled their horses for the night.

The following day was a repeat of the previous one, with a wonderful run down the Rio Uruguay, anchoring just after dark at the mouth of the small Rio San Juan. The Rio San Juan is the site of the first European settlement on the Rio Plata. A fort was built here in 1527 by Sebastian Cabot, son of John, but the Indians soon destroyed it. A tall stone tower marks the spot and the President of Uruguay has his official summer residence here. It is a relatively small, English-style country house, set in beautiful parkland with fine views across the Rio Plata.

After spending a day sheltering from a *pampero* in Colonia harbour, the main ferry port for Argentina, we sailed back to Montevideo. We decided to go into the main harbour and lie off the *Club Nacional de Regatas* as we had been told that they make visitors welcome. It was a big mistake. It is mainly a rowing club and has obviously seen better days. Situated in a corner of the harbour, it is the filthiest place I have ever seen. There are scores of laid-up deep sea trawlers moored in the harbour, and all the oil from their bilges collects off the Club. The water level was low and there didn't seem to be much room to anchor. We were hailed and offered the use of the one free mooring. This belonged to a heavy steel harbour launch, which persuaded us to ignore our normal rule of never picking up a private mooring. We tied up with a rope and shackled our cable to the heavy chain riser.

Our main purpose in coming to Montevideo was to stock up before going back to Brazil. We took on board a seamanlike quantity of wine — table wine in Brazil in undrinkable — and fruit and vegetables for the passage. We were treated to another *pampero* and a particularly vicious one, well over gale force. The harbour is well protected and as there seemed to be no problems we turned in, only to be woken a few hours later as we banged into a workboat tied up to the nearby jetty. The water had risen 6 feet and *Badger*'s buoyancy had lifted the mooring off the bottom. The wind pressed us firmly onto the oily tyres of the workboat's bow, but we managed to manoeuvre ourselves alongside it. The stanchions had been bent and the rubbing-strake was badly mauled, but we were lucky not to have landed on the ruined concrete jetty a few yards away. We spent the next day sorting ourselves out and trying to remove the ground-in oil from *Badger*'s cream built-up cabin. It turned out that the mooring had only just been laid and never used. Well, here was trouble number three and we hoped that we had got rid of the bogey. It took another bottle of detergent to clean off the dinghy and we couldn't leave Montevideo harbour soon enough. We sailed with a forecast of a south to south-westerly Force 3–4, but that shifted to the east by the time we had cleared the harbour. Within a day it was up to Force 6 giving us a chilly, wet beat to get back to Brazil.

Praia de Pinheira, Santa Catarina

The cold Falklands current runs north as far as Rio at this time of the year. Not only did it run in our favour, but the cold water attracted rafts of Magellanic penguins and the air was teeming with mollymawks and Cape pigeons; the odd sealion popped his head up for a quick look. After five days the wind shifted to the west and eased off and the next evening we came to anchor off Rio Grande, the southernmost port of Brazil. It was dark and we thought it prudent to wait until daylight before attempting the entrance. The river drains a huge area and consequently there is a strong current. We wanted to make sure that we entered on the flood and our tide tables would have to be the tidemarks on the breakwater.

At 0430 we were woken by *Badger*'s motion. The wind had got up, it was blowing south-westerly Force 5 and the glass had fallen. With a couple of reefs in each sail we tacked up to the anchor, but it appeared to be set in concrete. After much struggling the chain was up and down, but still the Bruce would not break out. We feared that the cable must part as *Badger* pitched into the sea, but it eventually broke out and we beat offshore.

Neither of us fancied trying the entrance in a *pampero*, so we bore away and made it a fair wind to run up the coast for Santa Catarina Island, another 350 miles to the north. We had a fast if rough ride, so much so that Annie commented in the log: 'Fed up of this bloody passage' — we ran 151 miles that day. We then ran 153 miles the next and the 'bloody passage' was over by noon, when we anchored in the shelter of Praia de Pinheira just south of Santa Catarina.

Overnight the wind shifted to the north and next day we beat up the Santa Catarina channel. It was a fine sail, with mountains close to port and the hills of the island to starboard. We anchored off the city of Florianópolis to clear in. After dealing with the authorities (an all-day job which included an interesting tour of the opposite ends of the city), we returned to *Badger*, our backs breaking under the load of provisions, our little faces beaming at the cheap prices.

We needed to find a sheltered anchorage to repair a batten which had cracked on our run north and to sew a few patches on the mainsail. The likeliest place seemed to be Enseado do Brito, which gave shelter from the north through west to south. Here we dismantled the mainsail and felt rather vulnerable, as though crippled. We had to shift berth several times to get better protection at either end of the bay; the weather was anything but settled. It was now mid-winter and the cold fronts were coming in quick succession. As soon as the sail and batten were repaired we decided to sail further north to Ilha Grande in the hope of finding some better weather.

A mixed bag of mainly light headwinds was our lot for most of the 400 miles, but the last twelve hours produced another cold front which rapidly concluded the passage. Baía de Ilha Grande is a large bay, 60 miles wide, dotted with small islands and surrounded by mountains. It is on the edge of the tropics 60 miles west of Rio. This is a delightful cruising ground, marred only by its general lack of wind. We spent seven weeks here, exploring the bay and attending to several jobs on *Badger*. I found enough teak on board to repair the ravaged rubbing-strake and the endless list of jobs was slowly reduced.

It is surprising how few cruising yachts visit Brazil. We only saw seven other foreign yachts whilst in the bay, the largest number since Salvador. I can only assume that tales of the crime and bureaucracy have frightened people away. Crime is only a problem in the cities (which are best avoided) and the bureaucracy is not much worse than in Portugal. A cruise to Brazil makes a good alternative to the crowded Caribbean and it will doubtless soon become 'discovered' in the same way as Venezuela.

We ended our stay in the bay by visiting the town of Paratí at the west end. This is an old colonial, gold-exporting town which has only recently been connected by road. The old town has some fine restored houses lining the cobbled streets, which flood at each spring tide, so that on more than one occasion we had to wade back to the dinghy.

We called at Ubatuba and Ilha Porcos on our way south to Paranaguá. The sun was about to set as we hauled our sheets and we could just lay the course up the channel over the bar. The ebb was against us, but we made up well with the fresh breeze and anchored for the night off Ilha do Mel. The next day we tacked up the bay with the flood to the town of Paranaguá. There is a thriving port here, with ships anchored offshore and in the bay, awaiting their turn to load. The small boat harbour is hidden up a creek off the old town. Here we anchored in front of the quaint, crumbling buildings

The old town at Parati

and watched the endless comings and goings of the *canoas*, the main means of transport in the bay. Their cargoes varied from building materials and gas bottles to cases of Antarctica beer.

Further up the bay is the port of Antonina, which now has lost its trade to Paranaguá. It was to here that Joshua Slocum was trading in his barque *Aquidneck* when she was lost on the bar. He then built a sampan-rigged dory (how seamanlike!), the *Liberdade*, and sailed his stranded family home to the USA.

Our ninety day visa for Brazil was soon to run out and as we didn't want to renew it, it was time to continue south. We called at Porto Belo on our way back to Santa Catarina and cleared out from Florianópolis for Uruguay. It took a week at sea to cover the 700 miles to Punta del Este, where they were getting ready for the arrival of the yachts in the Whitbread Round-the-World Race. We carried on up the River Plate back to Puerto del Buceo.

On 5 October we continued south for Mar del Plata in Argentina. Our course would take us close west of the English Bank, a dangerous sandbar in the middle of the Plate estuary. The wind was too light to overcome the east-flowing current, so we had to bear away and sail east about the bank. The wind all but disappeared for the rest of the day, but it eventually filled in from the north. It deserted us again within sight of Mar del Plata and we had to beat in against the afternoon sea breeze. We had met the yacht *Bastardo*, which came from Mar del Plata, in Horta the year before. They assured us of a good welcome there and this proved to be so. We were shown to a berth in the yacht harbour belonging to the Yacht Club Argentino, whose members made us most welcome. We stayed for a fortnight and made use of the sheltered berth, for which no charge was made, to go up the mast and replace much of the rigging, as well as giving the dinghy a much-need repaint. Mar del Plata is Argentina's number one holiday resort and its year-round population swells by over a million in the holiday season. I'm glad to say that we were too early to witness the crowds.

Sailing south, we called in at Puerto Madryn in the Golfo Nuevo. This large, enclosed bay is the breeding ground for the Southern Right whale and we were lucky enough to see one quite close to the town as we tacked up to the anchorage. It lay quietly on the surface with the occasional wave of its flippers; its distinctive breathing noises could be heard some distance away. Puerto Madryn is a small town that was founded by Welsh settlers in 1865. Apparently some people in the area still speak Welsh but there is little sign of their heritage in the town now.

We sailed over to Punta Loma to see a sealion colony and as we tacked along the shoreline we could hardly believe our eyes when we saw a flock of flamingos on the beach. It was a spectacular sight as about fifty birds took off, a mass of pink and rose, edged in black. We anchored off a shingle beach and, next morning, walked over to the point where there is a nature reserve. There were some run-down buildings and it rather looked as if it was abandoned, but a warden popped out of a house and asked us for £2 each to enter. We told him that we had no money on us so he shrugged his shoulders and waved us in.

While the nature centre wasn't much, there was an excellent view from the clifftops of the sealions and we spent some time watching the heaps of animals, with the large males making half-hearted threats to each other. Although it was a Saturday morning we were the only ones there.

In the afternoon we set off on the final leg of our voyage to the Falkland Islands. We had to pass through the Roaring Forties and into the Furious Fifties, although we did have the tip of South America to protect us to a certain extent. Fortunately the Forties didn't roar and the Fifties were not too furious, but just to show us that the Falklands are a windy place a fresh northerly got up overnight as we approached the islands. We sighted Macbride Head 15 miles off at dawn, and the wind increased to Force 7, necessitating a quick reef in the middle of porridge. We were soon in the sheltered waters of Port William, outside Stanley Harbour, with the wind blowing with some fierce gusts as we reached across to anchor at the west end.

We had arrived. It was a year later than originally planned, but looking back we have no regrets about turning our cruise on its head.

HAVHESTUR AU VIN

by W M Nixon

(The cruise for which the Founder's Cup was awarded.)

It is only about 175 miles from the Butt of Lewis to Akraberg on Suduroy, the nearest headland in Foroyar. A short passage perhaps, but it takes you to a different world. To places that appear higher than they're wide, where sheer cliffs of 2000 feet seem almost commonplace. To eighteen or so tightly-packed islands in an archipelago just 60 miles by 40 through which the tides move horizontally at ferocious speeds but scarcely go up and down at all, while the winds by contrast seldom move steadily in the horizontal but frequently go vertically up and down in sudden katabatic gusts. To a rugged environment where the humble sheep is king.

With just a fortnight to get to this extraordinary place and then back again to Howth we needed good luck, as it would involve sailing about 1200 miles. And our luck with the weather was uncanny, though we'd a hunch that by sailing up in June we'd get the best of any weather going. In the disturbed summer of 1993 this was certainly the case. The Atlantic lows were tracking so far south that we spent much of our time in relatively clear Arctic air, while Britain and Ireland were inundated. Certainly we had fog and mist as expected (it's fog when you don't know where you are, and mist when you do), but generally conditions were reasonable, while the passages to and from the islands could scarcely have been better.

With Aidan Tyrrell, I departed from Howth a few minutes before midnight on Thursday 3 June. Well laden with stores, we were also notably well equipped with charts and sailing directions thanks to the kindness of Christopher Thornhill and Oz Robinson, and also Captain Tom MacCarthy of the Irish Sail Training Brigantine *Asgard II*, which had been in the islands in May '92. Indeed, it was a pleasant and informative meeting with Tom in *Asgard*'s comfortable great cabin early in 1993 which finally made me feel we really were going to Foroyar, and we carried the spirit of that happy ship with us.

51

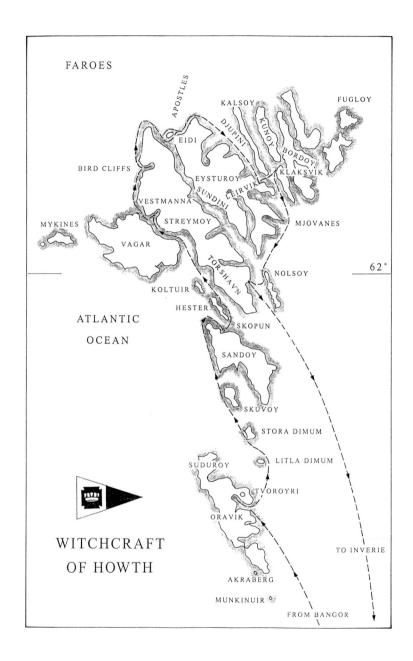

FAROES

APOSTLES

KALSOY   FUGLOY

EIDI

DJUPINI

KUNOY

BORDOY

KLAKSVIK

BIRD CLIFFS

EYSTUROY

LEIRVIK

VESTMANNA   SUNDINI

MYKINES   STREYMOY   MJOVANES

VAGAR

TORSHAVN   NOLSOY   62°

KOLTUIR

HESTER

ATLANTIC   SKOPUN

OCEAN   SANDOY

SKUVOY

STORA DIMUM

LITLA DIMUM

SUDUROY

TVOROYRI

ORAVIK

TO INVERIE

WITCHCRAFT
OF HOWTH

AKRABERG

MUNKINUIR

FROM BANGOR

We stopped off in Bangor to take on spirit of a different kind, and complete our crew. Thanks to Foroyar's relationship with the EC being only an associate one through its special autonomous status within the Kingdom of Denmark, our registered vessel was entitled to Duty Free, and this had been most efficiently organised at Bangor by a new but very welcome addition to our crew panel, Peter Minnis. His past experience as an officer in the merchant navy is an ideal background for cruising, for men of the merchant marine are used to making do with minimal personnel resources, which fits in very well with our kind of sailing.

Because of the distances involved, however, we reckoned four the ideal number for this cruise, so my partner Ed Wheeler also joined the strength in Bangor. As it's the place where we both spent our childhood, it was only after getting into all the usual scrapes that we took our departure shortly before midnight, and the following morning (Saturday 5 June) found us sailing fast out to the west of Islay in a sunny sou'wester.

We'd the usual bashing and splashing weathering lonely Skerryvore, but thereafter the passage through the Sea of the Hebrides and the Little Minch was a dream, with sheets freed and the distantly-glimpsed mountains of the Outer Hebrides going past at a very satisfactory rate. Shipboard routine was well established by the time we got to the Minch itself, with huge brunches, leisurely dinners, dolphins dancing past, and the big Autohelm doing all the work. As it was Sunday, Ed gave us a concert on his English Accordion (squeeze-box to you and me) which so astonished the wind it fell away altogether. So we motored for three hours while the Butt of Lewis faded astern on the port quarter, and this got us into the first hint of Arctic air, a breeze from the east which carried *Witchcraft* past the remote island of Rona.

A front went through during the short night to bring in a wet sou'easter which pushed up to Force 6, giving decidedly noisy going but in the right direction. They say that weather is all fronts and no backs, but the back of this front was fog, and on Monday afternoon we were bumbling through it on a dead run, approaching Akraberg with the genoa now boomed out to port.

Our approach was deliberately shaped to come in at Akraberg from the southeast, both to avoid the unmarked Munken Rocks, and also because The Red Scare Book indicated that this course would minimise our time in the inevitable tidally-disturbed water. In Faeroese (which is a sort of mixture of old Norwegian and Icelandic, as the islanders came from southern Norway despite their political links with Denmark) this remarkable tidal atlas is officially called *Streymkort fyri Foroyar*, or *Tidal Currents around The Faeroe Islands*. But we soon dubbed it The Red Scare Book, as the author Fischer Heinesen, from the great fishing port of Klaksvik, uses horrible big whirling red shapes with telling effect to indicate the more dangerous races and their hourly weavings as what seems like most of the North Atlantic Tidal Wave tries to push its way through the islands.

Heinesen's charts are based around the time of slack water in Suduroyardfjordur, which is approximately +0040 Reykjavik, but the man himself reckons that when it's really vital to know what's going on, for instance at Springs when tides can go from slack to 10 knots in minutes, then the real indicator is an adjustment around the time of the Moon's meridian passage. Needless to say, Ed our ace navigator — whom we reckon to be wired to the Moon in any case — had soon sussed out this business of the meridian passage. But we still approached Foroyar somewhat nervously through fog that Monday afternoon (7 June), grateful that we'd a hand-held Trimble Ensign GPS to back up our somewhat moody Decca.

Seabird numbers increased, and the water became distinctly popply. Then the fog wraithed away and there was Akraberg broad on the port bow, its clifftop lighthouse swirled with cloud. Ahead, there were glimpses of those steep islands, Litla Dimun and Stora Dimun. To port, the massive cliffs of Suduroy came and went in mist and rain. The place was all we'd expected, only more so. And then came the first human contact. A little Faeroese fishing boat, her Viking bow and stern jauntily clear of the dark and lumpy water, went past inshore, her crew waving cheerfully. The entrance to the fine inlet of Trongisvagsfjordur opened up, and we sailed in for the handy port of Tvoroyri as curtains of rain came in over steep hillsides, and brightly coloured little houses dotted the bare shore.

Although there are anchorages in Foroyar, notably in the half dozen or so 'winter harbours', in such places the seabed can be cluttered with abandoned ground tackle, while the ferocity of the wayward gusts can trip your anchor. The virtually nonexistent tidal range, so oddly at variance with the ferocious tidal streams, makes the many quays and piers very accessible so we tended to secure to them, or better still to berth alongside 'resting' fishing boats which wouldn't be expected to go to sea at some unearthly hour. We became quite expert at assessing which fishing boats were temporarily de-commissioned, while always keeping a wary eye out for longliners. Even an inactive longliner can have hook-filled reels along the gunwhale from stem to stern. A handful of hooks from over-enthusiastic hopping on board could ruin your entire day.

Another hazard is that, on both boats and quaysides, old tyres are universally used as fenders — often very old tyres. Inevitably your own boat will get somewhat mucky. Fortunately we carried a couple of litres of white spirit and this proved an effective cleaner. All this and more we learned in our first port of Tvoroyri, where we berthed outside an old fishing boat after averaging a comfortable 6.4 knots over the 449 miles from Bangor. Getting to Foroyar in no more than a long weekend was celebrated with the Mother of All Roast Wobbly Lamb Feasts cooked by Ed, and then we slept it out.

The morning brought a brief glitch in the weather. A front with a sou'westerly gale was to go through before the easterlies re-asserted themselves, so we'd a leisurely if damp time getting ourselves showers (for free) in the nearby fish factory, and concluding ship's business with Einar Larsen the customs

Looking across Skopun on Sandoy, the essence of contemporary Foroyar, with Hestur beyond and Streymoy in the distance   *Photo: W. M. Nixon*

officer. Tvoroyri is an ideal first port of call as you can clear customs there, yet it's a friendly little place without Torshavn's metropolitan notions. So Einar was able to come aboard and spend an hour or so over coffee talking of life in the islands. He was keen to know if we'd seen any small whales on the way up, as he pined for the *grindadrap*, the traditional whale entrapment and slaughter which used to be virtually essential to Foroyar's survival.

It was thought-provoking to see this mild man with eyes gleaming as he enthused about great kills in times past, and his drooping spirits as he reflected on the fact that in 1992 there'd been only one small whale taken in all the islands. We didn't have the heart to tell him that we'd recommended to the dolphins seen on the way up that they should take their holidays with Fungie in Dingle, where dolphins are treated like royalty, and stay well away from the Faeroese and their quaint habits. But if you're going to cruise to Foroyar, you simply have to suspend judgement on what should or should not be seen as food, for the tough struggle for survival over the centuries has meant that the only creature guaranteed safety from the pot is the *tjaldur*, the oystercatcher, the national bird of Foroyar, whose return to the islands each March heralds the spring.

Everything else has been seen as fair game for eating, and the vertiginous hunting of seafowl on the *fuglabjorg*, the mighty bird cliffs, is woven into the tapestry of Faeroese life as strongly as the *grindadrap*. As for farming, it is almost totally about sheep. In Foroyar, sheep farming is not one of life's gentler pursuits. Rather, it's the job for heroes — a successful Faeroese shepherd will know over which cliff there's a useful patch of grass, and how long it will feed a sheep. To get the animal there, and subsequently retrieve it, he needs the skills of an Alpinist. Cruising among the islands, we were continually amazed by the places where sheep grazed, and could only conclude that any successful Faeroese ram had to be sure-footed, and sure of his welcome. The Howth cartoonist Bob Fannin once cruised to the islands with John Gore-Grimes, and returned with a sketch which says it all.

This preoccupation with sheep will come as a surprise to anyone who associates the Faeroes with fishing. But while fishing was always important, in times past it was mainly only subsistence fishing, dangerous work from little boats. The vicious and unpredictable winds and the ferocious tides meant that it wasn't until the advent of the diesel engine that fishing from Foroyar could take off and develop as a real industry, with thriving exports. But once it got going, it rocketed. Thus the population soared from 30,000 in 1930 to 50,000 in the 1980s. By that time the islanders had the highest per capita income in all Scandinavia, with prodigious infrastructural development under way on roads and harbours.

Unfortunately, it all unravelled more than somewhat at the end of 1992 with the international currency crisis and the collapse in the price of fish. So we knew we were visiting islands with a real problem. But as far as we could

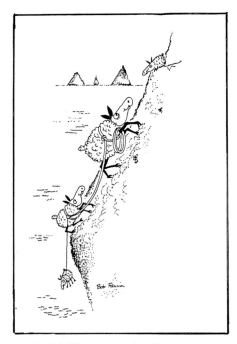

Sheep of Foroyar leading the high life, as seen by Bob Fannin

gather, the situation was serious but not desperate, or desperate but not serious. If push came to shove, the Faeroese could quickly convince themselves that historically the Danes have done so well out of the islands that they owe them a mint, and thus a postal order from Aunty in Copenhagen was the least they could expect. But in any case, the dark days of winter were over and the Faeroese were plodding on through life with their usual resilience, cheered by the anticipation of summer.

Even so, the utter dependence on the fishing industry is clearly a matter of concern, so the islands are trying to find additional ways of earning income and inevitably tourism is one of them. Thus in the autumn of 1992 they had relaxed their draconian licensing laws, so to ride out that day of bad weather, we took a taxi in the rain to visit the first pub in Suduroy, opened just three weeks earlier across the fjord in Oravik.

Don't expect a rose-covered Dog & Duck. It's pretty basic, and the price of a bottle of beer is £2.50. But at least it is a pub of sorts, and it provided us with the setting for a learned discussion of land tenure, on which Aidan proved something of an expert. Back in Tvoroyri we'd a party or two with some local citizens and the people on a French 34-footer which we'd beaten by four hours for the honour of being the first sailing crew to arrive in Foroyar in 1993. Then next morning (quite when we don't know, as the scarcity of darkness leads to confusion about the time of day, or indeed which day it is) we sailed in better weather and a sou'easter out round the hugely steep Litla Dimun (it's like an even steeper Ailsa Craig), and the larger Stora Dimun, which has the best farmland in all Foroyar.

The fact that, until the advent of helicopters, this farmland could only be reached by scaling an utterly vertical 360 foot cliff from an exposed westfacing landing place did little to hinder its development as a prosperous farmstead. Suitably awed, we went on through a bright if hazy morning round to the north coast of Sandoy and the little harbour of Skopun which was the very essence of Foroyar, with children playing around the colourful houses, a dredger improving the entrance, and the tiny village slumbering through the day while it awaited the return of the fishing fleet.

Summer had definitely arrived, but we found that the islanders of Foroyar think that their real summer is in July, so there was a sense of the place wakening up from hibernation. And we soon had a reminder of the weather's fickleness, for in the afternoon as we headed on across Vagafjordur after a quick look into the massively-constructed little harbour which has been built on the east side of Hestur, the Horse Island, we were back in a cold fog which wouldn't have gone amiss in December. The south end of Vestmannasund is distinctly spooky, more so in fog, but approaching Vestmanna on Streymoy there was a clearance astern and the peak of Skaelingsfjall appeared remote above the cloud, a magic mountain.

Vestmanna, the harbour of the western or Irish men, is probably the best winter harbour and has plenty of anchoring room, but the older fishing port in the northwest corner right under the main part of town had plenty of space to give us a convenient berth where we wolfed a very classy rocket-fuelled lamb curry from Café Aidan. This was a pity in a way, for on going ashore later we found there was a pleasant little restaurant, La Careta, run by an English girl in the hostel, which is the red building just above the old harbour. Unfortunately the shipboard catering was so good that any eating ashore was going to require real determination, and certainly at Vestmanna we weren't sufficient trenchermen to test the local food.

The colourful homeliness of the port was emphasised by the bare mountains all around, the contrast being underlined by the bright life of the Community Centre where of all things a bingo session was under way. Having anticipated a complete lack of trees, we were intrigued to find the little churchyard well-wooded with sycamores — stunted perhaps, but trees nevertheless. Reflecting on the challenge of trying some sort of afforestation in one of Foroyar's more sheltered valleys, we were surprised to note that it was after midnight as we read the gravestones by available light.

Awakening later in the morning, we found the weather further improved, albeit temporarily. There was bright sunshine and the colourful houses shone above their reflections in a harbour which was unruffled by a light easterly. In great good spirits we went off to see the Bird Cliffs of Streymoy. The exit through the north end of Vestmannasund between Vagar and Streymoy is dramatic. One moment you're in a steep and narrow channel, next moment out on the wide blue ocean with cliffs of the giant size marching away on either hand.

It takes some time to appreciate the scale. The *fuglabjorg* rises like a wall to 2000 feet, so assessing the range and number of bird life is wellnigh impossible as many of them are no more than dots flying at clifftop height. All of which is another way of saying that, after a while, you become blasé about seeing tens of thousands of puffins, guillemots and whatever. By this time we were even used to seeing sheep going placidly about their business on almost vertical and seemingly inaccessible greensward. So we turned ourselves to fishing, and although the easterly breeze meant we were able to wander at leisure around the majestic cliff inlet of Sakshovn, the very fact that it is noted for trout, but it wasn't the trout season, drove Ed to a frenzy of fishing further along the cliffs while the rest of us simply sat in the cockpit having early nooners in a state of awe, gazing in wonder at the huge rampart of the *fuglabjorg* which we could now see all the way westward past Vagar down to Mykines.

The fishing ended with two good hooks lost and nothing caught, but by this time we'd to move sharpish, as the weather was undergoing one of its Faeroese rapid changes. Cloud had suddenly started curling over from the top of Mylingur, the dramatic tusk-like 1847 foot north-west headland of Streymoy, and beyond there was a line of fog rolling out of Sundini, the passage between Streymoy and Eysturoy. Within minutes we were being battered by gale force katabatic gusts, but with a spot of cliff dodging we got ourselves the four miles round the corner to the handy port of Eidi, tucked inside the north point of Eysturoy.

The feeling of being in the far north of Foroyar was inescapable, with large snow patches on the bare mountains high above the bright little dots of villages. But away from the grim cliffs in Eidi's pleasant harbour it was summer again, and we found a berth at the fish quay rather than at the little 'marina' at the south end of the harbour. Central to Foroyar's harbour-improvement mania during the 1980s was the provision of marina berths for the little recreational fishing boats which are the nearest the islanders get to having yachts. Few of these craft are much longer than 20ft, so the marinas will seldom take anything bigger than 25ft in the unlikely event of a berth being free, although at Eidi there is berthing for larger craft along a main walkway. But provided there isn't a southerly gale, in Eidi it's more interesting to take a berth at the fish quay which, as in most ports, is near the centre of town, although Faeroese municipalities being of decidedly individualistic design you'd sometimes be hard put just to say where the centre is.

Eidi is famous for its 19th century Lutheran seamen's church, determinedly set on the windy neck of the isthmus (which is what *eidi* means, like *tarbert* in Gaelic). So while the others relaxed in the sun and took on water (very convenient at the fish quay), I was able to indulge in that special personal pleasure of going to an empty church alone. Eidi's beautifully kept little church with its ship models makes it a very special pleasure indeed. Then from the top of a nearby hill there was the view across the sunlit port to the

At the north end of the fuglabjorg of Streymoy, a sudden curling of cloud from the tusk-like headland of Mylingur warns of katabatic gusts of gale force. Photo: W. M. Nixon

cloud-swirled cliffs to be savoured while the *tjaldurs* piped their urgent song of the new summer. It turned out this particular pair were piping urgently because I was perched like an idiot almost on top of their nest.

Back at the harbour, the fishing boat *Byrgisnes* had come in with a very special catch — a 60 kilo halibut, well over a hundredweight of prime seafood. This is still the fish most prized by the Faeroese. Back in the days of primitive fishing from open boats, when a boy caught his first halibut he became a man, and the village flotilla would return to port to celebrate. Even today it still has a special meaning, and as this one seemed as big as a small whale it gave the crew of the *Byrgisnes* a good reason to return to port, which they welcomed as the weather was deteriorating rapidly.

This posed a problem for us, for much as we liked Eidi, our limited time made the thought of being isolated there in bad weather an irksome prospect. In severe weather we could possibly have headed south through Sundini, and thus got within striking distance of more sheltered cruising waters, not to mention the fleshpots of Torshavn. But Sundini is spanned by a bridge at the Sundelaget Narrows, and of the three heights we'd been given for it, two would have resulted in losing our masthead.

So before the weather went completely to pot, despite the fishermen's advice and the fact that The Red Scare Book indicated some pretty ghastly

Ship models in the 19th century Lutheran church

Eidi on Eysturoy has a small marina at its south end   Photo: *W. M. Nixon*

shapes off the north coast of Eysturoy, we went out to test the validity of our impression that it was sometimes possible to dodge inside the worst of the tide races. Distances are short in Foroyar, and while the passage round the fantastic weather-sculpted rocks known as The Apostles and close inshore under Wagnerian cliffs was increasingly grim it soon passed, and it was only for a couple of minutes at the very point of Eysturoy's northern headland of Rivtangi that we briefly got a real drubbing.

Soon we were proceeding serenely down Djupini between Eysturoy and Kalsoy in a moderate easterly. It seemed a completely different world, underlining the fact that you often get lighter winds on the weather side of the steep islands. Certainly the wind on the weather side of Rivtangi was nothing compared to the fierce squalls in its lee. But as we got further down Djupini, inevitably the squalls became more vicious as we got under the lee of black mountains. However, by this time the local forecasts were indicating that the expected front would bring a short, sharp, easterly gale. So after a quick look into the somewhat malodorous port of Leirvik we nipped across to Klaksvik on Borduy in search of a secure berth for the night.

Klaksvik is something else, the powerhouse of the Foroyar economic explosion. It is utterly devoted to harvesting the sea, and the variety of fishing boats used is mind-boggling. But despite its preoccupation it's a friendly place. The miniature fjord is just under a mile long, running north and south. Both sides are lined with quays, but the inlet is wide enough to make it worthwhile for a boat of *Witchcraft*'s size to seek a berth on the weather shore when bad weather threatens. We found a less-than-hyperactive longliner snug against the north side of a little nib running out from the quays of the eastern shore, facing east in the lee of a large shed. It looked like our perfect berth for a stormy night. It was.

The rain may have sheeted down, and the squalls may have roared down the mountainside and overhead as a vigorous front went through, but we were as snug as bugs in several rugs. With the heater doing its stuff, preparing supper was a leisurely affair of shirt-sleeved luxury. In due course, Mr Tyrrell created a dish so superb it was honoured as 'Red Boat Ragout'. Mr Wheeler gave an applauded rendition of hearty or soulful melodies on his squeeze box. Mr Minnis dispensed beverages with his customary efficiency. Mr Nixon was as usual at the consumer end of this continuum of delectation. Any citizen of Klaksvik foolish enough to be out and about might well have wondered at the sounds of hilarity emanating from the Irish boat on this night of climatic horror, but we were having one of the best nights of the cruise.

Klaksvik had a steam-cleaned look in the morning, but then as fishing ports go it's mighty clean anyway. Ed's splendid breakfast was in no way disimproved by Peter concocting Buck's Fizz with some sparkling wine, and it put us in the right frame of mind for a spot of decision-making. The gale-carrying front having gone through, we were now in the cold clear nor'easterly air coming round the Icelandic High. Further south, we knew the weather was bad (this was Friday 11 June, when much of Wales was almost rained into the sea) but the low which was causing that unpleasantness was forecast to move eastward into the North Sea.

Thus there was a chance of Foroyar's better weather pushing south to give a day or two of easterlies to provide us with an easy passage back to Scotland after a visit to Torshavn. Taking this opportunity would mean that Klaksvik would be the only place visited in Nordoyar, the spectacular northeastern islands which seem higher than they're wide under peaks which are like the Mountains of the Moon. But as we'd to be back in Howth by Saturday 19 June in any case, the possibility of a fair wind was too good to waste, for all the indications were of contrary conditions coming in on the back of the brief weather window. After consultation with The Red Scare Book, Ed reckoned the best time to leave Torshavn southward bound would be after 1700 on Saturday 12 June.

This left us a clear 32 hours to take a leisurely departure from Foroyar. We decided to approach the capital by stealth on a slightly circuitous route by way of Nolsoy, the island three miles east of it. But first we'd to make ourselves socially acceptable, so we moved across Klaksvik fjord to be handy for baths at the Seamen's Hostel, and after Peter had gone shopping to acquire four seafowl for the pot for that night's farewell feast (they were called *havhestur*, and we lazily assumed they were guillemot), *Witchcraft* headed down the busy harbour and outside found the air like champagne as the nor'easter strengthened, with a magnificent sunlit view through Kalsoyarfjordur between Kalsoy and Kunoy.

We'd a ripsnorter of a sail down past Mjovanes, that headland of evil reputation, and a swift run to Nolsoy across tumbling seas. The tide was

Sunshine in Norodoyer, looking through Kalsoyardfjordur between Kalsoy (left) and Kunoy.
Photo: W. M. Nixon

with us but the sea was restless nevertheless, and it was a spray-swept boat which scampered in past Bodin and rounded up into the ferry berth alongside the north-west pier in Nolsoy's little harbour.

If you were staying overnight you'd need to berth at the fish quay in the south-east corner, but with the ferry not due until 1830 we'd all the berth we needed for a poignant visit to what used to be the boatbuilder's island, but inevitably the advent of glassfibre has somewhat sidelined it. Little boatbuilding sheds clustered along the waterfront were an indication of a busier past. Between two of them, a whalebone arch gave access to the leprechaun-sized village square, where a group of Nolsoy men sat yarning and looking down the harbour, oblivious to a nor'east wind which would have cleaned corn. We were far from oblivious to it, and soon found our way to a warm café where sustaining sweet cakes and hot chocolate kept the cold at bay as Nolsoy slumbered on.

The contrast when we swept into the bustle of Torshavn harbour a couple of hours later could not have been greater. Quite the proper little capital city, is Torshavn. And it was very much a busy Friday evening, with the rowing skiffs of sports clubs and sea scouts, like updated Viking raiders, racing past in a flurry of foam as we trundled along the waterfront admiring the grass-roofed houses in the old part of town. You'll find houses with turf roofs in most parts of Foroyar, but the Torshavn ones are in a class of their own, so much so that we entertained the notion of a Torshavn office worker leaving early of a fine summer evening 'to get home to cut the roof'.

The old part of town is on the spur of land separating the inner harbour basins known as the Vestaravaag and the Eystaravaag. Both are almost entirely filled with marinas of the type encountered elsewhere in the islands, only more so. The easterly one in the Eystaravag has larger craft even unto gin palaces, but no spare space, so visiting yachts go to the north-east quay of the Vestaravag, where we berthed outside our French friends who had sailed 30 miles direct from Tvoroyri, while we had covered 116 miles via the scenic route.

It was quite a moment for Aidan, as he had last been berthed in exactly the same spot some 27 years earlier with the great Ninian Falkiner, having sailed up from Dun Laoghaire in the 36ft *Tir na nOg*. Even in 1966 the Faeroes economic boom was already well under way, but even so he remarked that Torshavn was significantly bigger. And then he went below to continue the preparation of the mighty feast, *Havhestur au Vin*, which he was giving four hours of slow cooking.

Although it was a cold evening, I dutifully went off to get photos of the old town in case there was rain in the morning. Virtue was rewarded. While ambling down a little street, a door opened in an anonymous building to reveal a night club getting ready for Friday night. Fully informed as to where our night on the town would start, I returned to the warmth on board, and all were comfortably settled in when a bump alongside announced that the Professors had arrived.

Summer comes to Torshavn. At centre in the somewhat limited visitors' berth are (left to right) the French 34-footer Vatna, Witchcraft, *and the slim* spitsgatter *of the three professors.*
Photo: W. M. Nixon

Their boat was just a slip of a thing, a *spitsgatter*, the 33ft version of Michael Pipe's even smaller *Stren*. You wouldn't expect to see such a thing sailing outside the Skagerrak, and in fact this was the first time this one had done so, having made a voyage from Norway direct to Torshavn with only a brief stop at Fair Isle.

Well, not quite direct. A person or persons unknown had put their little radio down beside the steering compass, and they'd made their landfall down at Sudoroy instead of Torshavn. Thus they'd just completed eight hours of superfluous and decidedly gruesome beating. They were frozen, but soon were thawing out in every way with hot whiskeys in *Witchcraft*'s warm saloon.

The party went merrily along, for their English was rather better than our Norwegian. Indeed, their English was rather better than our English. All three were professors. Their skipper was heading a delegation to a conference in Torshavn on Faeroese maritime history. "Notwithstanding the fact that my little ship had never been beyond the Skaggerak" he announced, "it seemed to me entirely appropriate that the leader of the Norwegian Delegation should sail to this first Conference of Faeroese Maritime History in his own boat".

By now there was the distinct flavour of one of Graham Greene's more comic novels. The second professor, as far as we could gather in the increasing conviviality, was the head of the Oslo Seafaring Museum, which seemed only natural in such a delegation. But the third professor apparently was the head of the Ibsen Institute. That stretched our comprehension more than some-what. But it was a grand little party nevertheless, and by the time the professors rolled off into town in search of their hotel the *Havhestur au Vin* had been simmering gently for five hours and more, which did it nothing but good — it made for a warming meal of strong flavours, gamey rather than fishy though with fishy undertones.

Then it was off for a spot of socio-political research and absorption of local culture which took in at least two night clubs and involved analysis and consultancy with the louche end of the social spectrum including printers, journalists, cartoonists, recreational chemists, Danish blondes and mysterious property dealers. Our mutual conclusion about why Denmark continues to be fascinated — nay, besotted — by Foroyar, was blindingly simple. The highest part of Denmark is just 537 feet above sea level. At 537 feet Foroyar has barely started. So now you know.

Next morning was unfair. Summer came to Torshavn with bright sunlight, and we weren't in a bright sunlight frame of mind. The mood was in no way improved by recalling that another piece of information garnered from our research group was the fact that *havhestur* is fulmar. Yes, fulmar. We'd been dining off a cousin of the albatross. Feasting on a harmless little bird which is the very symbol of offshore sailing. For all that the fulmar is now the commonest bird in Foroyar despite having only first appeared there as recently as the early 19th century, we felt that our offence against old seafaring tradition would finally see an end to *Witchcraft*'s luck.

So we'd a thoughtful lunch of grenadier in the Hafnia Hotel — grenadier is one of the 'new' fish the Faeroese bring in from the Stygian depths of mid-Atlantic; it's like extra-good monkfish. Thoughtfulness continued as the mood of the afternoon with a visit to the pleasant little maritime museum where the ancient little boats and their primitive equipment spoke eloquently of the harsh way of life which was the lot of Foroyar until very recently. A prize exhibit, the stuffed extinct Great Auk, drew fraternal glances. I felt like a stuffed extinct Great Auk myself.

It was a bright clear evening (Saturday 12 June) as we sailed away in a Force 4 to 5 nor'easter, down the harbour past a large Japanese 'Research Vessel' where they were burning whale blubber, and off to the southeast on a lumpy reach while the clouds melted away and the entire eastern seaboard of Foroyar was revealed in all its sunlit glory, so different from our foggy arrival. The miles reeled off, and away to starboard we could see the Faeroese Sail Training Schooner *Nordlysid* turning to windward past the Stora Dimun. As the short northern night drew on, there was a long sunset beyond the serrated skyline of these extraordinary islands. But as the sun began to rise again cloud cover spread from the east, and the islands were long gone as a grey morning witnessed our fast sailing southward, the seas regular at last with Foroyar far astern and *Witchcraft* eating the miles on a reach. Her luck was holding despite the *Havhestur au Vin*.

Slowly the cloud thinned through that Sunday (13 June) as the effortless

Homeward bound with a fair wind and sunshine ahead, Aidan and Peter (right) with the
Autohelm doing all the work.   *Photo: W. M. Nixon*

progress continued with the Autohelm working sweetly in the rhythm of the
sea. We were in sunshine by the time we found ourselves in the middle of a
NATO exercise. A Norwegian frigate came by rolling so heavily we feared
it might upset his Sunday lunch. Until we saw him, we'd thought the sea
calm after the pinnacle waves of Foroyar. *Witchcraft* closed in towards Rona
across a sparkling sea as the evening forecast warned of frost in northern
Scotland. We could tolerate frost if the wind stayed fair, and though the
brisk east by north breeze meant the landing place on Rona was unusable,
we sailed close inshore around that lonely island for a while, talking to seals
and enjoying the place before sailing on into a sunlit evening of cruising
perfection.

For there came one of those special little times that you remember long
after larger memories have faded. Aidan had set himself up in the galley to
start cooking dinner of silverside beef, baked spuds, cabbage and carrot. I
was on the other side of the companionway ladder writing up the log at the
chart table after getting the forecast. Ed was in the saloon reading a book.
Peter was on watch just outside the companionway while the Autohelm
down aft was doing most of the work. There was a very classy Benny
Goodman tape from Aidan's collection on the cassette player. Our glorious
big boat was thrusting southwards at a speed which promised some Scottish
cruising before we got home. And suddenly, there we all were, pre-supper
drinks in hand having mighty crack around the companionway for one hour?

two hours? who knows? — it doesn't matter, it was just the magic moment of the cruise, and as Aidan said, it was altogether typical of such a good party that everyone should end up in the kitchen.

From here Witchcraft *cruised her way home towards Howth, affording her four epicurean passengers the merest hint of pleasure along the north-west coast of Scotland.*

In fifteen days and nine hours our wondrous red boat had covered 1252 miles at an average speed of 6.3 knots with much splendid sailing, though engine use of 22 percent reflected the peculiar calms of Scotland and the need for an auxiliary close inshore in Foroyar. Of the fourteen places visited, eleven had been new ones, all had been interesting, and some were enchanting. Yet we still had two days to go before it was even Midsummer. It would seem that *Havhestur au Vin* brings good luck.

A JOLLY HAPPY BIRTHDAY

by Michael Richey

Following the singlehanded transatlantic race, *Jester* spent the winter of
1992–3 in Sheila McCurdy's backyard in Middleton which adjoins Newport,
Rhode Island. At the beginning of June I went out to prepare the boat for
the passage back and for the Wooden Boat Show which, sponsored by the
magazine off that name, was being held in Newport towards the end of the
month. There had been some ugly scouring of the mast from an unfendered
hauling parrel shackle which required professional attention and Frank
McCaffery undertook the necessary scarfing in his workshops at Narragansett
Shipwrights. I was able to carry out the remainder of the work myself and
in due course we launched and rigged the boat and carried out a few trials,
adjusting the self-steering gear and so on. Sheila had written an admirable
article about *Jester* for the issue of the magazine that would be published
during the show so that the boat attracted a great deal of attention. When it
was all over I sailed *Jester* back to the small basin belonging to the Museum
of Yachting at Fort Adams which had been her base in America.

I like to be afloat on my birthday which is on 6 July. It seemed a pity,
however, to miss the Independence Day celebrations on the 4th, particularly
as Fort Adams was to be the centre of the festivities at Newport. I therefore
postponed sailing until early on 5 July. The junketings at Fort Adams
included a firework display in preparation for which my fellow berth-holders
cautiously fled the basin whilst I, anxious to get at least some sleep before
sailing, shifted berth upwind of the launching pads and stood by with a water
hose. Things quietened down towards midnight and I turned in for a few
hours. I got up early, but with a northerly blowing found it impossible to
sail off from my berth without help. It was very much the morning after
with no one about. Finally a figure emerged and I was about to approach
him when I realised he was on roller skates. I then gave my old friend Joe
Davis a call and he was over straight away. Joe had been master of the
schooner *Bill of Rights*, another vessel without an engine but about 100ft

68

longer than *Jester*. We warped the boat to a more favourable position and I then sailed off, clearing the basin shortly before 0800. Joe with his inseparable companion Kelly, a labrador, motored down to Brenton Point from where, as I sailed past about an hour later, he hailed me shouting out, "Have a Jolly Happy Birthday Mike", each word distinctly pronounced. "*Les vrais voyageurs sont ceux là qui partent pour partir*" and departure sets the tone for any voyage. I was glad to be seen off by an American who knew the trade.

On the second day out I was buzzed by a US Coast Guard aircraft asking by VHF details of the boat's registry, destination, route and so on. My position may have seemed odd to him for I had gone well south of Nantucket to avoid the fishing vessels on Georges Bank which I so feared in fog. I wondered with some amusement whether my rig had excited his interest, since at about that time a boatload of illegal Chinese immigrants had been intercepted on the coast.

Rod Stephens used to say that he cruised at 80 percent of racing efficiency, and having navigated for Rod in the old days that level of performance would more than satisfy my requirements. But my modest aim nowadays is simply to make each passage as it should be made, irrespective of what anyone else is doing. On this occasion I thought a track south of 40°N until about 50°W and then direct for the Lizard should both keep clear of the fog and reap benefit from the Gulf Stream, although it would inevitably be longer

Jester leaving Newport R.I.

than a more direct northerly route. In the event I found no difficulty in following such a route and had favourable winds for most of the way and few calms. The passage was as a result surprisingly fast.

I lost my sextant with the original *Jester* and borrowed one, a wartime Plath similar to the one I had lost, to sail the transatlantic race with. For the present voyage I had borrowed a brand new sextant by a well-known English maker that was clearly designed to look similar to the Plath. I found it impossible to accommodate myself to it. Indeed I wondered whether it had been intended for use at all with its unwieldy telescope and a box that started to disintegrate almost as soon as we sailed. I had also been given on loan a Trimble Ensign hand-held GPS. It was the first time I had used GPS in the ocean and so convenient did I find it that, having first adjusted the sextant, I put it back in its box where it remained for the rest of the voyage. My practice now became to fix the noonday position by GPS and, once we had turned north, read off the great circle bearing and distance to the Lizard. The great liberation I felt with this simple procedure was not having to keep an accurate account of the direction and distance run between (Sun) sights, which can so easily, although it should not, discourage one from steering courses that are only roughly in the right direction to gain speed. Four AA batteries lasted me practically the entire passage.

I do not listen to weather forecasts in the ocean but tend to treat heavy weather with the greatest respect. South of the Grand Banks we were overtaken by a series of gales which followed each other in quick succession. Two things are generally in my mind. First of all, in anything approaching a full gale in the ocean there is going to be very little that can be usefully done in a 25ft boat beyond ensuring her safety. Secondly, each gale is going

Kelly gives Jester *the once over*

to be slightly different. I would hesitate to tell anyone how to behave in heavy weather but, at any rate with *Jester*'s rig which is so easily handled without going on deck, my preferred course of action at the onset of a gale is to heave-to for a while to see how things develop and what tactics will be appropriate. It sounds a leisurely enough procedure, but perhaps none the worse for that. Under the top panel of sail, with the yard peaked right up by the hauling parrel and the sheet strapped well in, the helm a-lee (or whipstaff a-weather), *Jester* will remain more or less motionless in the water, fore-reaching a little and of course setting down to leeward. I might see the gale out like this, or the worst of it, probably retiring to my bunk from where every movement and every noise can be interpreted. An alternative, of course, is to run before the gale under bare poles as we did on 1 August with a Force 8 westerly, averaging 3 knots for the best part of twelve hours.

I have often thought that the danger of sailing merrily alone into one's dotage is not so much that one might fall overboard or be unable to hoist the sail as that in mid ocean one will suddenly forget where one is going, or something of that sort. This was my tenth singlehanded transatlantic passage and one would have thought that the matter of catering would by now be almost automatic. On this occasion I ran short of food and from about halfway was counting the days down backwards in terms of daily rations. To some extent local difficulties in buying the kind of food I like to eat, by and large not canned, were to blame but I should perhaps have stocked up with tinned iron rations. In the event I ate well enough until the last few days, the very last of which, on 7 August becalmed off the Eddystone, passed in total fast and abstinence. The wine, predictably and as usual, lasted about half way but on this occasion I was rather glad to see it go. I had bought several wine boxes of a Californian red at the astonishing price of $12 for 5 litres. It tasted good enough but like many medicines had unpleasant side-effects.

On 3 August towards mid-day we were on soundings with some 230 miles to go. My plan had been to make a landfall on Bishop Rock and then use the inshore traffic zone of the Scilly Isles traffic separation scheme to the Lizard. On the 5th the Bishop stood proud and as the day dawned the islands themselves became clear. At 0400, just before I turned in for a while, I had reckoned that we could just about lay the Bishop, but the wind was veering northerly and towards 0800 I found myself at the western end of the west-going traffic lane about 1½ miles south of the separation zone.

I was anxious not to lose ground to windward and, short of a drastic alteration to get into the east-going lane, which would cost many sailing hours, the best course seemed to be to try to cross the separation zone into the inshore zone. There was no shipping about but as I attempted to effect this plan a merchant vessel, German so far as I could make out, appeared on my starboard bow coming up the lane. Clearly I should not hinder him and, since hard on the wind I should only just cross ahead of him, I opted for a port-to-port passing and paid off, sailing safely if illegally eastbound in the west-going lane. By the time he had passed I was virtually through the separation scheme. Had my VHF still been working (it had suffered a fall) I would have explained the situation to him. I suspect he reported me, for some hours later a helicopter flew out from the mainland and circled me several times, I imagine taking photographs. I took the precaution when I got ashore of writing an account of what had happened to the Department of Transport, and heard no more.

At 2040 that day the Lizard bore due north, distant 5 miles, and so far as I was concerned the voyage was over. A flat calm descended which lasted until the 7th when at about 1300, having ghosted past Plymouth breakwater with the idea of anchoring in Cawsand Bay, we picked up a local breeze and sailed through the Bridge to the Cattewater where Alec Blagdon, having spotted *Jester* through binoculars, came out in the workboat to meet us and put the boat on a mooring.

EX AFRICA SEMPER ALIQUID NOVI

by Johnny Bourne

Claud Worth suggested that accounts should begin with a brief description of the yacht. Since then yachts have tended to be described by class, but as *Yara* is not what John Power calls a 'Super-Dooper 55' I shall return to that tradition. She is a three-quarter decked gaff yawl, 25ft 5in LOA, 7ft 9in beam, 4ft 9in draught and with no engine. Her stem is straight (at least it is in the plans) and her counter is short. She is carvel planked in pine on grown mulberry frames (battleship size) fastened to a pomegranate keel and — in traditional fashion — floats slightly below her marks. Despite all this tradition she was designed as a dayboat and has fine lines and a moderate displacement. The basic hull was built in 1992 in Damietta, Egypt, to a design by Fabian Bush who most skillfully attached the lead keel, fashioned the spars and provided some internal strengthening over the winter of 1992–93 at Rowhedge. I intended to keep her at Mylor on the River Fal and so had the choice of either transporting her there on a lorry or using the winds that Nature provides. The latter seemed more suitable although I recognised that the cost of marina fees would probably be greater than that of a lorry as work would not permit me to take off sufficient time to make the trip in one. To attempt the voyage early in the season made sense as the chances of a high pressure system were greater and harbours would be emptier.

A few trial sails suggested that there were no major problems, so on 15 May Fabian and I hoisted ourselves and our gear on board in the Pyefleet for the crossing of the Thames. Fabian had nobly agreed to accompany me on the basis that he ought to see how his design fared at sea. He had made a cover for the forward metre of the well and this was to provide our cooking and navigating station as the foc's'le has lying headroom only. Navigation was by chinagraph on a chart inside a plastic cover. Compass, trailing log and leadline were the instruments. The day was sunny but windy with a forecast of south-west Force 5–6 occasionally 7, decreasing. We set off at 1300 under double-reefed main, staysail and jib, and found we could lay our course out of the Colne, passing as we went a sight to gladden all sailors eyes in the form of a smack tearing along in the opposite direction under reduced canvas. We rounded the north of the East Barrow sand at slack tide but with the wind blowing hard so that we had to take in the jib. The wind was on the nose for the Barrow Deep but with the tide under us it was not long before we slid to leeward across the Sunk Sand by the beacon with the lead sounding at 3 metres. In the Black Deep the Force 6 was throwing up the short, steep sea that the estuary is famous for in wind over tide conditions, but *Yara* coped well until a squall forced us to spill the wind as her low freeboard, narrow sidedecks and low coamings failed to keep the water out. We had elected for the South Edinburgh Channel and as soon as we were sufficiently far uptide we lowered the main and reached across under staysail.

The wind then fell so, despite an ominous black cloud to windward, I raised the main again as I feared being swept sideways onto the North Shingles by the tide. Before I had finished coiling the halyards the squall struck and *Yara* heeled to the blast; out went the mainsheet and down came the main and for the first time Fabian and I became anxious as the spray flew round us: Force 7 plus was more than we had bargained for and when we compared notes afterwards neither of us could say whether it had rained or not. We just knew that it had been wet. But it was only a squall and it was not long before we were raising sail again, although bailing the dinghy which had filled with water, followed by lying on my stomach to re-attach the mizzen sheet block to the bumkin, was more than my stomach could cope with. The wind continued to vary in strength but the overall trend was down and Fabian even managed to boil the kettle in one lull, no mean feat as at that stage this involved hugging the Primus to stop it sliding about. After a peaceful final few hours in light winds we slid into Ramsgate at 0200, extremely pleased to have made it but also satisfied that *Yara* had passed a searching test.

The bottom boards may have been hard but, apart from a brief disruption to let another yacht escape, neither owner nor designer stirred early the next day. The forecast was for more strong winds from the south-west and R & R was obviously called for. However time was short and the next leg was a long one, so if we were not on the move by Monday evening we were going to have to retreat to the inner dock. Monday morning was spent fixing a radar reflector to the top of the mizzen and improving the cooking arrangements. The 1350 forecast was south-east Force 5–6 occasionally 7, but as the wind appeared no more than Force 4, Dover and the next forecast beckoned. With the aid of the oar we escaped from the shelter of the harbour walls, and a fair wind and tide pushed us south at seven knots across the ground under all plain sail and a sunny if cold sky. Off the South Foreland a lumpy sea persuaded me to take in a reef, although we then had too little sail as we played the usual dodgems with ferries and hovercraft off Dover. The 1755 forecast was south-east Force 4–5, occasionally 7; since the land forecast referred to thundery showers we assumed the worst would be under them

Yara *becalmed.... 'old ships sail like swans asleep'.*

and therefore shortlived. Dover was not a particularly attractive proposition so we decided to keep going. In the event a sudden squall from west of south with only sufficient warning to take in the mizzen caused a scramble to release sheets that were under water, and a certain amount of sea invaded the bilges before we could take off the jib and tuck in another reef. Even then we had to jill along in somewhat unseamanlike fashion with the main and staysail spilling wind. Fabian had once had to be rescued from a 16ft dinghy which capsized off the Dutch coast in a squall so he had a healthy respect for black clouds, and he insisted quite rightly that in an open boat caution should take precedence. As a result we were pushed inside Dungeness and had a struggle to round it, not helped by the inevitably foul tide. The night was cold and uncomfortable for the off duty watch as it was too rough to get out of one's oilskins and the cuddy made hard lying.

By contrast Tuesday 18 May was beautiful and sunny, oilskins were stripped off and the crew generally made hay. The downside was the light wind from dead ahead — not what gaff yawls like — and the background to this idyll was a view of the South Downs notable for its constancy. By supper we were in Pevensey Bay three miles north-west of the Royal Sovereign and the foul tide had brought progress to a halt. From the chart we appeared to be in about 50 metres so we lowered all sail, bent two warps together and anchored. It was a curious feeling being anchored in such calm solitude but as we ate our supper and watched the sun go down behind Beachy Head below fluffy grey clouds in a watery blue sky we both agreed that we were mighty glad not to have an engine — although there was speculation on how long calms could last. Fortunately after we had washed up supper an air disturbed the water and, as the tide was shortly to be in our favour, we weighed anchor. Once the wind had decided where it was coming from we had a pleasant run close in past Beachy Head and headed down the coast. Our decision to be greedy and go for Brighton rather than Newhaven looked foolish as the wind died on us, but we crept into the marina at 0400 on 19 May with the help of the sweep on the very last of the tide, before packing up and catching the train as a stiff westerly blew white horses against the pier.

For the weekend of 12 June Charles Bird, a work colleague, joined me as crew. Some years ago he had introduced me to the delights of desert cruising in Jordan with a hair-raising drive down a desert track from the heights of the mountains of Moab to the floor of the Dead Sea Valley. This occasion turned out to be less biblical but more uncomfortable as the north-westerly gradually increased (there was a local gale warning but I put this down to Round The Island caution on behalf of the weather men) so that as we approached the Looe Channel at dusk we were down to staysail and single reefed main. Conditions were wet and I could not persuade the Primus to stay alight. Even so Charles maintained that he was enjoying himself, a statement which I felt lacked objectivity.

I chickened out of the Looe in the dark so the early and rather uncomfortable hours found us with a second reef down making no progress up the entrance to the Solent. In the gusts *Yara* had as much canvas as she could take, but life started to look better as the sun came out, the wind decreased, and the Primus did its stuff. We were back to full canvas by No Man's Land Fort and ended up with a lovely Sunday sail up the Solent so that we were tempted by Lymington although the tide was against us. Having crossed to Beaulieu to get out of the worst of it progress became slower and slower until we were stationary. Offices beckoned, pride was swallowed (not difficult) and we cadged a tow which kindly took us into the Lymington Yacht Haven.

A week later (19 June) I returned to *Yara* with the prospect of a full week free. My cousin Richard Bott was to join in Poole, so with the help of the marina launch I set off down the river by myself into a stiff westerly breeze. Once past Jack-in-the-Basket I hove-to, reefed the main, set the staysail and dropped the jib. The tide swept us down past Hurst and into the North Channel where there was a horrible short sea that stopped her completely. Progress was very slow and although the wind was only Force 5 *Yara* was digging her leeward side well into the troughs: it was obvious I was not going to make Poole on the tide. I bore away for the Shingles buoy passing a large blue ketch flying the Club burgee and enjoying the conditions under full sail: rather galling. Morale was low as I anchored behind Hurst, had supper, and retired to the foc'sle feeling peaky.

There is nothing that the sun won't cure, however, and a leisurely start

Johnny at the helm

on a glorious morning put things in perspective. As it turned out, from now on it was downhill. I beat gently across to Poole until abandoned by the wind off the entrance at 1600. Threatening the gods with the sweep did the trick, and I slipped up the channel arriving off Town Quay with the first of the flood in a light north-westerly. Sunday evening was not the best time to choose as the area between the quays was crowded with boats waiting for the bridge and a rather harassed Harbour attendant told me that it was against the byelaws to progress under sail in that area. This was the one harbour where I felt less than welcome. Richard arrived on his motorbike and at 2300 we drifted down the Main Channel with a light ebb under us. Off Swanage the wind veered to the north-west and slowly increased so that we were soon making good progress. By dawn on 21 June the Bill was well astern and the log spinning merrily. A perfectionist would have requested that the scene be a bit less grey, but I was not complaining and nor was Richard. He had brought with him one of those self-inflating air mattresses, and this converted the 'burrow' forward into a feather bed so that it now became a highly desirable spot.

The land came out to meet us at Berry Head and then stopped moving at Dartmouth; indeed it started to retreat again as the ripples vanished. We were several miles off but with the new 100m warp I had purchased in Brighton we kedged successfully and I enjoyed my second deepwater anchorage. Again the timing was perfect for a happy hour and supper spent watching a gentle pink sunset with Berry head as the backdrop, and again the breeze filled in as dusk fell and the tide turned. We were soon scooting past Start Point with the topsail set, although we took it down in the early hours of 22 June. Richard had to get back to the farm so I closed the coast off Rame Head for fear of being becalmed offshore. The Cornish cliffs were at their most spectacular with the sun glinting on wet rock and green pasture; what had at one stage seemed akin to an endurance test had become a sybarite's dream. It was no hardship to be in the open. As we passed Udder Rock at 0830 I woke Richard telling him the world was wonderful and we would soon be at Fowey. At 1200 we were still off the entrance rowing hard. In the meantime the topsail halyard had unrove from the masthead and while I was contemplating what could be done with a bosun's chair Richard stated that he was in need of mountaineering practice and shinned up the mast. Perfect crew. We could make no progress against the ebb running out of the entrance at some strength and were towed in by a kindly yacht. We celebrated with a shower and beer, before lunch at the Lugger. Richard caught a bus and I returned to *Yara* for some horizontal meditation.

After supper a gentle northerly wafted *Yara* to the entrance. Off Gribbin Head a sea breeze set in and blew stiffly out of St Austell Bay, enabling her to put her best foot forward with the dinghy surfing along behind. We were becalmed under the lee of the Dodman, but the breeze came true again out of Veryan Bay. A spectacular red sunset and a crescent moon against a scattering of stars floated above the familiar cliffs and I fell to thinking that in the right weather there was nowhere better in the world. By 2330 we were becalmed off Zone Point, before some fitful gasps propelled us to the mouth of the Helford. I was congratulating myself on recognising the outline of the hills against the night sky when I noticed that someone had taken all the fun out of a night approach by lighting the Gedges, and then as the river slowly opened behind Mawnan Shear my illusions were further shattered by the blaze of light from one of Seacore's drilling barges that lay anchored just inside the mouth with the VHF blaring. For some reason they felt it necessary to produce more light and noise than all the other boats in the Helford combined. Against the ebb *Yara* could barely make way, and recourse to the sweep was needed before at 0230 I could drop anchor off Carwinion in 5 metres.

Another beautiful morning greeted me. *Temptress* (RCC) was anchored off Grebe, friends lunched me on their Twister, and a tan sail well heeled over to seaward proved to be *Squail* (RCC) with the Admiral (as my mother is known in the family) and my uncle James on board returning from a cruise to St Ives and Padstow. They were also engineless so we swapped experiences over supper. The Admiral accompanied me across the Bay the next day and we admired *Temptress*, stiff as a church, as we slowly overhauled her. A walk round Zone Point while waiting for the tide and then we were at journey's end, sailing *Yara* straight onto the foreshore up Mylor Creek, rather to the Admiral's consternation.

ONWARD TO SOUTH EAST ASIA

by Hugh Merewether

This is the third year of Blue Idyl's *progress through the southern hemisphere; for ninety percent of the cruise Hugh was singlehanded.*

January 1992 found *Blue Idyl* at the Royal Yacht Club of Tasmania, Hobart, where balconied Victorian houses and an attractive waterfront afford an aura of historic charm. Though Hobart is well known as the destination of the annual race from Sydney, it is not so widely known as the centre of some wonderfully sheltered cruising grounds. A few of these I sampled, notably Cygnet at the time of a music festival there, and later Port Arthur where the old penal settlement is preserved as a reminder of those dark days when deportation could result from the theft of two sheaves of corn.

From there I day-hopped up the east coast of Tasmania, mostly by motor because of calm conditions, to Lady Barron on Flinders Island, where I had to replace a failed engine water pump bearing. Two days of favourable winds then took me on to Gabo Island, at the south-east corner of Australia. It was here that Sir Francis Chichester's *Gypsy Moth IV* met her unfortunate end.

I was now faced with the uninviting prospect of a 1600 mile slog up the east Australian coast, much of it in the face of adverse seasonal winds and current. By taking my time however and waiting for favourable conditions I eventually managed to get blown most of the way to Townsville over a four month period.

The coastline en route can be tricky as gales, when they occur, tend to blow on shore, and safe havens can be few and far between. Early on I experienced some anxious moments during a fully fledged onshore gale from which I was relieved to gain shelter at the friendly fishing port of Ulladulla on the south New South Wales coast.

I revisited Sydney for five weeks, staying at the CYC Marina in Rushcutters Bay, then Brisbane Water off Broken Bay, some 20 miles north of Sydney. This was to visit a newly discovered second cousin, Alan Lucas, whose well-

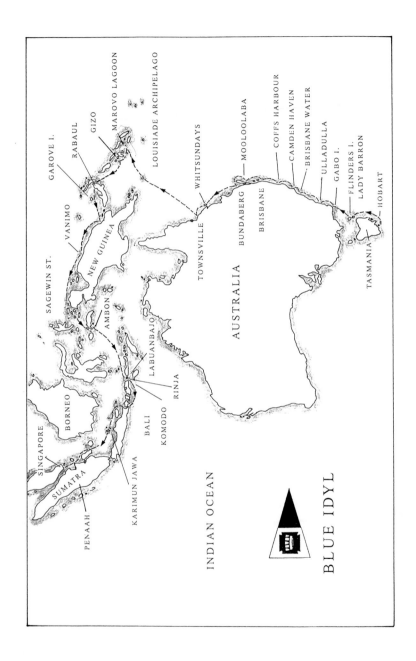

BLUE IDYL

The old convict settlement at Port Arthur

known coastal cruising guides I was using. A visit to Camden Haven followed. It has one of the typical east coast river entrances, across a sand bar which must be taken well into a flood tide to avoid breaking waves even in settled weather. In bad weather such bars become impassable.

Next came Coffs Harbour where I became friendly with an interesting Perth yachtsman who has spent much of his life pursuing and catching great white sharks, principally off Albany, South West Australia, and Mossel Bay, South Africa. He had a bizarre travelling exhibition featuring any number of shark jaws, photos, relics, bitten surf boards and so on: not to mention a freeze dried and somewhat smelly great white itself!

Across the border in Queensland one soon comes to Brisbane (up the river), Mooloolaba (where I hauled out) and Bundaberg: all places where international cruising boats tend to hole up during the tropical hurricane season. Next one comes to a scenic strip of islands, starting with Lady Musgrave, and stretching all the way up to the Whitsundays, a much favoured cruising ground. For this stretch I was joined by Kristina, an American physical fitness fanatic who soon found life aboard a yacht too confining, and Jennifer, a delightfully well adjusted young German who accompanied me to Townsville before resuming her land travels.

From Townsville the westbound cruising boats invariably carry on up to Cape Yorke inside the barrier reef, a long trip restricted to day hops for safety, then west to Darwin. Once again I elected to take a different tack and

headed 660 miles north-east to the little visited Louisiade Archipelago, a
large group of islands inside a 50 mile by 100 mile barrier reef to the south-
east of Papua New Guinea.

Once through a well marked gap in the Australian barrier reef I picked
up a strong wind from south-south-east to south-east which over the next
four days carried me to uninhabited Duchateau Island at the south-west end
of the Louisiade Archipelago. It was wonderful to anchor off a sandy beach
in crystal clear waters once again, after the murk of coastal Australia where
nothing is visible below the surface and eyeball reef dodging is out. Next
day I moved 18 miles north-east to Moturina Island, off a village where my
anchor chain got trapped 65 feet down. Fortunately free diving to this depth
is nothing to the locals, who sorted things out without any trouble and then
saw off a litre of my rum.

To clear Papua New Guinea Customs one has to visit Misima Island, just
outside and to the north of the archipelago. This I did next before returning
to the archipelago a few days later and making my way south-east, with
several overnight stops along the Calvados chain, to Wanim Island, the best
of all. Here a small and friendly group of mainly Australian yachts had
foregathered off a village with a sandy beach and scenic backdrop of green
hills. Thanks to a British Colonial past the locals speak good English. The
whole area is delightfully unspoiled, friendly and law abiding, unlike mainland
Papua New Guinea where the towns can be very tricky. It was in the

Post anchor recovery party

anchorage at Wanim that an Australian boat caught a huge tiger shark, which made me pension off my swimming trunks for a while. Before leaving the Louisiades I made one more stop at Nimoa Island where there is a Roman Catholic mission and a nearby exit through the outer reef.

I was now headed for the New Georgia group of the Solomon Islands, some 360 miles to the east-north-east. The wind, though shifting a bit from side to side, averaged east-south-east Force 3–4 and by staying hard on the wind for four days I just managed to lay my destination. This was the Marovo Lagoon which lies between peripheral islets and central Vangunu Island, to the south-east of New Georgia Island. It is said to be one of the most scenic areas of the Solomons and certainly looked it. My arrival was greeted by a school of sailfish which leaped and splashed with abandon, far from the lures of any fishermen. The lagoon is dotted with many beautiful islets and is the home of some extremely skilled woodcarvers, keen to sell their wares but apt to be a bit pushy. Children, too, of all ages come by in dugout canoes with fruit and vegetables for barter.

I gradually worked my way around the central island of Vangunu before heading north-west for Mburuku Harbour, Rendova Island, and then Ringgi Cove, Kolombangara Island. Both of these harbours are exceptionally well sheltered and the route from one to the other is via a long, narrow and interesting passage between New Georgia Island and one to its west.

From Ringgi Cove it was only a short run west to Gizo, the capital of the West Solomons. Here I joined a party of visiting Australian scuba divers for

Wanim anchorage...

some fascinating diving on various coral walls, a sunken Japanese freighter and a US Navy Hellcat whose aluminium surfaces are still perfectly preserved and growth-free in 30 feet of water. Included in all this was a visit to the island where JF Kennedy took refuge after his patrol boat was cut in half by a Japanese warship during World War II.

It was now mid August and time to head for Indonesia over the top of New Guinea, a route I had committed myself to with some reservation as there have been some nasty incidents along the coast in the past. My first stop was Rabaul, at the north-east tip of New Britain, some 470 miles north-west of Gizo. Getting there took four days, with Force 3–5 winds from abaft the beam. I was pleased to have a recently acquired GPS as my landfall took place in continuous rain with low cloud and minimal visibility, as well as a current in the opposite direction to that predicted. Rabaul is completely landlocked and surrounded by mountains into which the Japanese tunnelled so effectively during the war that they were never dislodged and had to be bypassed. After an agreeable four days of sightseeing I rounded the north-east tip of New Britain and headed west to the partly sunken volcano of Garove Island, some 250 miles distant. A mainly light following wind got me there in four days, to an inside anchorage off Balangori village where some mindless vandals cut my genoa furling line in two. Next day I moved to Widu Harbour at the south-west end of the island and was met by Dicky Doyle, a local character of Australian extraction who took me on a visit to

Marovo Lagoon, Solomon Islands

his nearby plantation. He is said to race outgoing aircraft on his Harley Davidson, at the local airstrip. He told me that a number of yachts had in the past had trouble with some of the locals at my previous anchorage.

From Garove I headed another 230 miles west to Madang on the north coast of Papua New Guinea, assisted for the three day sail by moderate winds from abaft the beam. Though I checked in at Madang itself I had previously been warned not to stay in its harbour overnight and so proceeded to the safe haven of a small resort in Nagada Harbour, 6 miles north. Apart from the resort there is a marine research establishment there and excellent scuba diving lies within easy reach. This strip of coastal water lies inside a long stretch of reef and used to be a favourite haunt for Australian yachtsmen before the youth unemployment cum law-and-order problem got somewhat out of hand in Papua New Guinea.

Ahead lay a long 850 mile, eleven day stretch to the Sagewin Strait at the north-west tip of New Guinea. Light winds came and went, mostly from the port quarter, and there was a slightly beneficial current to help the boat along. I made a brief victualling stop at Vanimo, a quiet port on the Papua New Guinea side of the border with Irian Jaya (the Indonesian half of New Guinea), and stayed mainly in sight of the coast which was mountainous and impressive. Muddy waters from many large rivers discolour the sea in places and floating logs can present a hazard.

Once through the Sagewin Strait, Ambon, my first Indonesian destination, lay 320 miles to the south-west. For the first two days the wind came and went, mostly from the south-east, the third day involved a certain amount of tacking and the fourth day twelve hours of motoring, to an anchorage off Amahusu village, Ambon. Along the coast a notable feature was the first sight of onion-domed mosques glinting in the sun, and blue sailed *praus* heavily laden with families, their goods and their chattels. Indonesia is an extremely friendly place and in Ambon one is forever greeted with cries of 'Hi, Mister' from every hand.

By now the Darwin to Ambon race had been and gone — I was very much the tail end Charlie — and the advent of October meant that it was time to move on. The Dragons of Komono were beckoning from 620 miles to the west-south-west. Indonesia is noted for its light and variable winds so I was lucky to have six days of wind from abaft the port beam, moderate to begin with — then easing to light before eighteen hours of motoring at the end. I checked in at the town of Labuanbajo at the north-west end of Flores Island before moving to a sheltered inlet at Rinja Island between Flores and Komodo. Rinja is the site of a national park from whose hillsides wonderful views of the surrounding area can be obtained. After being shown around by a park ranger next day I moved on to Soro Lia Bay, Komodo, where I caught up with some friends on the only Turkish yacht I have ever seen. Komodo is the home of the 'Dragons', giant and prehistoric looking relations of the lizard family. These can be seen lying in wait for the luckless goats

Madang, Papua New Guinea　　　　　*Nagada harbour, Madang*

that occasionally get slaughtered and then cast into the shallow ravine below a rickety viewing area, from which one is well advised not to topple.

Wanting now to visit Bali, some 300 miles to the west, I took the route south of Sumbawa and Lombok. After about sixteen hours of motoring, light to moderate winds arose from the southern quarter and I sailed for all but the last eight hours, making Bali in four days. Along the Indonesian chain flow strong currents (up to 6 knots), which run up and down between the islands causing dangerous tide rips at times. The harbour at Benoa, near the southern tip of Bali, is well protected by reefs but unexciting and quite a long way from supermarkets and the like.

The southern tip of Bali is overrun by tourists and best avoided. One needs to get upcountry to experience its true magic, which happily still exists. The cultural centre is at Ubud where I spent about four days, taking trips into the surrounding countryside, a mountainous land of temples, villages, lakes and beautiful vistas of rice terraces. Ubud is the home of artists and craftsmen of every description and above all the exotic and wonderful spectacle of Balinese dancing. This is a place one could return to again and again.

On 30 October I left for Singapore, some 1000 miles to the north-west. After some initial motoring to round the southern tip of Bali I set sail in light airs for an overnight passage to the narrow strait between Bali and Java. Fortunately my timing worked out right as the tide gave me a favourable current, peaking at 6 knots, between the islands. My first intended stop was at the island of Karimun Jawa to the north of Java. The 436 miles from Bali took seven days, mostly under sail with light following winds, occasional overcast skies and one heavy shower. Motoring was restricted to the equivalent of about one day. Potential night time hazards are large numbers of fishing boats, but fortunately these are always well lit for the purpose of attracting fish, and so comparatively easily seen and avoided.

Idyllic Bali...

Karimun Jawa is a pleasant and unspoiled island with a large village where I was taken in hand by a friendly young man. He kindly cast my garbage bag onto the beach when given it for disposal, and couldn't see why I had troubled to bring it ashore! Way back in Ambon my engine cooling water intake had been blocked by one of the many plastic bags carried to and fro, like old friends, by the tide. After an overnight stay at Karimun Jawa I set off again for the Baur/Gelasa Strait between Bangka and Billiton Islands. It was another seven day (506 mile) haul to an anchorage off Tanjung Tuing at the north-west end of Bangka Island. To begin with there were three days with a lot of low cloud and rain. Then light following winds gave way to winds that were mainly contrary and I ended up with the equivalent of two days motoring.

From Banka is was an overnight sail — then motor — to the south-east end of Lingga Island. Winds which had earlier been mainly from the east to south-east were now becoming north-west to north and it became more and more a matter of motoring, in order to make night stops at some of the many small islands on the final stage to Singapore. These stops were at the islands of Penaah, Kentar, Mesanak, Karang Besar and Buan in the Riau Strait immediately to the south of Singapore. The pick of these was Penaah Island which is the site of a small, seldom visited fishing village on stilts. Here I was given a royal welcome and supped cross-legged on the floor of the headman's abode. I was shown over two *kelongs* (offshore fishing huts on

Fish drying at a Kelong, Penaah islands

stilts) below which nets are lowered for the catching of what amount to overgrown sardines. One of the *kelongs* was devoted to the culture of a small red fish known locally as Kerapy Sonu, which the locals can sell to Singapore for the incredible price of £14 per kilo, some ten times the going rate for other fish.

The final crossing of the Singapore Strait to Changi was uneventful except for the need to negotiate a way between the multitude of ships which continually pass through this marine crossroads of the world. Thus ended another interesting and enjoyable 7800 miles of wandering that had commenced the year in Tasmania.

THE SWAN'S ROAD

by Wallace Clark

It was, I believe, the *Saga of the Ynglings* that implanted in our family the idea of sailing round Europe.

> *The Earth's Disc has many deep bays and inland seas. We know that a sea goes from the Norva Sound (Gibraltar) all the way to Jorsala (Jerusalem). From this The Black Sea extends far to the northeast. It divides the three parts of the world... North of the Black Sea lies Svithjoth the Cold... In it there are many races, languages, giants and dwarfs; Out of the north, from the mountains ... a river runs through Svithjoth whose correct name is Tanais (a confusion perhaps of the Don and the Volga). Its mouth is in the Black Sea... This river divides the three continents. East of it is Asia, west of it Europe.*
>
> Snorri Sturlusson. 13th Century

My son Milo and I read that Saga together about the time he was starting to sail *Wild Goose* as skipper aged seventeen, perhaps the Viking blood in our veins turned the account into a challenge. The Vikings for centuries crossed Europe by water but always had to make portages. The way through was often opposed — by Bulghars, Mongols, Volga princes or the Tatar Khans. They were the guardians of the watersheds; so the *voloki* or portage points became the bastions of the inner continent. In peacetime, crossing from one headwater to the next involved little more than hard labour. All you had to do was leave a bag of squirrel skins at the local kremlin. The system of tribute was universal.

Aged thirty-two, Milo perceived the possibility of a waterborne passage from the White to the Black Sea for non-Russians for the first time in history. The two essential links were created by Stalin; the White Sea-Volga Canal in 1933 and the Volga-Don in 1952. Since then all foreigners had been barred from all Karelia, not just the canal, and remained barred through the Gorbachov era. But the failed coup in 1991 seemed to open a door. Three

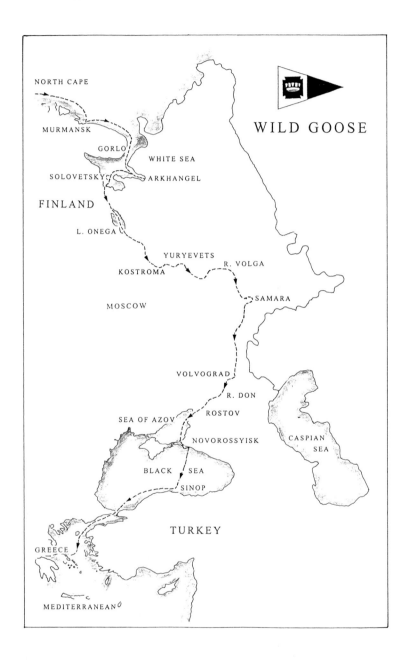

WILD GOOSE

NORTH CAPE

MURMANSK

GORLO

WHITE SEA

SOLOVETSKY

ARKHANGEL

FINLAND

L. ONEGA

YURYEVETS

KOSTROMA

R. VOLGA

MOSCOW

SAMARA

VOLVOGRAD

R. DON

ROSTOV

SEA OF AZOV

NOVOROSSYISK

CASPIAN
SEA

BLACK   SEA

SINOP

TURKEY

GREECE

MEDITERRANEAN

trips to Russia in the winter of 1991/92 were needed to seek KGB and Government approval. With powerful assistance from our other son Bruce, the *Time*'s man in Moscow, Miles met Mr Fixit — Nikita Schparo, President of the Moscow Adventure Club. He'd helped Ran Fiennes towards the Pole and with his guidance the necessary permits were issued. A condition was the fiction that the fifty-eight year old *Wild Goose* would be on charter to the Adventure Club and fly the Russian flag; two members would have to act as skipper and mate and be armed against brigandage. Miles would officially be their guest.

Timing was critical. The White Sea is blocked by ice in an average year up until mid June. Crossing the Black Sea after mid September with less than 18 inches of freeboard is not done in the best circles. That leaves eleven weeks for 3000 miles of ill-charted river, lake and fifty-two locks from the White Sea to Rostov-on-Don; and one week for 500 miles of Black Sea to the Bosphorus. Miles had to be in the White Sea by 15 June.

John Gore-Grimes (RCC), the icicles scarce melted on his beard, lent charts, checked gear and told us "North Cape's a doddle!". We got our old friend Jim McGarry to install a new Sea Panther diesel and, having found every plank and fastening sound, to apply a skin of Cascover nylon sheathing. Stainless tanks gave a 500 mile range under power. We shortened the mast by two feet in the hope that the remaining 45 feet would pass under all bridges en route. Sails from Gowen were the first new ones made for *Wild Goose* in twenty years. These and numerous other modifications and additions were completed in a hectic three months before May 1992.

Rarin' to Go

On 12 May 1991 cousin Stephen Clark, Milo and I sailed direct from a fitting-out berth at Coleraine. It blew Force 7 from astern on the first night when the cabin sole was still two foot deep in unstowed gear.

The biggish following seas proved that the old *Goose* with new gear was dangerously low aft, so we landed the mizzen at Barra to bring her up a vital four inches. Stephen flew home from Stornoway where Bill Spears (RCC) replaced a missing burgee staff with his own from *Aeolian* and filled us with drams. I peeled off from the Shetlands. "It's a big adventure, Dad," said Milo as we parted with some pangs, but I knew I was leaving him prepared as thoroughly as our combined efforts could devise and in the best of company — Justin Smallwood whose three years with the Royal Marines at Harstad had given him a detailed knowledge of the north-west coast of Norway and its inhabitants (male and female). With him came John Hodges, full of laughs and practical help with engine teething troubles. Add husky-handler and Highland galley shipmate Alastair Scott and the crew was A1 throughout.

First landfall was at Ålesund where the local yard helped cure some deck leaks and a bottle of Bush was bartered for tankfuls of diesel. After a dirty night the weather became calm and cold, the coast ever more beautiful as they took the Vikings *Swan's Road* north to Harstad. The Shetland joiners left in turn as RCC 'ice-eaters' Hugh Clay (who had made his name by painting the whole of *Wild Goose* at Easter) and Willy Ker joined at Tromsö and Hammerfest. There a 6 foot packing case, food for four men for three months, awaited collection — shipped from Ireland to minimise reliance on Russian sources.

North Cape hid his head in mist to frustrate photography, but off it Willy caught three fine cod. Barents Sea blows enforced a couple of short stops as the coast declined from Norway's icy mountains to Russia's tundra strand. Dodging a bigger gale for two days in an exposed berth between two islands at Vardo gave a chance to bunker and clear Customs. From there it was only 120 miles to Murmansk. An extract from the log reads:

June 8: Filled up every container with diesel. Slipped at noon with 80 miles to go to Kolskoy Inlet. The weather fine and sea down. At 1500 the Russian coast came in sight.' Later Miles wrote: *There was still something imaginary about the lost grey land which began to emerge from the sea. The sun had descended from yellow into pink before climbing into yellow again without bothering to set. For a time it grew brighter, floodlighting the underwings of a skua. The cold began to lose its grip and then, as though by the flick of a switch, the floodlight was extinguished. The sun was swallowed by a layer of grey cloud and the land took on the same sense of weary hopelessness that I had felt in the winter forest around Moscow.*

At 0730 on 9 June, as Kolskoy opened up, a rusty tender came bouncing

Under the watchful eye of the Russian navy off Murmansk

over the swell and almost rammed *Wild Goose*. She launched a boat, rowed ineptly by conscript sailors with makeshift oars. Six pistol-packing matelots climbed on board *Wild Goose* and took station at bow, stern and midships. The officer took Milo and Willy below to examine charts and log. A cruiser appeared amid clouds of black smoke. Her four escorting gunboats formed a ring while the inquisition went on. Milo protested a little when ordered to enter a bay marked on the chart 'PROHIBITED', with only dots for shore-lines, but it was calmer in there and things proceeded faster when he lent a radio as the Russian's was defunct. At last the officer broke into a smile; "Your peppers are in order. Welcome to Russia. Have a best voyage".

It then took until 2045 to get past rows of anchored warships to the Polar Sea Terminal in Murmansk and be told that harbour dues would be US $300 per day, but vodka supplied behind a shed by a pier policeman steadied the nerves. Later Boris, a smooth shipping agent, helped get the fee halved and drove the crew round the city. Several yachts have come here from Norway in the last two years but before that there were none. It appears that much of the to-do about *Wild Goose* was because her attempts, with no Russian speaker on board, to report progress off the coast had not been understood.

Russians sunbathing along the shore at midday emphasised Murmansk's unique situation in 71°N as the only Eurasian port not ice-bound in winter. This is due to the anti-freeze effect of the North Atlantic Drift pushing warm water round North Cape. The port was created from tundra in 1915, and a Royal Navy base established to ship in military stores. Murmansk was under heavy assault when used similarly again in World War II. With the German army only 30 miles off, 15 million tons of weapons and munitions were brought in.

The next leg was 450 miles to Archangel along a coast where gales are endemic and shelter could only be sought in extreme emergency. But no gale appeared, and since the spring had been relatively mild they didn't see an iceberg or even a teeny-weeny polar bear.

The White Sea

On Friday 12 June at 1700 *Wild Goose* reported to Svyaty Nos ('Sweaty Nose') at the western entrance to The Gorlo or 'The Throat', the 30 mile wide entrance to the White Sea. The prevailing wind blows from the south and floes during the breakup can pile 40 feet high along the shore.

For the run in it was a fine sunny evening and the wind in the west for the first time since Murmansk. A big whale blew alongside. There was a curious visual effect all round with the horizon appearing to unfold and twist like a breaking wave in slow motion. After a period of calm *Wild Goose* was motoring against a headwind once more and anchored during the foul tide which runs up to 7 knots in the lee of Sosnovets Ostrov (Island) to the south-west of the channel. The sea was brown and full of debris with menacing tree trunks and swirling yellowy eddies.

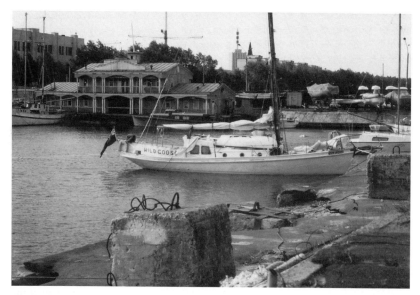

Wild Goose *at Archangelsk Yacht Club*

The log noted: *June 15: Passed outer buoy, Dvina River, 0130. Low scrub covered hills. 0815 — Tied up at the Arkhangelsk Yacht Club. The grey gabled building looks decayed but the welcome has been enthusiastic. Customs slack and underwhelmed. Elsewhere surprising amount of normality. People in short skirts and bikinis rubbing on sun oil and draped on sand just like anywhere else. Everything wooden. Wooden piers, wooden houses, wooden walkways, wooden ships. Sorry to see Hugh off. Vitali Chanksali, Russian interpreter from Omsk, joined looking like a football supporter.*

June 17: Left Arkhangelsk at 2100. 250 miles to Solevetsky. Changed to Russian flag. Heavy rain, leaden skies. Two yachts accompanied us at first, and naval vessel followed astern for twenty miles. Many deadheads and hefty floating logs. Stiff nor'west wind in teeth. Decided await improvement; anchored at 0115 south of big dredger, beside low thickly wooded island. Tide-girt, stern to wind. 0730 — Still blowing hard; decided to take another look. Short uncomfortable seas. Vitali in bunk looking deathly. 2150 — Passed close to huge Russian sub. on surface. Changing weather ahead. 0200 — sky different everywhere; behind us blue with moon rising over sea. We sail in pitch black.

June 19: Beam reach through night, at dawn wind fell. 1220 — anchored in small cove north of Anzer, ten miles long, second largest of Solovetsky Islands. Great feeling of satisfaction at first chance non-urban run ashore. Vitali alarmed by 'Landing Prohibited' notice. No one around so hid sign in bush and walked up to monastery. Row after row of cells, windowless, decayed and haunted, seem to emit a permanent sigh. We had read that frozen bodies of dead prisoners were stacked upright in the nave of the church to save space. In contrast are peeling frescoes to remind of earlier glories.

Here thousands of monks had lived for centuries before the community was wiped out by Stalin. Later political prisoners were imprisoned in the monastic buildings, kept on tiny rations and made to work on the land and at times on the canal. No-one now lives on this island on the excuse that it is a wildlife reserve — the true reason may be that some of worst of all *gulag* atrocities were committed here.

June 20: 20 mile passage SW to reveal magnificent kremlin with cupolas on west side of Solovetsky itself, the largest island. Warm and pleasant; scent of pine off land. Best sailing for days. Clear calls home by Autolink on Skanti SSB set as we anchored in golden light below kremlin. Certainly the most memorable anchorage in my or Wild Goose's life. Somehow seems unbelievable that this link with the past should have survived close to the largest nuclear submarine base in the world.

Up until World War I this was one of the holiest places in all the Russias. Granite walls 30 feet high, a mile long, immensely thick, with towers at the corners 35 feet above the walls, still guard the islands. The pilgrims were housed in temporary wooden guest houses erected outside the wall after being fetched from Archangel and Onega. Luggers manned by monks and later grey steamers flew the monastery flag and a golden cross at the masthead. Then it became one of the most notorious places of banishment off a coast so stark and savage that it could not fail to strike gloom and horror into the souls of those navigating off it. *Wild Goose*'s crew were not unaffected. Today pilgrims are beginning to be allowed access once more.

Into the Waterways

Log: The glass was falling hard at noon as we prepared to leave, the forecast indecipherable. Squalls and heavy rain cut visibility to less than a mile, the wind rose from SW right in our teeth. The GPS, without which it would have been imprudent to set out, brought us 30 miles past a horde of reefs and islets to the outer buoy on the Channel leading WSW to the canal entrance. The last 10 miles between shallows barely buoyed seemed endless. Luckily the wind was far enough on the port bow to give a fetch, or we couldn't have made it in that wind strength. Extreme concentration required at the tiller by Willy, spray splashed but showing no signs of noticing the cold. Twelve icy hours brought us at last to the lee side of a long wooden pier at the canal entrance.

The journey now ahead through Russia consisted of six sections, amounting to a total of 2122 miles.

The White Sea Canal

(Built 1931–33. Maximum height 335 feet, nineteen locks, 150 miles.)

The first and least travelled leg was the White Sea Canal. This link was dreamed of by Peter The Great, and built by Stalin 1931 to 1933, by hand labour only, at a cost of from forty to 100,000 lives.

In the late '20s Stalin managed to sell to the Russian populace the myth that forced labour was a matter of honour, glory, and heroism. Work on the canal was reported in newspapers, and in a disinformation book *The White Sea Canal* (English edition by Anabel Williams-Ellis, Bodley Head), to have reformed hardened criminals as they marched out joyfully to cut paths through forests (there were no roads), build camps, dig channels in frozen peat, dam rivers, inundate villages and blast rocks. The results of their efforts is 50 miles through canalised lakes, 60 through flooded rivers and 30 through artificial canals. The casualty rate was enormous even by the standards of Russian forced labour schemes. When told of it, Stalin's comment was that men were mortal while the canal would be there forever.

At 0600 as rain drummed on the deck voices were heard alongside. Nikita Schparo, son of the president of the Adventure Club, had arrived to assist yet another crew change — the sixth — Nikolai Litou came to join as skipper. Willy was told he had fifteen minutes to pack up his kit to make use of a scarce pre-booked seat on a train to Moscow. He made it riding to town on a timber crane and was off to Antarctica not long after!

Nikolai, aged thirty-eight with film star good looks, soon showed himself an energetic and capable amateur yachtsman. As the crew soon learned Nikolai stood out among Russians as a model of common sense, affability and quiet competence, with a pleasing twinkle in the eye. He acted as Master, helped with pilotage and made the arrangements at locks and other stopping places, while Miles decided when and where to go. They got on well. As Nikolai said, "Between myself and Miles there was a calm, good-hearted relationship. I'm not a great expert on language, but we could communicate with a single word whenever it was anything to do with the boat. Miles used to laugh at the peculiarities of Russian speech. Perhaps English has peculiarities as well, I don't know. Anyway when an old crock of a boat would come up to us and ask: 'Where are you from and where are you going?' I would say 'Belovo Na Chornoye'. Miles would ask whether they had understood, and I would reply: 'What's so difficult?' I am saying 'From the White to the Black!'".

The radio on the first lock was defunct and raw hands had to move ship in a vicious onshore wind to an un-warned lock crew. By 1130 *Wild Goose* was berthed beside a rusty tug at the Inspector's dock. It took the remainder of that day, 23 June, and all the next one to complete formalities. This was the 'Secret Canal' — no-one must query or look sideways. Petty officialdom demanded lengthy inspections, treating *Wild Goose* as a big merchantman. The Fire Authorities demanded hoses and pumps, the Health Authorities to see a sealed sewage system. Nikolai and Vitali sweet-talked them all, payed a nominal fine of 20 roubles (about tuppence) to the firemen and assured the sanitation squad that the crew would always squat on the bank. (Milo, very much of a green man, did so).

June 25 saw the first of many early starts with a bridge booked to open at 0730. It really did too, only an hour late. And then a second bridge lifted, and beyond it the channel led through endless birch forests.

L to r: Vitali, Miles and Nikolai   *Photo: James Blair, © National Geographic*

Seeking an anchorage in a cove at the south end of Shavan lake the *Goose* ran onto a bottom hard enough to lift her bow high out of water. The crew shifted weights aft and into the dinghy (which was towed astern for the inland passage) After much hard work on a cold grey day in water below 40°F and clouds of killer insects they managed to winch her off. Gain for the day had been a respectable 50 miles. There was little incentive to go ashore in the beautiful but untouchable forests.

June 26 involved climbing slowly up locks made entirely of wood and operated as all on this canal by ladies — only 15 miles made good. The anchorage that night was just short of Lock 11, a magnificent piece of engineering cut out of granite, at the north end of Lake Vyg, the largest lake in the canal. On the shore was the village of Nadvitsky, one of few to be seen as most had had been drowned by the damming of rivers to raise water levels.

Lock 9, 150 metres long, was equally impressive but in poor condition, a rocky canyon with splinters of ancient wooden piles and rusty spikes protruding from the sides. Three quarters of the length was filled by Volt-Balt 181, looking more rust than ship. Her 13 metre beam gave only ½ metre to spare on either side. As *Wild Goose* tucked under her stern her engines running ahead made eddies so powerful that if Milo's crew had lost control for a moment and let a gunwhale get jammed under one of the many projections the consequences would have been horrific. The lock filled with extraordinary speed.

A stop at Himpeski Island halfway along Lake Vygon on 27 June extended to twenty-four hours, so fascinating were the yarns of a couple of islanders who had survived there childless for thirty years. Aleksey and Nastasia lived in one of a dozen tumbledown log cabins, chinked with moss, set in a meadow of buttercups and cowslips. They fished for a living, by rod in summer and with special tube nets when the lake froze over metres thick for five months in winter. The worst time of year was summer because of the extraordinary ferocity of Arctic mosquitoes. But in general things had not changed much since 1960. The only thing Aleksey wanted was insect repellent so Milo gave him a bottle. "How did it do?", he was asked in the morning. "Harroch!", he said, "but a bit strong. Vodka is better". He'd drunk it!

June 28. The afternoon was passed at Stara Kalikina labour camp. 2000 prisoners were held here up until 1977. A row of punishment cells stood dark, tiny and horrific with relics like a mug under a bed, scraps of clothing and calendar on the back of the door. This part of the canal had cost one life per metre of progress.

Anchored that evening above Lock 7 to endure a cold night, rendered sleepless by the whine of mozzies outside face nets. At Povonets, nestling among low coastal scrub where the canal ended, there was a visit from the President of the White Sea Canal Company, "You are indeed the first foreign vessel to pass through", he said. "Twelve ships a day once used to come by but now not more than three". Submarines made the passage during the War until the canal was bombed and put out of action for months.

Lake Onega

(1500 islands, 150 miles.)

Having collected the inevitable lapel badges, the crew made sail in late afternoon on the dark green waters of Europe's second largest lake. '*A wonderful middle watch*' Milo noted. '*A clear sun at dawn flashed off the golden domes of Kizhi island's churches.*'

Kizhi, whose name translates as the 'isle of games', was an important station on early trade routes, and later a defence post against Sweden. The Transfiguration Church, 120 feet high with three tiers and twenty-two cupolas, compares with St Basil's Cathedral in Moscow.

In the afternoon an intricate passage through a few of the lake's 1500 mostly wafer-thin islands to the shabby docks of Pretrozavodsk. This city has many traces of its former Finnish status. Jim took a room ashore. With four up, and his mass of gear, the boat was overcrowded as never before. The Russians slept in the forepeak, firearms by their side, Milo and Jim aft; the narrow saloon floor was piled high with photographic boxes leaving hardly room to walk fore and aft, let alone set up a table. Meals, all cooked by Milo as the Russians couldn't understand the labels on packets, were eaten off knees.

Leaving in blustery weather, Milo had a worrying night in steep 6 foot waves of brown water. As the wind rose he decided to shelter in a bay called Rog Ruchay (Horn Stream). When leaving at midday *Wild Goose* grounded on the gable of a sunken house. It took most of the day and help from a fishing boat to get off.

The Volga-Baltic Canal

(Completed 1964 as an improvement on 18th century Marinsk. Length (Onega to Cherepovets) 229 miles, seven automatic locks, ships up to 5000 tons.)

To make up for lost time Miles worked out a 24 hour, 100 mile passage over the Vytegra river bar and and through the seven modern automated locks of the Baltic-Volga Canal and to Lake Beloye. The weather was very cold, 10°–11°C with a big chill factor and the traffic alarming with three or four ships sharing the vast locks. Orders came impersonally from high control towers. Gates slid up alarmingly from lock floors. The landscape was now much more cultivated with long meadows, unsettlingly English-looking at times, Douglas fir growing out of red devonian type soil. Lock 6 took them to the highest level of the voyage having climbed 280 feet during the day.

July 5: 0015 — Motored on in dark as we saw nowhere suitable to bring up. Hard on the go for 24 hours, through seven locks. Pick down off small island north-east corner of Lake Byelo. Barometer falling and winds very strong. Anchor watch. Big fry-up to keep Russian bear from the door and decided to stay until weather improved.

July 6: 0800 — Blue sky but still blowing hard. 0900 — set reefed main, jib and staysail. Straight down into Sheksna River. Temperature 11°C. Rain squalls and never more than 4 metres under our keel. 1300 — passed Krokino sabor (Orthodox church) in 60°N. We last passed this on 19 May in Shetland. Each lake brings you south into a new world; now copses, houses better built. Some degree of pride in gardens, vegetables growing in strong soil, handsome barns and outbuildings in neat rows, a bit like Canada. Passed Goritsky monastery in ornate red brick.

And so they came to the great Maloga Triangle, a 60 mile long reservoir at the confluence of several rivers, covering the city of Maloga with only spires and cupolas showing and endless villages. At the end of that they came to Cherepovets — '*Much like the deadeningly similar Soviet cities I had imagined.*'

The Middle and Lower Volga

(Once a river, now a series of reservoirs: Ivanko, Uglich, Rybinsk, Gorky, Cheboksary, Samara, Volvograd. Eleven locks, 1200 miles.)

On 9 July they saw a yacht, the second only since Belomorsk. Then at midnight came arrival in the Volga, ('*What a terrible name for a river,*') and celebrated with Black Bush.

July 10: Motored to Tutyaev, one of the loveliest evenings afloat I ever remember. Cupola-topped sobors all round. Vigour of nature and consumption of churches. Nuns came to paddle in the river. Wooden izbas (decorative peasant huts) on river bank.

Yaroslavl, the nearest point to Moscow, reached on Sunday 12 July was memorable for a moonlight meeting with one familiar and welcome sight — brother Bruce came laden with edible luxuries, encouragement and news from home. His fluent Russian broke down many barriers as he travelled on with them for twenty-four hours, all he could spare from the demands of journalism. There were endless sunbathers and colourful crowds on park-like river banks by the famous Tolga nunnery where Mother Barbara showed off her 120 nuns, grown from ten a few years ago.

At Kostroma a baking hot day was spent in trying to cure an expensive sound in the engine. It was traced at last to bad diesel and minimised by keeping revs down to under a thousand. At Plyoss were holiday camps, sanitoria, and on the river pedalos and swimmers with motorboats dangerously speeding among them.

July 18 at Yuryevets was marked by another meeting. *Sailed all day in a featureless wall of grey, then saw big white sails on horizon. A 40ft schooner, Betelgese, beat up alongside. "We are private yacht. We have good meat and French wine. Please come on board".* She had been locally built ten years earlier. Captain Vadim Romanov of Tsarist descent was an excellent host and full of advice on every subject.

At Gorodets, Arkadi Gershuni, forty, arrived to take over as skipper from his friend Nikolai. He also combined a good state-sector job in the Moscow area with a strong interest in sailing.

July 23, Nizhni Novgorod: Visit of Director of Okay River Yacht Club with present of traditional Russian shoes woven from reeds. Water filthy. Paint all blistered along water line. Engine sounding rough but keeps driving well. Passed three ski jumps. Six days now to Kazan and then we will be heading south. Rain all morning.

July 23, Makarief: Sick fish basking on surface. Brought Wild Goose alongside meteor ferry in an extraodinary manoeuvre after much miming and drawing of diagrams by Russian skipper. Lovely sunny morning. Some organised forestry for first time and tended meadows. Still no visible pollution. Have not seen a single piece of litter in 800 miles other than around towns. Visit convent. Nuns' cells, 18th century hospital, witches hat towers. Conversations ashore. "There is no comparison between the Volga in my young days and now, it used to be fast flowing forty-five days from source to the sea. Now it is stagnant. It used to clean itself and used to flush out and thaw lakes on either side, now they remain stagnant". We returned laden with fruit we had been given.
2200 — anchored in a strange place off an island near Fukino after deciding against anchoring off the north side where girt by the current. Dinghy banging, swarms of white flies. Our chain was covered in tiny snails as we got the anchor. Expedition ashore in dinghy, first to swamps and then through drowned forests and then to a dam wall. Once it was very rich grazing but now poor and in time will get worse.
1200 — the beginning of ten miles of flooded trees on either hand — called The Floating Forest. 1340 — at the confluence with the Sura river near Vasil Yursk.

Steep hill with houses looking out from among trees. Beautiful day with fresh ENE *wind. Passed a cruise ship at 1400 at the village of Soomka, not mentioned on chart, seemed dead. Passed Yurino behind its wall.*

July 26: At Cheboksary. Water from spring. Very modern lock with sliding tower and thousands of tons of concrete. Jim and I went into control room. Lock is in size like two football pitches 300 x 30 x 10 metres deep. Empties 90,000 cubic metres of water in six minutes. When we got away had lovely sailing at nearly 5 knots. Never tire of looking at right bank, now cliffs. Left bank is low sandy islands. In the evening on the right bank the sunlight lights the tops of the trees on the hills leaving the land falling away to the river in shadows in folds of light and dark, quite different where the river turns south you get this lovely play of light and shadow. This is exactly the half way point between Belomorsk and Rostov. Vodka and Bushmills to celebrate.

The great confluence where the Kama joins the Volga and the combined rivers are 20 miles wide came up on the last day of July.

Samara, where the river takes a dramatic panhandle eastwards round a spur of hills, gave *Wild Goose* her outward point — 50°10'5E on 7 August. A boatman gave a present of a Soviet style sledge hammer and a case of Vodka. Like a Scots friend of mine he thought, 'a bottle doesn't go far amongst one!'

The view from up on the neck of the bend was *One of the most memorable of the whole voyage — a deserted Tolstoyesque landscape, with only eagles, sparrowhawks and magpies for company, and a view of the Volga spread out below, 8 kilometres wide in places.* The Volga, which had appeared clean in its upper reaches, became fouler with every city passed and shoals of filthy scum as thick as paint were not uncommon.

At Volgograd (ex-Stalingrad) Jim Blair departed. Now came came the twisting ascent over hills in the Volga-Don canal.

The Volga-Don Canal

(Built 1948–52. Rise of 289 feet from the Volga, then descent 144 feet to the Don. Fifteen locks, 63 miles.)

By 12 August *Wild Goose* rode at sea level below Volsk; gulls became commoner and meals duller as the Hammerfest case ran low and attempts had to be made to shop every other day. The mast had been kept up all the way, but not without some worry. Some bridges had looked within inches of the masthead light.

A stop at Saratov, *revealed a city with a real heart, interesting architecture and wonderful Art Galleries.* A young surgeon friend of Bruce's took Miles home to his flat and arranged several visits including one to a nuclear power plant.

Arkadi commented on the Don water: *In the Saratov reservoir, the water was blooming with algae, a thick, bright verdure, opaque, and out of that vegetation there were some fungi growing, a blue mustiness, an absolute swamp. When you anchored there, there was continuously a dream in Miles' head to get quickly to the island of*

Syros, to put out the anchor and see how the anchor chain lies on the bottom, on sand, in clear sea. That was the dream, because this water was not for a seagoing yacht. The reservoirs sometimes leave a very dispiriting impression, air heavy with rotting seaweed presses down on you, especially when the wind drives it to the shore, our anchorage was between about 20 metres from the shore and there was a terrible smell.

The River Don to Rostov

(330 miles.)

August 29: Thalassa, Thalassa! Rostov on schedule. The city offered shopping for food on a scale un-heard of further north. "I am very exciting", said Arkady, as a taste of salt water marked his first sea voyage; but his initiation was not to be gentle. A fair gale drove the old *Goose*, rolling her side decks in, across the shallow Sea of Azov. In the Kerchensky Strait dolphins a-leap welcomed her to the Black Sea and her natural element.

On 3 September Novorossyisk, a big commercial harbour in a deep bay under mountains, saw yet another crew change, the eighth. A call here was compulsory to clear out of Russia. Officials were effusive. It was sad to say goodbye to splendid Russian shipmates but good to welcome Molly Ronan from Cork and Calum Graham from Rhodesia.

* * *

A blow halfway across the Black Sea compelled heaving-to under trysail, then making an unscheduled stop in Sinop on the Turkish coast. Four days later I sighted the *Goose*'s distinctive raked wooden mast as I drove down a spiral track to a tiny concrete harbour called Roumeli Ferrari at the north west end of the Bosphorus. Miles had picked it for an rendezvous as he had been there in the *Argo* with Tim Severin. To celebrate, Molly produced the best scrambled egg for breakfast that I've ever eaten, and Calum helped wash it down with Pusser's rum.

Wild Goose with white deck and topsides over blue boot-top looked her smartest, unscarred by the journey. The Russian crew had looked after her well. Milo was in the effervescent form of a man just out of prison; due to his extraordinarily thorough preparations and remarkable diplomacy en route there had been no major mishap or delay. Perhaps the strain placed on him in keeping up the momentum as skipper of different Russian crews of limited English and varying temperament and an elderly American journalist had been more severe than any of us realised.

A happy ship we were in September '92 as we dodged traffic between the bonnie banks of the Bosphorus and arrived at Karima Marina at the south end of the Anatolian side. Apart from a kiss on both cheeks for Miles by the Minister of Sport as he presented a plaque the visit was uneventful.

So by the Dardanelles to Syros in the Cyclades where Dick Musgrave had offered us his matchless clifftop House of the Winds in which to rejoin Sarah and June. We left our ship ashore at the island's capital in the yard of Stavros. There she well survived the heat and dust of winter.

Milo had some fits of worry and depression during the winter, totally unlike his usually creative jocular self. But this seemed to be over when he and I arrived in March '93 and spent a 'paint-till-you-faint' week getting ready for sea. He went home to write. I stayed on.

Then came the sudden heartbreaking sadness of a sort not usually related in these pages but it is part of, and happened because of, the voyage. We received in Evvia the news that Milo had been 'called by the gods' — departed this life, as the delayed action result, I am convinced, of a chemical infection picked up in the White Sea or Volga.

June and I, with help at different points from brother-in-law John Deane, from old shipmates John Fishbourne, Richard Butler, Lewis Purser and Colin Gall, sailed *Wild Goose* homewards. That was just as Milo would have wished and *Wild Goose* made us enjoy it in spite of his absence. We left her at Povoa de Varzim, a fishing harbour 15 miles north of Oporto and a suitable place to lay up.

A summary of distances, anchorages and place names in the Russian waterways can be found in the Club library. Members may also like to note that an illustrated account of the voyage will appear in the June 1994 issue of the National Geographic Magazine.

THE MATERNITY CRUISE

by Charles Nodder

People kept telling us that the birth of our first daughter would change our lives. For a time it did; we took an unprecedented three months off work and went sailing. The idea of a 'maternity cruise' had evolved some years before, and inasmuch as these things can be organised, Suzanna's arrival was timed to allow Elizabeth to take her maternity leave *post partum* in the early summer months of 1993. I persuaded The Game Conservancy Trust to give me twelve weeks leave of absence and so at last we had an extended period in which to go to sea.

A cruise round Great Britain had always appealed, and had the added advantage that if sailing with a new-born baby in a 27ft yacht proved quite unbearable, the voyage could be abandoned at almost any stage without undue complications. *Acorn* was fitted out with appropriate care, although the final coat of varnish was never finished owing to urgent business at Odstock Hospital. We eventually left Christchurch on 1 May with 154 charts (mostly RCC), a forepeak full of nappies, two sets of earplugs and sundry toys. Suzanna was thirty-three days old.

My decision to go anti-clockwise was based on arriving off the north coast of Ireland late enough in the cruise to go inside or out depending on weather and the time remaining. Beyond that we had no plans other than to maintain a modest average of 25 miles a day. We wanted to see as much of our native coastline as we could and we hoped that *Acorn*'s shoal draught and ability to dry upright on her triple keels would allow us to visit parts which others cannot reach. The roller jib and Autohelm would compensate for the light crew. We also carried Decca, although my intention was to navigate principally by dead reckoning and eyeball.

We spent our first two nights rolling gently at anchor off the south coast in pleasant northerlies. The baby wasn't seasick, which was encouraging. Straightforward weather shore anchorages such as these had the advantage that one of us could anchor or get away singlehanded if the other was preoccupied with 'domestic duties'.

Further up Channel stronger winds veering on to the bow encouraged us into the narrow river at Rye. Here we found excellent new facilities two miles inland alongside the pretty but drying Town Quay. At Dover we rode out a near gale in the outer harbour, only to be pinned in Ramsgate for four days while a strong north-easterly bored into the Thames *Estuary*. *Acorn*'s 27 feet became rapidly more claustrophobic as the rain beat down on the coachroof and I ruefully recalled the words of those who had said we were going the wrong way round. Eventually we escaped for a magical night sail across the swatchways to the River Deben, full of birdlife, and thence to bustling Lowestoft.

Acorn's ability to windward is pretty desultory, and when the fuel pump failed as we left Lowestoft we faced a long beat to the next safe haven. Elizabeth was feeding Suzanna one hour in every three. When she wasn't, each time we tacked one of us had to check that the baby hadn't rolled onto her face and suffocated. After thirty hours we copped out and sneaked across the shipping in the Humber mouth to anchor behind Spurn Head for a rest. Eight hours later a backing wind made the anchorage uncomfortable, but once clear we could free the sheets for the first time in eleven days, and reach away up the Yorkshire coast into unknown territory.

Off Whitby at dawn the next day I made a bad mistake. We were all tired, so I tried to beat into the harbour despite an old onshore swell still rolling in off the North Sea. What we didn't know was that overnight rain inland had caused the River Esk to spate. Swell met spate-water in the narrow harbour mouth and the sea was on the boil. Fortunately, a departing trawler warned us of this before it was too late. Brought to our senses, we retreated to anchor off, and *Acorn* was ignominiously towed into her Port of Registry by another fishing boat on the next tide.

The engine was quickly repaired and we found Whitby a hugely enjoyable place; an unusually successful blend of working port, seaside resort and historic town. Our plan was to make good speed up the east coast, however, so we pressed on.

Overnight stops within the entrances to the Tees (industrial) and the Tyne (imperial) took us on to a delightful anchorage among the seabirds of the Farne Islands. At Holy Island we dried out under Lindisfarne Castle in the Ouse, rather than contend with the very strong tides of the deep water anchorage. The fly of our burgee had all but disintegrated, and after a grave discussion we sacrificed our old red ensign so Elizabeth could fashion a new one.

We were now to enter the realms of deep granite fish docks whose slimy ladders provided an obstacle course for Elizabeth, with Suzanna precariously suspended in a sling on her front. Being thus encumbered proved a boon, however, when it came to persuading dour east coast hoteliers to allow us baths. The baby was a talking point, and we made many friends among

Elizabeth giving Suzanna her check up

harbourmasters, fishermen and other cruising yachtsmen, most of whom humoured us with the sort of helpful tolerance normally reserved for the faintly mad.

Our relatively undemanding sailing schedule left us plenty of time for shore leave. Some of this was inevitably spent watching nappies going round in the washing machines of Britain's coastal launderettes, but there were many trips to see more edifying aspects of our maritime heritage. Berwick-upon-Tweed and St Andrews were especially worth visiting and we also thoroughly enjoyed threading the shoals into the River Ythan just north of Aberdeen (best water in 1993 well north of the old leading line, the wreck against the small shelter on the beach).

In Fraserburgh Suzanna had her eight-week check and injections, while I 'phoned the Met Office to see whether we were going to go round the top or through the Caledonian Canal. The man at Bracknell was surprised to hear from a yachtsman; it seems that these days this personal service is reserved for ships. Nonetheless we had a useful chat and with nothing ugly brewing I elected to head for Wick and the Orkneys.

Despite the benign forecast I was anxious about the Pentland Firth and reading descriptions by Macmullen and Belloc did nothing to reassure me. As so often happens, though, when the time came all was well. We had a gentle wind and a flat sea with a mere knot of cross-tide and only the odd tell-tale swirl to remind us of anything more unpleasant. Elizabeth made new cushion covers and the baby slept peacefully as we sailed across.

Lush Orkney, with its red sandstones and abundant birdlife was delightful. We particularly liked Stromness, our most northerly anchorage; its winding main street was filled with the music of the Orkney Folk Festival. We tore ourselves away, however, to take a fair north-easterly to gloomy Loch Eriboll, where we anchored next day in pouring rain behind the peculiarly symmetrical Ard Neckie peninsula. Elizabeth was shivering from the onset of mastitis and unusually the baby was wailing. It was our fifth wedding anniversary!

Having a GP among the crew is a distinct advantage when you are faced with a medical problem fifty miles from the nearest doctor's surgery. Elizabeth sorted herself out within twenty-four hours, and the rain even cleared enough for me to exercise the trout rod. We left Eriboll in excellent spirits on 1 June, one month into our cruise.

Round Cape Wrath we found the coast we had been dreaming of but never sailed. Dream weather too, as the sun shone for a fortnight on distant mountain tops and fresh blown billows. With detailed charts and the excellent pilotage provided by the Clyde Cruising Club, we explored the remote sea lochs of the far north. Without the need to hurry on, we sailed only by day, often finding that a few hours with a fair tide would give us a respectable run. Even in this short time, though, the wind could change dramatically. Sailing south from Lochinver we reefed *Acorn* deeper than ever before, only to restore full canvas by sunset. It was active, enjoyable and scenically splendid.

Loch Kanaird, next to the main road just north of Ullapool, provided an excellent anchorage in preference to the dubious shelter of adjacent Loch Broom. It was here, by arrangement, that we met friends on holiday from the south, bearing a replacement for the contact lens I had lost in the Moray Firth. While the girls gossiped, Frederick Graham-Watson and I sprinted up Stac Polly, for the clearest view I have ever known in the Highlands.

And so the islands; the Summer Isles, Raasay and Skye, all abounding in excellent anchorages but cursed with increasingly prevalent fish farms. On Soay, below the Cuillins, we revelled in the solitude of North Haven, entered over a drying boulder bar with the best water indicated by two tiny white posts on the shore. A mile away on the south side of the island a dozen families manage to eke out a living.

On Muck, to my delight, we not only heard a corncrake, but were able to tell friends about it by means of a Button A, Button B, public telephone. Old 10 pence pieces were provided by Stella Stephen, who also cooks excellent meals for visitors (telephone in advance, 0687 2363). Thence to Tobermory for stores, before cruising the west side of Mull. In the northern end of the gut between Gometra and Ulva we found our own idyllic anchorage (shoal, but with water clear enough to see the underwater rocks). This wonderful haven was surrounded by seals and red deer, while merlins darted overhead. Fingal's Cave and Iona lived up to expectations but had the tourists to

Acorn among the trawlers in Ilfracombe

Anchored between Gometra and Ulva on the west side of Mull

match, while Colonsay was both quiet and attractive. Here *Acorn* dried out in the tiny harbour at Scalasaig as we examined the next folio of charts to plan our route south. It was a tricky decision and it took nearly two bottles of wine, but eventually we elected to carry on at a dignified pace down the Irish Sea, rather than scamper round Ireland's west coast.

Next day the fastest tidal set of our cruise swirled us down the Sound of Islay to Aros Bay, where bizarrely there is no tidal range at all. The day after it was the 'Sound of Bukh' which dominated as we chugged past the Mull of Kintyre in a calm. This was another day of wonderful visibility, with Malin Head away to the west and Ailsa Craig on the eastern horizon. While the Autohelm did the work, I read last year's far-flung *Roving Commissions*, in contrast to which our family voyage in well-charted seas felt very parochial. Yet the green glens of Antrim on an evening of sunshine and showers would challenge many a coastline, and we ended the day with a brisk reach into Larne of the sort which makes one revel in the quality of British home waters.

In Carrickfergus we borrowed a detailed chart of Strangford Lough, a unique and wonderful stretch of water, full of interesting pilotage and friendly watering holes. Our favourite anchorage within it was Audley's Roads, below the Gothic facade of Castle Ward. The First Earl and his wife could not agree on a style and the farther side of this building is neo-classical. In contrast to their disputes, our own life on board was proving remarkably harmonious, despite our occasionally wailing crew and the general lack of space.

From Ulster we sailed to the Isle of Man and from there to north Wales. Conwy is rather off the usual cruising route through the Irish Sea, but well rewards a visit as you can moor afloat right up under Edward I's castle. At Beaumaris, the Royal Anglesey YC got our award for the friendliest we encountered, while the Menai Straits themselves provided an interesting sail down to another wonderful anchorage just inside the shingle spit at Abermenai. Crossing the Carmarthen Bar the following morning we found ourselves surrounded by dolphins playing at who could get closest to our bow. Porpoises, too, were abundant all the way down the Welsh coast.

Taking advantage of a settled easterly, we cruised deep into Cardigan Bay, closing Aberystwyth at lunchtime on 30 June. Following the advice in *Macmillans*, we waited for half flood. Nonetheless the seas over the bar seemed surprisingly short, so I asked Elizabeth to turn on the echo-sounder. "Don't look!" she said, and at that moment we surged round the pierhead to see most of the fishing boats in the harbour still dried out. High water entry is recommended!

Fishguard next, and then some intriguing sailing among the sounds and islands off Pembrokeshire. Skomer — a nature reserve — was superb and we rowed ashore through water so thick with puffins that they opened up before us and closed in again behind like crowds around a police horse. Why this coast doesn't attract more yachts is a mystery. We enjoyed it so much that it lured us well into the Bristol Channel. Here we paid the penalty, being trapped in Ilfracombe for four days by strong north-westerlies, which made the north coasts of Devon and Cornwall an unattractive prospect. In the end we had to abandon thoughts of Bideford and Padstow to sail well-reefed past their foaming entrances and straight on to the Scilly Islands.

The following week, with the sun shining and Lands End behind us, an end of term feeling began to pervade the boat. An increasingly social time was had with various friends as we dawdled in the Helford, the Fal and the

Anchor below the Cuillin in Soay's North Haven

Yealm. We then made our way up Channel with a good old fashioned south-westerly, pausing for a night in St Mary's Bay, just south of Brixham, before creaming across Lyme Bay with twin genoas and no oilies. We finally re-entered Christchurch a day ahead of schedule on 22 July after 83 days away. For the statistically minded, we had sailed 2031 nautical miles, visited 28 different harbours and 45 splendidly varied anchorages. Hours under way totalled 513 of which the engine ran for 138.

Cruising with a baby had proved remarkably easy and the principal factor which made it so was having plenty of time; to pick our weather, to catch up on the inevitable lost sleep, and to 'recharge the batteries' by enjoying the places we visited. In addition to time, the other key requirements were a deep, narrow sea berth for the baby, a decent carrying sling, and an unflappable mother. Given all of these, I would recommend a maternity cruise as the perfect introduction to parenthood.

A LOST CORNER OF THE CARIBBEAN

by John Woodhouse

John and Val Woodhouse are in the process of a two year circumnavigation aboard Caraway GB, *their 43ft GibSea 126 sloop. This section focuses on the San Blas islands of Panama.*

Curaçao, West Caribbean. We headed into Willemstadt on the first opportunity following two days of public holiday. While our honeymooning guests (sister Hannah and her husband Will Denniston) visited the floating market for

Sister Hannah

vegetables and fruit, Val and I drove a rickety little hire car across the island to the airport. We were not deserting ship, it was just that the only working public photocopier in Curaçao is in the airport café. We had been lent a much-copied set of notes and chartlets for the San Blas islands and had set our sights on this remote Panamanian archipelago.

With our fifth generation copies and several hot hours later we were also equipped with some lino offcuts for our home-insulated fridge, distilled water for the batteries and some frozen meat for the voyage. Emigration requirements were completed with usual Dutch dispatch and our final boat preparations filled the afternoon. As a departure treat, we took steaks ashore at Sarifundy's Marina, a relaxed bar and club run by a Dutch expatriate family in a corner of Spanish Harbour.

Next morning saw *Caraway* sailing out through the narrow neck of Spanish Harbour, leaving behind the fleet of expensive Dutch motorboats and sleepy long distance cruisers. A brisk north-east trade was blowing and, running west in the protected coastal waters, we passed the giant bridgespan of Willemstadt at 8–9 knots. The comfort diminished as we cleared the western tip of Curaçao but the speed remained good. In a rising swell we set a course north of Aruba and settled into a two-on, six-off watchkeeping routine. Our honeymoon guests are working for their passage! Hannah had some Mediterranean sailing experience but Will was quite new to it all, so it was a relief to see him settling in so easily. His windsurfing prowess showed in a ready understanding of sail trim and helming.

Today is the skipper's birthday so teatime produced a few extra treats. Foremost among the gifts was a dangerous looking harpoon gun. The crew are either losing faith in my normal fishing methods or they are worried about piracy in the forthcoming Columbian waters!

So started a five day passage of fast sailing but lumpy seas. The Force 5–7 trades kept up, generating large surfing swells that kept us on our toes and tested Stanley (our vane steering gear) to his limits. Appetites, though small to start with, soon recovered and activity increased as the crew settled into the daily rhythm. As to course, we stuck initially to the 13th parallel to keep clear of the Columbian hazards, only turning south west at a point (13°00′N 76°00′W) that held us 70 miles or more off the coast. Even this far off we were 'buzzed' by a USAF patrol aircraft carrying out spot checks for drug traffickers. As we entered the Columbian Gulf a series of spectacular electrical storms all around us provided good entertainment. Dawn found us untouched and becalmed.

The swell died away in a matter of hours and the sea became glassy. Conscious of our newly-weds' limited time aboard, we switched on the faithful old Perkins and chugged across the millpond. We approached 09°00′N in boiling sunshine, disturbing a pair of sharks and a pilot whale from their surface slumbers. Flying fish burst from under the bows, razoring the water with their long tails before skimming above the untouched mirror ahead.

As the day wore on we looked at the chart and weather. Continued calms seemed in prospect and our destination, Puerto Obaldia (the southernmost port of entry into Panama), was still a long way off. If we diverted west into the San Blas islands today, on the other hand, we could island-hop north-west to the next entry point instead. A daylight landfall would be essential in these little charted coral waters: we raised the revs and turned west.

Even so, it was touch and go. We identified and aimed for an offlying sand-and-palms islet, Isla de Pajaros (09°04′N 77°46′W). This can be found four miles due north of the distinctive Isla de Pinos, with its 400 foot high whale-back profile.

With the last usable sun we 'eyeball navigated' around the northern fringing reefs of the island and probed inshore towards a sandy cove. Suddenly the depths shoaled from 30 feet to one foot in the course of one boat length. We dropped back as our bows overhung the menacing coral outcrops. Soon we found a safe patch, and dropped the anchor in 15 feet over sand. The adrenalin drained away with the last of the sun, now beneath the yardarm, allowing due celebration of our safe arrival.

Our sketchy notes and photocopied chartlets showed the Isla de Pajaros as a tiny mark on a field of unsurveyed white. They did, however, give good and detailed advice on the locals. The indigenous Kuna indians are an almost unspoilt Central American race that has negotiated semi-autonomy for its territories along the eastern seaboard of Panama. Due deference must be made by a visitor to each village chief or *sila* and on no account should

Val and Kuna in a canoe

coconuts be collected without permission, even from outlying and uninhabited islands. Copra forms the basis of essential trade with traditional Columbian coastal vessels and supplements the Kuna's mainland cropping of fruit and vegetables. All the Kuna communities are resident on specific village islands, a scattered few among the 365 distinct isles of the San Blas chain.

Our first experience of the San Blas idyll was delightful — a postcard scene of palms leaning out over untouched sandy beaches, bordering azure waters full of brightly coloured fish and ornate coral gardens. The snorkelling proved excellent and the speargun was used to good effect. After a fresh fish lunch, we motored the four miles south to the Isle of Pines with Val and Will perched up on the bow rail to provide guidance through the reefs.

Again bounded by a half-mile ring of coral, our next anchorage warranted a slow approach but we found a clear sandy bay on the leeward western shore. Soon after the anchor was down a dugout canoe paddled over from the nearby tiny village. We were presented with smiling faces, pidgin Spanish and an evident sales pitch for *molas*, intricate appliqué panels that form the fronts and backs of traditional Kuna women's clothing. Our two visitors came aboard and a warm-hearted and partially understood greeting followed. We declined their wares, however, being determined to see a wider range before committing ourselves.

As the first ambassadors left, another canoe appeared — perhaps our tea supply could be smelt ashore? This time it was a wrinkled old man (mid-70s?) and his two-year-old grandson. They too proved charming and the elder explained in patchy Spanish that he was the *sila* of the nearest village, Mamimulu, a cluster of some six to eight grass thatched huts under the coconuts. We were accorded the freedom of his domain in return for a second cup of heavily sweetened tea.

The next morning we made a leisurely start by dinghy to the main village of the island, Tupak (Kuna for 'whale', after the island profile). Landing in a squalid fringe of plastic, glass and worse detritus, we feared the place might have already been ruined by North American consumer products. Thankfully the village itself proved well-swept and welcoming. A visit to the palm thatched 'congress hall' yielded permission to walk around in return for a US $2 'tax'. This was payable to the *sila* and seemed also conditional upon our purchasing Molas from the ladies of the village. We soon found that the community followed an enviably harmonious and well ordered pattern of existence; resources are willingly shared around, village policy is decided democratically in the congress hall and both sexes share equally in the work and responsibilities of daily life.

Down every tiny path between the bamboo-walled huts we were greeted and followed by chattering children. We bought bread at a tiny hut that contained nothing but a Calor gas oven and sacks of weevilly flour. As we explored, the Mola vendors assembled their wares. We had pressed for old examples rather than the lurid new stitchwork produced from modern

Kuna, digging a dugout

imported threads. After lots of good natured haggling we settled on two excellent traditional pieces and made our way back to the dinghy.

The Tupak *sila* had declined permission for photography but the tiny village closest to *Caraway*, half a mile to the south, seemed less camera-shy. The ancient *sila* of Mamimulu showed us around his little community of six families. Each had a hut with a bamboo-fenced courtyard for children, chickens and the occasional pig. Breadfruit, mango and banana trees grew all around and the plentiful fish of the surrounding reefs meant that all looked well-fed and contented. In an unusual display of early marital priorities, Hannah bartered a pair of Will's shorts for a fish-tooth necklace.

Our next departure northwards, later the same day, involved negotiating a narrow pass in the reef before a relatively clear run of 24 miles. The reef patches closed in again as we approached the islands of Mamitupu and Achutupu. A brisk nor'easter created sufficient surf to mark the biggest dangers and, at times, it seemed that we were sailing through ever narrowing gaps in the foaming barriers. We zigged and zagged in concert with our sketchy sailing directions and the bow lookout's instructions. Around us, picturesque sailing canoes fished the reef edges or set their patchwork lateen sails for the trip back to their nearby village islands.

We had chosen a tiny protected triangle for that night's anchorage. 'Islandia' seemed an appropriate name for the little group of islets set in a broad band of fringing reef. The approach was particularly tricky, however, and soon highlighted the need to treat our photocopied material with extra caution. Following a 'charted' gap, we found it narrowing to nothing. Again our bows overhung dangerous coral heads and we had to reverse carefully out. Will found that a windsurfer mast provides an excellent fend-off pole in such cases. Our second attempt proved unsuccessful also: 10 fathoms shallowing to surface coral with no apparent gaps. We tried again, half a mile further west, and found a healthy 40 foot channel through to the lagoon. In the narrow confines between three small islands, we placed fore and aft anchors. The sun set behind the mountainous Panamanian jungles and we toasted our isolation and 'gunkholing' success.

Sunday 10 May. While Val and I scrubbed and tinkered, Hannah and Will took off in the dinghy to explore. The immediate waters were mildly disappointing; a strong current scoured the lagoon and stirred up the sand. Nevertheless the beaches yielded some beautiful shells and intriguing old concrete fixtures (copra processing sites?). The honeymooners ventured further afield after lunch — to investigate the apparent small airstrip beside the neighbouring village island of Ailigandi (09°14′N 78°02′W). Our guests hoped to find a local method of flying out so that island-hopping could continue as long as possible. They returned against a stiff and splashy chop, soaked but bearing gifts and good news: a daily 0600 flight to Panama City and fresh chicken, bread and potatoes.

In the meantime, Val and I had moved on from boring maintenance jobs to prepare a secret 'wedding breakfast'. We planned a beach supper for the setting sun, complete with smuggled champagne and even napkins! Hannah and Will were sent ashore to light the bonfire while Val put the finishing touches on our house specialities: 'caviar' pancakes, tikka-marinaded chicken and mangoes soaked in lime juice. All was transported ashore to join the roasting potatoes and then the festivities began. The only interruption came at high tide as we had to move the bonfire clear of the highest waves.

The next day we motored carefully out through the reefs and west to Ailigandi. Between the village island and a mainland rivermouth there is a 400 yard wide passage that shoals to the north. We entered the muddy waters from the south, forced to rely on the echo sounder until we met suitable anchoring depths. These we found opposite a small jetty that serves the village and regional medical clinic. The surroundings were a mass of contrasts. On one side of us, the raw rainforests of Darien grew to the water's edge. On the other, a smartly whitewashed medical facility, a slightly seedy school building and tightly packed indian huts bulged over the island boundaries.

Ailigandi itself maintained the incongruous mixture. Despite the efficient clinic, carved wooden *uchus* still guard some of the dwellings against disease. A nominal police presence exists but Kuna congress discipline exerts a much greater influence. Fishermen paddled up to us to give lobster, fish and fresh picked avocados yet the popular items in the village 'shop' were imported bubble-gum and tinned Spam.

Our first visit was, of course, to the *sila*. This time we also wanted to enquire of the flight out to Panama. Fortunately the skipper's schoolbook Spanish was augmented by the local schoolteacher — the only Kuna in the village who could speak any English. It transpired that, although the flight existed, it was only for lobsters. Our lack of proper immigration procedures also worried the local policemen. Both problems would be solved, however, by travelling 40 miles north-west to Nargana (or 'Rio Diablo') where flights and formalities could be dealt with.

We considered our timescales. To meet Hannah and Will's booked homeward flight from Panama, we would need to sail more or less directly to Nargana. The police 'chief' offered an alternative. For US $30 (to cover fuel costs) he would take us by motorised canoe; a six-hour journey instead of two days of careful reef-dodging. The only stipulation was that all four of us must go, leaving *Caraway* at anchor (as surety?) in front of the *sila*'s house.

Our last evening together was spent in the dim light of a surging paraffin lamp in a grubby little 'restaurant' near the quay. The darkness hid untold health dangers but the food was very good and very cheap. The schoolmaster appeared, clutching a letter he had written to our Queen. He wanted to know the postal address of Buckingham Palace. We guessed at something suitable and hoped the letter was not a complaint about the current representatives of Great Britain. It transpired that he just wanted to send his kind regards and suggest a pupil exchange scheme between Ailigandi and some (similar?) school in England. We gave him the address of the British Council as well. He was delighted.

The next morning came all too soon as we had to be ready at 0500. Speculating about the likely size and (dis-)comfort of the canoe, we waited a full extra hour before anything appeared. The dugout was around 25ft long, about 4ft wide, powered by the borrowed 25 hp medical outboard and, to our slight dismay, already holding four people. It was quite a squeeze to add four more plus luggage but we managed. A plastic sheet was passed over us all as a spray deflector and we were off.

In the protected lee of the first 10 miles of reef the going was speedy and relatively comfortable. As the solid wood of the seats began to make an impression, so too did the sea state. Travelling at around 8 knots across the swell, we developed a long and persistent roll. Waves slapped the long sides of the canoe and came aboard, keeping the assistant boatman-cum-police trainee busy with his coconut shell bailer. Eventually our stolid and unmoving driver indicated that the next island would be Nargana. A big double island, linked by a high spanning iron footbridge, greeted us with all the trappings of western exposure including concrete and brick housing.

We found the local police chief in the concrete shed. He was surrounded by henchmen and clearly modelled himself on Telly Savalas playing *Kojak*: bald head, wrap-around dark glasses, black leather jacket and constantly chewing (not lollipops thank goodness!). He was an intimidating sight and soon proved up to the image. We explained our case but might have been talking to the concrete wall. Despite the assurances of the Ailigandi policemen and confirmation in our reference books, Nargana is NOT a port of entry for Panama. We feared a wasted journey. After some patient persuasion, however, Hannah and Will were given permission to catch the air taxi to Panama for inward clearance there.

The air taxi flew in, gathered up our two guests and whipped them away to the world of traffic jams, mortgages and married life. They seemed to have enjoyed a taste of coral escapism. Meanwhile Val and I had to face a second six-hour 'ordeal by sore bottoms' back to *Caraway*.

Next day we asked the *sila* for permission to paddle up the river opposite the Ailigandi jetty. He gave us the okay, so after lunch we rowed the inflatable across the muddy shallows and followed the intermittent traffic of small dugouts into the encroaching forest. As the banks closed in we passed clearings planted with taro, banana, mango and avocado. A small group of huts and a few thin plumes of woodsmoke marked one of the rare mainland dwellings of the Kuna.

After a mile or so the river narrowed rapidly. We could just row between the root entangled banks while ripe wild mangoes made loud 'plosh' noises as they fell around us. With the splashing dives of large kingfishers, the similar noises of larger fish, and the background screeching of treetop parrots it was a noisy but magical trip. We beached the dinghy beside a hauled out canoe and followed a jungle track up a small hill. Climbing among fig trees

A jungle village

and cropped banana plants, we emerged above the level of the surrounding forest canopy. An unbroken carpet of rich green rolled and folded away into the hazy mountain backdrop.

Then the mosquitoes found us. It was time to go so we scrabbled down the hill and paddled back downstream. We soon reached *Caraway* and were enjoying a quiet cuppa in the cockpit when we noticed a pair of eyes sticking out of the water just ten feet astern. A young alligator was out looking for scraps! We were glad not to have run into its daddy while paddling around in the inflatable.

Our departure on the morning of 13 May was marked by typical Ailigandi treatment. A host of waving and laughing children watched from the quay and a fisherman paddled up to give us a pair of small lobsters. It was difficult to tear ourselves away but we felt we should press on and sort out the paperwork as promised.

The route onwards was now familiar as we loosely followed the track of our canoe trip. Eventually we passed the wide beach and village of Playon Chico and entered the dangerous mosaics of light blue and brown that guard the aptly named Snug Harbour. This is a wide, deep and totally protected haven reputedly much used by 18th century buccaneers. With an exit clear to the north-west and a tortuous escape route to the south-east it seemed a natural pirate's lair. Our own requirements were more modest and we found a beautiful spot in the north corner for the night. We dropped the anchor in 20 feet between a group of small tree-covered cays and the dense mangroves of the outer rim. We leapt overboard and swam to a sandy point. A short walk along the beach triggered hundreds of tiny crabs into frenzied scattering while the sun set in romantic splendour. Our return to a lobster supper completed the feeling of real paradise.

What had been planned as a simple overnight stop was changed the next morning with the appearance of 'Charlie Smith'. A wizened indian of indeterminate years appeared in a dugout with two of his adult sons. They were on their way to fish the outer reef in the prevailing calm conditions and wondered if we would like to join them. Charlie had been a deckhand on one of the old tea clippers and had 'bin many country'. There was certainly no room for five in the canoe, so we gathered our snorkels and flippers and took Charlie in our dinghy while the two sons paddled ahead.

Once through the shallow gap between islands, Val and Charlie looked after the boats and put the world to rights (at least that is what she thinks they discussed) while the three of us dived among the crevices of the reef face. Half an hour yielded a large octopus to the speargun and a big crab that had to be winkled out with a wire noose. This was ample for the *Caraway* crew so we rowed home with Charlie, leaving the two fit and wiry fishermen to do the day's real work. They returned three hours later with a boatful of fish. They gave us back our harpoon and flippers and we split the octopus with them as a parting gesture. Taking Charlie, they paddled off back to

Playon Chico shouting goodbyes and invitations to stay in their house 'next time'. We are sorely tempted to cancel the circumnavigation and settle here! The postscript to today's adventures comes from the galley. While Val turned the crab into a wonderful hot salad, the octopus was another story. We boiled it, and boiled it, and boiled it, but no amount of cooking or bashing with a winch handle seemed to touch its india rubber consistency. Having spent another peaceful night in Snug Harbour, we then left the San Blas altogether. A natural gap in the offshore reefs provides a safe exit route and we knew that the northernmost islands are much more westernised and 'discovered'. A number of cruise ships stop in the Golfo de San Blas on their way to or from the Panama Canal so tourism and its attendant commercial impact has already been felt.

APPENDIX

The San Blas are covered in part by the following charts: (BA = Admiralty, DMA = US Defence). Isla de Pinos and surroundings — BA 1278; Ailigandi to Playon Chico — DMA 26042 (no soundings); Golfo de San Blas — DMA 26042, 26063, 26064 and four charts privately published by Kitt Kapp, c/o Bluewater Books, Florida. Our navigation was largely based on a typewritten *Sailing Directions to the San Blas Islands of Panama* by Tom Zydler.

BISCAY STORM

by James Burdett

(The cruise for which the Sea Laughter trophy was awarded.)

La Coruña in late summer resembles something of a motorway service station on the main route to a holiday resort. Some boats are at the end of a summer cruise provisioning for the passage home, while others are heading south to warmer waters and have barely started their adventures. My cousin, Tom Hasler, and I were heading home after a six week cruise of north west Spain in my Laurent Giles designed Vertue *Mary*.

I bought *Mary* two years ago and she is the first 'big boat' I have owned. She was built just before the war and had been owned for most of her life by the couple who sold her to me. When I bought her she had been laid up for twelve years in a yard on the Tamar river. Her surveyor reported that there wasn't a spore of rot in her pitch pine planks or oak frames and was in most respects a thoroughly sound boat.

I spent many weekends and holidays getting her up to scratch and preparing her for commission. The main jobs were the renewal of the galvanised strap floors, selective refastening of the planking, building a self-draining cockpit and stripping down all her varnishwork. The floors were done by the same yard where she lay but the other three jobs and endless other small tasks I did myself. Eighteen months and £120 worth of silicone bronze screws later she was ready for her first ever voyage outside British waters.

Although *Mary* had spent most of her life racing she is remarkably well equipped for cruising — including two mainsails, ten foresails, three spinnakers, and 55 metres of anchor cable. I only needed to hire a liferaft, borrow a VHF and buy a small outboard to get in and out of harbour.

By Friday 10 September we had been sitting in La Coruña for nearly a week and despite the many attractions of the town we were both sick of *tapas* and were getting itchy feet.

The day before I had telephoned my parents to get a long range Met Office forecast. This was uncharacteristically vague and spoke only of a low pressure system moving in from the west and creating gales over North Biscay. We had already sat through the first of the autumn gales earlier in the week and knew only too well that the longer we stayed in Spain the more likely we were to get stuck there. So when on Friday a Danish skipper gave us a synopsis from the Danish Met Office which totally contradicted the British one we latched onto it. The Danes predicted that the weak high pressure ridge over South Biscay would fill and push any depressions further north and out of the way. One of the forecasts had to be wrong; after lengthy debate between us, forever the optimists, we decided it had to be the British one.

So at lunchtime on Friday we weighed anchor, sailed round the massive Digue Abrigo breakwater and headed north-eastwards on a beeline to the Raz de Seine, Brittany, 360 miles away.

The outward passage had taken us sixty-two hours and now with a Force 4–5 behind us we expected a repeat performance on the homeward leg. After twenty-four hours at sea we had covered 120 miles and could almost smell the freshly baked *croissants* that awaited our arrival in France. We were brought sharply down to size by the 1800 shipping forecast on Saturday, the first we had tuned into since our departure: '... Biscay, North Finisterre, southerly violent storm 11 imminent ...' the announcer read it out with the same emotion as the talking clock. I wondered if he could imagine the sense of disbelief and acute apprehension that had suddenly gripped me when I heard those words. Tom and I stared at each other in amazement. How could we have been so foolhardy as to have ignored the long range British forecast, scant as it was? And why on earth were we in the middle of the Bay of Biscay in a boat that was older than our combined ages waiting to be hit by a near hurricane? All those questions flew around my head. Still, it was too late to try coming up with answers.

We were undoubtedly too far from land to make a dash to shelter. The Spanish coast was 120 miles to windward and the French 270 miles to the north-east. There was nothing for it but to ride it out as best we could.

We had to act fast and make use of what little fair weather we had left. The first priority was to get as much searoom as possible. By heading north-west we came onto a broad reach and began to make valuable miles out into the Atlantic and further away from land. The two prime dangers were the lee shore of South Brittany and, close at hand, the line of the Continental Shelf. This runs roughly from Ushant in a south-easterly direction to the French-Spanish border, and the depth of water rises from over 200 metres to less than 100 metres in the space of 15 miles or so. It has the potential for creating huge and confused seas as the deep water swell piles up over the shelf.

We handed the sails and lashed the main tightly along the boom. I put extra lashings over the pram dinghy which stowed on the cabin roof. I had brought along two 150 foot heavy warps for trailing astern, as a more

Mary *25.3ft LOA built in 1939*

manageable alternative to a drogue or sea anchor. We got these into the cockpit in readiness for deployment.

By dusk on Saturday *Mary*, Tom and I were as ready as we could have been for what lay ahead. The wind was rising steadily and by midnight it had reached an estimated Force 6. We streamed the warps in two large bights, one from both the sheet winches and the other from the large bronze cleats on each quarter. The warps undoubtedly held the stern up to windward and slowed us down. They weren't as effective at checking our speed as a drogue or sea anchor would have been as we were still moving through the water at 3–4 knots.

By dawn the true scale of what we were in became apparent. The wind by now was a steady Force 10 from the south. It was extremely difficult to look to windward to see where the next wave was coming from as the spume and spray hit you full-on like a sandblaster. The waves had built up overnight. It was difficult to gauge the wave height but when we were in a trough the crests would tower well above mast height and create an unnerving lull in the wind. These lulls were shortlived though, as the next crash would arrive from astern carrying us upwards like a piece of flotsam back into the teeth of the storm.

Shortly after daybreak on Sunday while I was in the cabin — the motion was too violent to sleep — Tom shouted down to me for a white flare. It had to mean only one thing. I shot up the companionway and looked round behind me to see the outline of a ship emerging out of the mist and spray.

She was headed straight at us and no more than $\frac{1}{4}$ mile away. Luckily, after Tom had set off the flare, she altered course and passed a couple of hundred metres to port of us. I managed to raise them on the VHF and got an accurate GPS fix from them. Encouragingly, we were only 10 miles out on our dead reckoning since La Coruña. They asked if we were okay. I answered 'Yes', because although our situation was far from pleasant I still felt in control and expected the centre of the low pressure system to move through quickly, taking the strong winds with it. In any case there was little that they could have done for us even if we had needed assistance, the seas were so short and steep as completely to rule out any sort of rescue attempt.

By now the wind had veered to the south-west and our original hope of being blown northwards far enough to be clear of Ushant was no longer realistic. The South Brittany shore was now directly downwind and about 150 miles away. Although that was well over a day away at our speed, the 100 metre seabed colour change was less than 75 miles away, and this posed the most imminent danger.

The waves gradually grew larger and more menacing. Where before there had been smooth crests, many were by now breaking. It was virtually impossible to avoid a breaker when it came down on you, you simply had to try and align the boat to minimise the damage. We started by steering directly down the front of each wave in the belief that this was the best way to avoid broaching or rolling. In theory it makes sense because you are presenting the smallest surface area to the wave, but it only works up to a point. Naturally the course directly down the wave is the steepest and fastest route, and when each wave is a good 60 feet high, a 5 ton boat can reach quite a speed down its face even with warps trailing. We learned this the hard way and had spectacular sleigh rides down the face of some waves. *Mary*, though, was as forgiving as ever and her long keel tracked so perfectly that one barely had to exert pressure on the tiller to prevent her from screwing round at the bottom.

Mary has no self-steering (not that it would have been much use in these conditions) so when on watch one was constantly on the helm. This took a lot out of me and by mid-day on Sunday fatigue was settling in. We were both soaked to the skin and unable to keep warm despite having the cooker burning constantly in the cabin.

The wind showed no signs of letting up; instead it grew stronger and stronger. Just when we thought it couldn't possibly get any fiercer it did, and with each passing hour the seas became steeper and more unpredictable. Virtually every wave crest was breaking and you couldn't see for the spray and spume on the surface of the sea. Breakers regularly swamped the entire boat, filling the cockpit instantly. After each swamping it took a good ten minutes to pump the boat dry as inevitably a large amount of water found its way down below through the cabin doors and cockpit locker lids.

With the now dreaded 100 metre contour getting closer and closer it was only a matter of time before we would be unable to keep pace with the

L to r: James Burdett and Tom Hasler

onslaught of the seas. It was decision time. We had a stark choice of attempting to continue into what was a rapidly deteriorating situation or swallowing our pride and calling for help. I was acutely aware of the fact that *Mary* might not be able to stand up to the punishment we were putting her through for much longer. When I eventually sent a 'Mayday' no one responded. Realistically though I shouldn't have expected anyone to hear, as my handheld VHF probably had a range of no more than 10 miles in these conditions. In retrospect we were extremely fortunate that no-one did hear us since any attempt to abandon *Mary* and scramble up the side of a heaving merchant vessel would have been suicidal.

The Mayday was a turning point since we now realised that we were totally alone and entirely dependent on our own resources. Our only hope was to keep *Mary* afloat at all costs. The liferaft wasn't an option. Even if we had managed to go forward to cut its lashings, the chances of launching it, getting in and keeping it upright were close to zero.

As night fell on Sunday all hell let loose. The night was pitchy black and the only warning of the next wave was the glowing phosphorescence churning up in its breaking crest. There was spume and spray everywhere. We both had stinging and bloodshot eyes from looking into the wind. We both remained in the cockpit, harnessed in, as I was convinced that if *Mary* did go down she would go down fast.

Thankfully Tom had discovered that the best way to tackle the unrelenting onslaught of breaking seas was to steer so as to take them on the quarter. This meant that the line of descent down the face of the wave was not at its steepest. Although it did not prevent *Mary* from being completely swamped it did reduce the amazing acceleration and speed we had encountered when going straight down the waves. This 'Hasler Oblique Storm Steering System' also meant that we could put more east in our course and avoid heading for the nearest part of the French coast.

Midnight Sunday. The storm had been raging for twenty-four hours, it had been blowing a constant Force 11 and gusting stronger for at least twelve hours. Neither of us had had any sleep for over thirty hours. We were soaked through, tired, hungry and becoming more and more despondent. I found myself thinking that it might be altogether simpler if the next wave took us to the bottom. It was all too easy to huddle in the corner of the cockpit and doze off into semi-conciousness, although this could never last for long since a shout from Tom on the helm would alert me to the next swamping and then what seemed like hours of pumping to empty the boat.

We had a go at singing and stamping our feet to boost morale and keep alert but even Tom, the doyen of singers, had forgotten all his tunes.

The waves had totally lost any pattern and were coming at us from all directions, and we needed to pump almost continuously to have any chance of preventing the boat from filling. The louvred companionway doors were woefully inadequate at keeping the water out of the cabin and it regularly filled up to the level of the bunks.

During one of my spells on the helm I looked back and saw high above and behind me something that seemed like a cloud. I was mistaken only for a second — the next moment it plummeted downwards towards us and hit *Mary* full on from above with enormous force. We were both pinned down into the cockpit, green water above our heads, and then with the most almighty acceleration we took off down the face of the wave, completely out of control. *Mary* smashed from side to side as she flew down the face like a bob-sleigh. Something had to go, and it would only have taken one plank to spring or the coachroof to stove in for the whole lot of us to go down. Somehow we survived it though.

Sometime in the early hours of Monday morning I was again on the helm battling to control her. Almost by accident I discovered that the most effective way of slowing us down was to hold the tiller hard over to port and effectively lie a-hull. The warps still kept the stern into the wind to a certain extent, but it meant that the wind and the majority of the waves were coming from just aft of the beam. This seemed to reduce the frequency of swamping as the waves tended to wash over the coachroof rather than fill the cockpit from astern. Although it increased the risk of rolling we were both too tired to care and, because pumping was reduced to once every twenty minutes or so, we decided to lash the helm to port and turn in.

I crashed out onto the leeward bunk and slept, and woke to find that Tom had resurrected the cooker (which had jumped out of its gimballs) and was warming up the cabin.

By daylight the wind had dropped to Force 9–10 and we spent the rest of the day lying in our soaking oilskins hoping that the worst was now over. By Tuesday morning the wind had moderated enough to consider sailing, although the seas were still big and occasionally breaking over the coach roof. I got an RDF fix at 1000 which put us 70 miles west of La Rochelle. We had been blown over 200 miles in the previous fifty hours under bare poles.

Before setting sail we assessed the damage. The only breakage was the topping lift which had been cut through at the top of the mast by the radar reflector (which had merrily spun its way up the backstay during the storm). The rigging and mast were intact. Ironically this may have been due to the lightness of construction (the mast is hollow spruce) and small surface area of the spars which would have presented less resistance to the waves than something more heavily built.

We set sail and headed north-east towards Isle D'Yeux, only to find some hours later that I hadn't brought any charts of the island. When I discovered this, and after a serious humour failure on both our parts, we headed for the next closest landfall, Belle Isle, about 40 miles further along the coast. Eventually we entered La Pallice at 1900 on Wednesday 15 September, but not before being pooped twice in the tide race off the southern tip of the island — a final reminder from the Bay of Biscay of our mortality.

I later discovered through the coastguard that a Danish yacht and another British yacht had left La Coruña shortly after us. Both were lost.

DOWN UNDER DOWN UNDER

by Michael Pocock

While others are attempting to circumnavigate in under eighty days, Pat and I now seem unlikely to complete our voyage in as many months. Prompted by a strong desire to cruise in Tasmanian waters and a wish to call on some relatives in Perth, we opted to go 'down under down under' and explore South Australia on the way.

There is a very strong element of maritime history to be absorbed in such a passage and in addition to James Cook, whose track we have crossed in many places, we are now much more familiar with Tasman, Flinders, Vancouver, D'Entrecasteaux and Nuyts. All of these remarkable men left their names and records of their exploits in these waters.

We made our landfall from New Caledonia just north of Australia's widest point at Gladstone and worked our way south in easy stages. In the Pittwater we were delighted to welcome Ronnie and Jill Andrews (RCC) on board. We were for ever after in their debt for the introductions that they gave us both at Lady Barron and in Hobart.

We made a non-stop passage from Sydney to Eden, the traditional jumping off spot for crossing the Bass Strait. On 17 November we sailed from Eden and this was where the cruising took on a special quality that will long be remembered. The forecast spoke of north-east winds of 25–30 knots which seemed acceptable, and we passed Gabo Island and entered the Strait as the sun went down. We later came to learn that Australian forecasters are accurate in direction and conservative in strength and this time was no exception. The north-east winds steadily rose to 40 plus knots and we ran with ever increasing speed on a south-south-west course aiming for the west coast of Flinders Island. There should perhaps be a special prayer, 'O Lord preserve us from heavy weather gybes on old mainsails'. Ours had already passed the 40,000 miles mark and with two gybes in the strongest conditions it was a wonder it survived. The Bass Strait is notoriously rough and we would have no argument with that assumption. The bottom comes up from a great depth to less than 50 metres with steep fronted seas. All of which is more bearable with the sun shining.

In Mooloolaba we had succumbed to temptation and installed GPS. The price was so low that it seemed stupid to sail without it. Now was the chance for this wonderchild to show its worth. As the evening came closer visibility became reduced and a policy for the coming night had to be chosen. On dead reckoning we would have had to steer for the widest gap in the string of islands ahead of us. With GPS we could feed in a waypoint that would lead us into a sheltered bay on the south side of Inner Sister Island and with thirty minutes of daylight left we dropped our hook for an unexpected night in, after an exhilarating run.

It remained windy, sometimes extremely windy, while we worked our way round Flinders Island to Lady Barron. At this stage we were bound by our schedule and we sailed for the Tamar River 90 miles to the south-west with entirely the wrong wind and much more of it than we would have liked. Like all things unpleasant they are so nice when they stop and we sailed into the Tamar in lovely sunshine with a fair flood tide that swept us up to Beauty Point like an express train.

We picked up a mooring off the Port Dalrymple YC and were amazed when someone pulled out from the shore almost immediately. Imagine our delight when we recognised Hugh Clay (RCC) whom we had imagined was well on his way to South America. We overlapped with him for 36 hours and did what we could to help while he forced a good deal more than a quart into the proverbial pint pot. *Aratapu* was looking remarkably short of freeboard when he left for Hobart the following evening.

In two easy days we made our way 35 miles up the Tamar to Launceston and this was where the true nature of cruising in Tasmania showed up. Firstly the Commodore, no less, of the Tamar YC rowed across to bid us welcome, something that has never happened to us before in our travels. Secondly, we called at the boatyard to say that we were lying to their deep water mooring and would like to stay for five days, and how much did we owe them? They dismissed the notion with the comment that it was only a mooring!

In Launceston we were joined by Pat's stepmother Mary Barton (RCC), for the passage round Tasmania to Hobart which was achieved without a night at sea, with only one morning of strong head winds and with a series of delightful stopovers. In Port Arthur we visited the old penal settlement, now restored, and enjoyed the spectacular rock formations around Tasman Island and Cape Raoul. Mary left us in Hobart to fly north to join Pat's brother in Phuket and we settled down to enjoy the delights and excitements of Hobart at Christmas time. Just before the Sydney-Hobart fleet arrived we transferred from Constitution Dock to a berth at the Derwent Sailing Squadron. What marvellous facilities overseas yacht clubs have; during our visit we were hauled out on the club lift and we antifouled for a sum way way below any other that we have ever enjoyed before.

In the middle of January we sailed away down the Derwent, and down the D'Entrecasteaux Channel, enjoying attractive anchorages and sheltered waters. From Recherche Bay we embarked on the most significant passage when rounding south-west Tasmania. The winds recorded at Matsuyker Island are said to average 35 knots from the south-west and we should presumably be thankful that the day we chose was no more than average. It was a long hard slog and, although we did not reach Port Davey, we did get a peaceful night in Louisa Bay and finished the passage in relatively windless conditions next day. Port Davey and Bathurst Harbour are only accessible by some rugged bush walking or by air or water. There is therefore a great feeling of escape from civilisation when one reaches this true wilderness environment. Because of our draught (2.12m) we could not take *Blackjack* up the Melaleucca Inlet which leads inland. We were, however, determined to meet Peter the Pom and so mounted an expedition in our sailing Tinker, plus outboard, on what turned out to be one of the wettest days of our time in Tasmania. Peter and his wife, Barbara, mine for tin in the moorland basin at the head of the inlet. They have a 33 ton barquentine rigged vessel and twice a year they sail to Hobart with a cargo of 6 tons of tin ore and return with an equivalent load of stores, fuel and new equipment. They are a remarkable couple, totally independent and dedicated to their mine.

To be honest we enjoyed Macquarie harbour, the only other refuge on the wild west coast, even more than we did Port Davey. There is road access to the old fishing harbour of Strahan and therefore a steady flow of tripper boats serving the constant stream of land-based tourists. There is, thankfully, room for everybody. Once safely through Hell's Gates there is plenty of delightful sheltered cruising to enjoy, with the opportunity to go some way up the beautiful Gordon River even with our draught.

Nobody spoke well of Port Phillip and the approach to Melbourne and, having dallied long enough in Tasmania, we decided to head futher west. We re-crossed the Bass Strait to Portland, which proved a useful place for minor re-stocking after the very limited opportunities on Tasmania's west coast.

Once again we took local advice and made no attempt to reach Adelaide, instead we visited two anchorages on the north coast of Kangaroo Island on our way to Port Lincoln. Port Lincoln is at the centre of the best cruising area on the south coast with a wide variety of sheltered anchorages within easy reach. In the Sir Joseph Banks group we found a colony of sealions on a sandspit. When we rowed in closer for better pictures, the younger generation were filled with curiosity and came and swam playfully all round the dinghy.

It should be said that South Australian cruising is not without its drawbacks. The first of these is the poor holding in many of the anchorages. Local yachtsmen carry large fisherman type anchors with the flukes ground to sharp points. Our faithful CQR was not ideal. The second caution is that onshore winds come straight off the Southern Ocean and have a sharpish bite to them.

Finally a combination of cold water and white pointer sharks makes one reluctant to spend much time in the water.

The weather system is such that in February and March a series of high pressure systems move eastwards south of Australia with fresh easterly winds between them and the shore. They are interrupted by small fronts that upset the pattern bringing south-westerly winds of fairly short duration. The weather forecasting from Melbourne and from Perth, which overlaps in South Australia, is excellent and with reasonable patience, which we sometimes lack, it should be possible to cross the Bight on entirely fair winds.

From Streaky Bay on the west side of the Eyre Peninsula to Esperance in Western Australia is around 600 miles and is the longest jump without a good refuge that it is necessary to make. Arrival in Esperance is not without its excitement. The Recherche Group of islands spreads for just over 100 miles to the east and makes the last night's navigation interesting to say the least. GPS may tell you exactly where you are but the chart (the latest available) carries cautionary notes stating that large areas are still based on the surveys of Lieutenant Matthew Flinders in 1802. His measurement of longitude was exceptionally good in 1802 but actually varies by as much as two miles with the satellite-derived positions now obtainable! Unfortunately the islands are mostly sheer sided rock and temporary anchorages are not easily found.

We lay in the yacht club marina in Esperance and again further west in Albany and were made very welcome in both places. In contrast to the east coast of Australia visitors are a rarity in these places and we met a number of very interesting and delightful people. In Albany there are several owners with first hand experience of sailing in the Indian Ocean and we picked their brains at every opportunity.

From Albany we had an easy passage round Cape Leeuwin to Bunbury which, if nothing else, has a very sheltered small boat harbour. In a long day from there we reached Fremantle at midnight and groped our way into the Fremantle Sailing Club marina, in spite of the lights and not because of them! Be warned, the approach is only lit by two amber flashing lights that are indistinguishable from those guarding a hole in the road.

NAVIGATORS OF THE GREAT BARRIER REEF

by John Webster

'Sunday 3rd June 1770 winds between SSE and SE a gentle breeze and clear weather'. So wrote Lieutenant James Cook in his journal on the day that he navigated and named Whitsunday Passage in latitude 20° South, off the coast of what is today Queensland. 'Among the many islands that lay upon this coast', he continued, 'there is one more remarkable than the rest ...'. He named it Pentecost Island but, having passed to the west, he never saw its even more remarkable eastern side.

Cook was passage-making, sounding as he went. The islands off the coast of what was then New South Wales were virtually uninhabited so there was little inducement for him to tarry. He observed smoke from fires on the mainland and on one occasion an outrigger with two natives putting out

H.M. Bark Endeavour. *Whitsunday Passage and Pentecost Island*

from an island. But it was all very different from his experiences elsewhere in the Pacific where native populations had greeted him variously with wariness, hostility and friendship, where he and his crew had acted as diplomats as well as colonists. The Australian aborigines had been on this coast for forty thousand years, since before the Barrier Reef was formed, but these shy people were little in evidence as Cook sailed north on his way to Batavia and home. Cook was in fact unaware of the existence of the Barrier Reef, which in the latitude of the Whitsundays lies between twenty and thirty miles offshore, and unaware that he was sailing into a funnel where the reef converges with the shore, where on 11 June 1770 *Endeavour* struck coral and was stranded. Cape Tribulation and Weary Bay are names which suggest the struggle which followed to save the ship. Superb seamanship achieved this and after seven weeks of repair in the Endeavour River Cook resumed his passage, passing out through a gap in the reef before rounding and naming Cape York. Technically he did not complete the full inner passage of the Great Barrier Reef. The first professional navigator to do this was Lieutenant Philip Parker King RN with the cutter *Mermaid* and the brig *Bathurst* in 1819 (Flinders surveyed portions of the reef in 1802 but passed out to seaward in latitude 18° South).

The distinction of being the first Europeans to traverse the whole inner passage goes to a truly remarkable couple, Mary and William Bryant, escapees from the penal colony at Port Jackson. Mary was a sailor's daughter from Fowey, transported for seven years for stealing a cloak. William was a Cornish fisherman and smuggler. They both sailed with the First Fleet and married in Australia. On 28 March 1791, with their two children and seven other convicts, they stole the Governor's six-oared cutter and sailed it to Timor — 3250 miles in ten weeks — arriving on 4 June. This epic voyage rates with Bligh's to the same destination exactly two years earlier. (Bligh had previously sailed with Cook in the *Resolution* on his second voyage of exploration and had clearly learned well.) After a spell of freedom the Bryants were taken prisoner by Captain Edwards of the frigate *Pandora* who had been searching

... stole the Governor's six-oared cutter ...

for *Bounty* mutineers. George Bryant and his son died in Batavia but Mary eventually reached England where, thanks to the intervention of James Boswell, whose imagination had clearly been stimulated by her courage and resourcefulness, she was pardoned and returned to obscurity in Cornwall.

I first became acquainted with the passage inside the Great Barrier Reef in 1956 as the navigating officer of a destroyer bound from Singapore to Melbourne for the Olympic Games. The navigational task was considered sufficiently testing to justify the payment of pilotage money, three ha'pence a foot draught every 10 miles, which my Captain kindly shared with me — not all did! A few years later I returned to the Barrier Reef while serving with the Royal Australian Navy and contributed in a minor way to their hydrographic survey work in that area. Now, after an interval of over thirty years, I was able to go back to the Whitsunday Islands for a ten-day charter with my family.

By a happy coincidence of travel plans Dick and Sheila Trafford (RCC) were able to join us, which give the afterguard equal voting power. Our boat was a Northshore 46; apart from the lack of a chart table or navigatorium of any sort, and a rather cramped main saloon, it was perfectly adequate for our purpose and sailed quite well. Distances are not great and the cruising ground permitted to charter boats covers little more than forty miles in a north-south direction. This contains a multitude of islands, continental in origin, and many beautiful anchorages. The South East Trades had largely

The Whitsunday Group

faded but we experienced sufficient strength of wind from various directions to make the choice of overnight anchorage important — it only needed one roly night to give rise to a string of complaints from a sleepless crew. There are three main 'resort' islands, generally to be avoided though we nearly lost Dick to the delights of Hamilton Island during a brief refuelling stop. He returned just in time clutching eight ice creams.

Up to 5 metres tidal range and strong streams make it necessary to plan ahead, always with the book, *100 Magic Miles*, close to hand. It is an outstanding general guide and pilot book though it is perhaps a little casual when advising on the need for experience in order to charter — 'someone in the crew should have a few clues about handling a boat!' Perhaps because of this minimal requirement charter boats are kept on a tight rein — not underway before 0800, at anchor by 1630 and a twice daily radio schedule. And the penalty for missing two chat shows in succession is a helicopter search at charterers' expense.

Notwithstanding these restrictions we had a ball. The distaff had victualled to a very high standard — eight people for ten days totally from scratch in an empty boat is no mean feat in an unknown port. The booze was easier and like the food did not run out. Most of the serious cooking was done on the gas-fired pushpit-mounted barbecue and the presence of two *cordon bleu* trained younger crewmembers added a certain quality to the menus. Fishing lines were trailed but the sea yielded very little to this approach. However,

A ship's company of Websters & Traffords

the oysters off the rocks were delicious. It was wonderful to see the turtles —
the precision with which they bury their eggs a few inches above the high
water springs mark is impressive — and the natural world provides few
sights more thrilling than a pair of fish eagles swooping down from their
eyrie hundreds of feet above an anchorage in search of their supper.

The islands themselves offer little beyond the beaches. In most cases the
scrub or forest is impenetrable and there are no inhabitants except in the
resorts. This lack of local colour is disappointing, perhaps the reason why
Cook passed without stopping.

Sharks are not a menace though the book warns about stonefish, stingray
and at certain times various forms of jellyfish. We had no problems from
these. Coral heads or 'bombies' can be a threat which demand a good lookout
when coming in to anchor. Underwater visibility can vary and on one
occasion we anchored near high water only to find ourselves embayed by
bombies as the tide went down.

After the first couple of days when it rained and rained, the weather was
very kind, with breezes up to Force 5 and warm sunshine. Our ten days
passed all to quickly in a routine of early morning swim, breakfast, sail,
anchor, swim and snorkel, lunch (zizz), sail, anchor, swim, tea, happy hour,
dinner and bedtime.

Our final evening was the 188th anniversary of the Battle of Trafalgar
which we celebrated in suitable fashion in an open-air restaurant at the base
port of Airlie Beach — not quite Greenwich's Painted Hall but exactly right
for the occasion. His Lordship would have approved.

LIFE WITH THE FORTRESS

by Geoffrey Nockolds

If you judge a chap's cruising intentions by the weight of his anchor, then mine are scarcely beyond harbour. On the principle that the only way to try equipment is to use it, we have had a season with a Fortress anchor. It is made from high tensile extruded aluminium and weights just 6.5 kilos. It is the largest model that would fit in our kedge anchor well, and even then I had to saw 6 inches off the stock to make it go in.

It had its inaugural plunge in Studland in a 25 knot south-westerly breeze

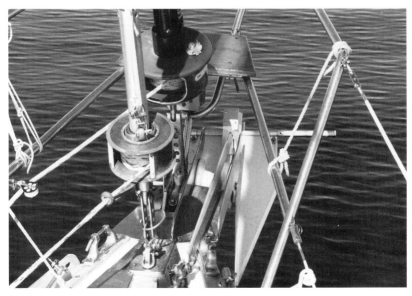

The Fortress

with plenty of chain. I was amazed the next day when I came to pull it up; I thought it was fouled, as with the chain taut up and down the bow started to sink before the anchor broke out. When we used it again in Castletownshend it was blowing much harder and it repeated the same performance. In the Aran Islands, where they were relaying the lifeboat mooring ahead of us, we were convinced when we came to weigh it that they had laid their heavy chain over our anchor and that we were there for the season — but wrong again — it was the Fortress.

'Miraculous', we said, 'why bother with heavy old conventional anchors?' We then used it continuously in mostly the same sort of weather up the west coast of Ireland, reinforcing its maker's claim 'strong as steel — half the weight, three times as resilient and no welds' each time we anchored! Only when we anchored in Golam harbour in a gale, too near the rocks for comfort and, feeling really rather disloyal, I put down a second anchor about the same size but twice the weight which incidentally came up much more easily.

Flushed with its (we've not yet christened it!) seeming invulnerability, we rafted up with the Thornhills in Ventry Bay using the anchor again. After a shellfish feast was consumed, we went to bed in a flat calm only to be woken up when we had dragged about a quarter of a mile across the bay. We motored back to our anchorage and plonked the anchor down with more care this time. The wind rose during the day to Force 6 or 7 but the anchor held both boats until it was getting really quite uncomfortable. Time to part company. We had another couple of dud anchoring episodes but it was thick weed that did for it and the CQR did no better.

The only disconcerting thing about the anchor is that it flutters down like a piece of silver paper! And therein lies the only fault we have found. Sometimes it doesn't seem heavy enough to dig in straightaway. I intend to buy a 14 kilo model as a main all-purpose anchor and we look at the 60lb CQR on deck and wonder when we will be using it again.

GIANT KELP, MASSIVE SEAS AND HUGE NETS

by Christopher Lawrence-Jones

The pretty girl looked up from her shrimping net. "No, I don't live here, but we do own it — of course, you can land at the boathouse and walk up". We had moved gingerly up to the highest reaches of Kilmakilloge Harbour, Kenmare River, low water enabling us to see the drying rock (Carrigwee) whose beacon has long gone. Dereen Garden is a riot of overgrown rhododendrons and secret paths — well worth visiting.

It was 6 July and Gail and I had left Lymington three weeks before. We had made for Cork and thoroughly enjoyed all the Irish harbours along the south-west coast. Our plan now was to sail up the west coast of Ireland to Scotland, and then home via the Irish Sea. We had been warned of giant kelp, massive seas and salmon nets extending almost across the Atlantic, but so far all had been well. We discovered that fishing boats converse on Channel 6 so would call up as follows:

Call:	'Red fishing boat off Stags, we are sailing yacht *Mermerus* approaching from the south — over'. (Repeat several times)
Answer:	'Yeah'.
Call:	'Red fishing boat — please advise — are we clear of your gear on this course?'
Answer:	'Ah, you're foine as you are'.
Action:	Proceed with caution.

The forecast was for strong northerly winds and by the time we rowed back to *Mermerus* from Dereen, the wind was already gusting down the harbour, which is exposed to the north. Just across the Kenmare River is Sneem, and to this snug and wooded inlet we now went.

As we rounded the point, there was *Golden Harvest* RCC. We hadn't seen Michael and Rosalind Snell for ten years, since we had sheltered together in stormy weather in the Isles of Scilly. Michael hoisted the RCC burgee, but it wasn't long before he had to perform a hurried restoration of the ICC flag, as their Commodore appeared in the entrance.

Michael and Rosalind were intrigued with our Freedom 38. *Mermerus* was built for us in Rhode Island two winters ago, after we had been entranced with the sparkling performance of a similar boat we had chartered. She has a single tall carbon fibre unstayed mast, and is rigged as a sloop. The mast is fairly well forward and the mainsail, with its large roach, does most of the work. The small jib has an integral camber spar and is self-tacking. With her wing keel she is very responsive, and easy for a husband and wife crew to short tack, reef and manage generally.

Mermerus has been modified for longer range cruising — extra fuel, water and battery capacity. A powerful alternator with 'Stirling Booster' produces a good charge with very little engine running.

It was not until 10 July, four days later, that the wind moderated enough for us to leave Sneem. On the radio-telephone we had heard the calls of the 'Round Britain and Ireland' contestants, including some distinguished RCC members, bravely battling it out against strong north-westerly winds and heavy seas. When we did leave at 1130, we certainly shot down the Kenmare River at speed, but then had quite a hard beat in still rough water round Valentia and across the bay to Dingle, arriving at 2130, with 60 miles on the log.

As we approached the entrance it was growing dark, but sure enough, a snort and a gurgle on the starboard quarter told us that Fungie, the Dingle dolphin, was still meeting boats and escorting them in. He led the way for at least ten minutes.

In Dingle, we had a new experience — a bookshop/restaurant. While you wait for your food, you browse in the bookshop. We deduced that the attractive girl who served us our whiskies with a slice of lemon must have been recruited for her knowledge of books, and so it proved. We wanted a history of Ireland, and among others, she brought us Robert Kee's '*Ireland — a History*'. It is very readable and was endorsed by Irish people we met later. Apart from the excellent ICC '*Sailing Directions*' (new 1993 edition) the other obligatory reading is the delightful '*Sailing round Ireland*' by Wallace Clark (RCC).

Having stocked up, witnessed the curragh racing in the Dingle Regatta and met up with John and Alison Wiltshier in *Moonbeam*, a forecast for lightish southerly winds encouraged us to leave. We hoped to reach the Aran Islands, some 80 miles on, by evening, as we were not attracted to the Shannon.

The southerly wind brought drizzle and mist as we passed through the Blaskets. The ICC pilot says Ireland has little fog, but we often had very poor visibility, especially when the south-westerlies blew in from over the gulf stream. Perhaps this is why the ICC says that the Irish go round Ireland anti-clockwise — they know about using the northerlies that bring clearer weather. We saw schools of dolphins as we ran steadily northwards, often in torrential rain, but had no sight of land until we saw the breakers on Inishmaan in the evening light. We passed through Gregory Sound and round into the peace of Kilronan Harbour, totally sheltered from the south, as dusk fell. We were the only yacht, and there was a great feeling of remoteness as we anchored, peat smoke wafting across the bay in the twilight mist.

We knew that it was possible to visit Inishmore from the mainland, but we were not prepared for the way in which the tranquility of the morning was shattered by the arrival of several large and fully loaded high-speed tripper boats. It was as if a plague of brightly coloured locusts had descended on the island. By late afternoon, Inishmore seemed deserted again.

Nevertheless, the ancient fort of Dunaengus, dominating the great cliff to the south, must be seen. What we should have done was to move the boat very early to Portmurvy, a little cove with a sandy beach, and walk up to the fort from there. This looked an excellent anchorage in winds from the south.

From here, the charts look like a cruising paradise — offshore islands, and long inlets with modest depths and tides. We made first for Kilkieran Bay. It was still misty, but we were able to make out the conspicuous tower on Golam Head and make it on one tack from Kilronan in a south-westerly Force 3–4. A sheltered spot was an anchorage inside Dinish Island — no other boats to be seen, and the only people on a fish farm float waving in

Kilronan Harbour

yellow oilskins, turned out to be 'scaregulls'. Dinish Island has one or two abandoned houses but is deserted, and has carpets of wild flowers.

In the morning we were delighted to see a sail. It was the tanned lugsail of a hooker tacking bravely out into a fairish west wind, which had set up quite a chop in the entrance, though it was perfectly calm where we lay anchored. Soon another and another sailed out past — a race? Too spread out. We reefed and followed as we all tacked down the 'inner channel' to Bertraghboy Bay. Now all became clear, as the hookers anchored in the sound behind St MacDara's island, where there is the oldest, and possibly smallest church in Ireland. It was St MacDara's day and — being the patron saint of sailors — the hookers would have probably braved any weather to get there. We surfed on up the bay, altered course to starboard at Inishnee, passed (we hoped) between the unmarked oyster banks towards Canower Point, and followed with extreme caution the winding ICC recommended course, often with little water, to the lovely anchorage off the quay at Cashel. Again, we were the only yacht.

The well known Cashel House Hotel was not far away, but somehow with rain teeming down we were not in the mood for launching the dinghy and struggling up the road in wet oilskins. Not that I mind how often we eat aboard. Even in mild but damp weather, it only takes a moment to fit the chimney and light our Taylor paraffin stove. Soon the saloon is warm and

St. MacDara's, possibly the oldest and smallest church in Ireland

dry, there are candlelight reflections in the cherry wood panelling and Gail is preparing one of her gourmet dinners.

The next morning was brilliantly sunny and we were up early to return to St MacDara's Island for breakfast. We were the only boat in the little sound, perfectly sheltered. From the top of this tiny deserted island we could see the whole of the bay and to the east the Twelve Pins of the Connemara Mountains clearly behind. To the north-west Slyne Head snaked away towards the horizon.

We were able to lay Slyne Head close hauled on a single tack, the fountains of spray caused by swell over various covered rocks, aptly called 'bellows', conspicuously marking the dangers so that with the large scale chart, it was easy to pick our way out of this island and rock strewn bay. Rocks have names like Mullauncarickscoltia, which we passed close by.

After rounding Slyne Head in uncomfortable seas, we ran between High Island and Friar Island to reach the harbour of Inishbofin. We loved it, especially the traditional fiddle and accordion music provided by the O'Hallorans and friends in the pub. The days were sunny and warm.

On Monday 19 July, we had a splendid sail across to Clare Island, except that the very expensive Quik-Vang parted at the attachment to the base of the mast when the bolt sheared, bending the mast fitting as it did so, so that a replacement bolt could not be fitted. After some fruitless hammering I had to put the whole thing in the cockpit locker where it languished for the rest of the voyage.

Wallace Clark warns about running up into the bays on the west coast — generally a lee shore — as you have to get out again. But, we wanted to see Clew Bay, which on the chart looked a fascinating maze of islands and channels, and so it turned out. Sure enough, the next day was a long beat out in light winds, so this was a rare moment for using the engine a bit to get round the dramatic cliffs of Achill Island, inside Eagle and the other islands to deserted Inishkea. We anchored in the lagoon and went ashore to the abandoned fishing village. There was no-one there, but we felt we were being watched and were glad to leave.

Broadhaven had looked a good place for the night, and we anchored in the little bay on the west side, just north of Gubaknockan Point. However, it is a rather desolate place, though the holding was good in the strong westerly winds which blew in the night. The following day the forecast was for fog, mist, drizzle, rain and strong south-westerly winds. We stayed at anchor.

Next day was better. We surfed our way up Donegal Bay to Killibegs — 60 miles in nine hours. The harbour looked as if it would be sheltered, but we had one of the most uncomfortable nights we experienced on this coast, anchored off Gallagher's blue fish processing shed. There were only one or two yachts in the entire harbour, which is dominated by enormous Atlantic fishing vessels. Luckily, we met Patrick Gallagher when we went ashore, and he offered us his mooring in the old harbour, where we were beautifully

The Killibegs

sheltered and surrounded by immaculate fishing vessels dressed overall in readiness for the annual blessing ceremony by the Bishop.

Endless depressions marched over, and while looking at the rainfall map in my atlas, I could see that Killibegs had one of the highest rainfalls in the whole of the British Isles and that in fact it was never going to stop.

So it was out of Donegal Bay in steep seas and head winds, through the sound of Rathlin O'Birne to head for Aranmore Island, where we anchored in the sound. Here, we found we had no water. One of the inaccessible connections in the pressurised water system had come adrift in the rough waters of Donegal Bay. With tremendous efficiency, the water pump had pumped all our fresh water into the bilge, from whence the automatic bilge pump had sent it overboard. Water ashore is of course available, but words like 'from a well in the village three miles uphill' are not encouraging.

It was now that our electric Power Survivor 35 watermaker came into its own. The seawater in the anchorage was beautifully clean and in a day or two we had a full tank again — and delicious water it was too. This gadget is light and quiet and not much drain on the battery.

Thursday 29 July was fine and sunny with a westerly wind Force 3–4, excellent for sailing through the delightful channels amongst the islands of the Rosses. First you go through Owey Sound with beacons to help you, and then it looks as if you can go up the Carnboy Channel between Carrickfin and Inishfree. As there are rocks just covered everywhere, I was relying on seeing the leading marks shown on the chart. No sign of them. We stopped the boat and searched diligently with binoculars. Nothing. I looked hurriedly at the ICC text — 'in daylight it is impossible to see where they are'! Discretion prevailed and we tacked round the outside of Inishfree then passed inside Gola, Inishmeane and Inishirrer, which is a very pretty trip and quite feasible with the large scale Admiralty chart. Now Tory Island lay ahead and we knew that as soon as you say you have sailed in Irish waters, you will be classed as a wimp if you haven't visited Tory Island. The south-westerly wind was sending a fair swell into the main harbour, so we sailed round to the east side, where there are two 'anchorages'. I didn't like the look of Port Doon — rather cramped — and too much swell to go alongside the quay. We went on to Portnaglass, a rather desolate and deserted inlet between high forbidding cliffs. 'There is a small jetty and steps up the cliffs where the lighthouse stores used to be landed. Anchor in 10–18 m.' (ICC). This we did and had a fascinating walk to the old village. Wallace Clark says that if the islanders have hauled their boats up, look out for bad weather. Was it my imagination, or were they hauled up especially high? We walked rather quickly back to the anchorage and were relieved when the burgee appeared over the top of the cliffs.

Thankful for the electric windlass, we got away and sailed off in the evening light for Mulroy Bay, crossed the bar and anchored just outside Fanny's Bay. The bay itself is full of moorings now. Here we spent some days — the only visiting yacht in the whole of these beautiful miles of water. A friendly local asked us to join a party of friends he was taking on his boat to the head of the bay. He was a Protestant from Northern Ireland, and his friends were a Catholic family from the Republic, including a nun on holiday. They all came on *Mermerus* for drinks, and the next day we all went to their home for lunch. There was such an atmosphere of friendliness that one began to believe that a peaceful future was possible.

This was our last port before heading for Scotland. What a wonderful experience is a cruise along the west coast of Ireland: unspoilt, dramatically beautiful, fascinating wildlife, friendly people, excellent anchorages free of swell, and coastal radio operators who sign off by saying 'God Bless You'.

TO PROVIDENIYA

by Willy Ker

As *Assent* approached the Aleutians, I could not help thinking of Captain James Cook in his ex-Whitby collier *Resolution*. In late June 1778, he was making his way north towards the Bering Strait, on what was to be the last of his great voyages of discovery. He was in thick fog, just as I was, but without any idea of what lay ahead and only lead-line and lookout to warn him of danger. He wrote in his log, '... a mist, so thick that we could not see a hundred yards before us. We were now alarmed at hearing the sound of breakers on our larboard bow ... a few hours after, the fog having cleared a little, it appeared we had escaped very imminent danger ... there were several breakers about them and yet Providence had guided the ships between these rocks, which I should not have ventured on a clear day'. The *Discovery* was following close astern and her commander, Charles Clerke, wrote with some irony 'very nice pilotage, considering our perfect Ignorance of our situation'. I, by contrast, had excellent charts, the *Admiralty Pilot*, the tidal stream tables as well as GPS and radar. Why should I feel apprehensive?

When approaching Dutch Harbor, which is on the north coast of Unalaska Island, there are three main passes through the Aleutian chain from the south-east. Streams can run in excess of 8 knots, and all can be turbulent if not taken at the slack, with 'rips and whirls', as the *Pilot* warns. The first ship passage south-west of the Alaska Peninsula is Unimak Pass, but this carries a good deal of traffic, since it is the fastest route to Japan and close to the great circle course from Seattle. I had no wish to be run down by a container ship (a problem which fortunately would not have worried Cook) and I was therefore making for Unalga Pass, 50 miles to the west. Only 1.3 miles wide, it is the narrowest of the three, but favoured by fishing vessels since it is clean, the current sets fair with the pass and in thick weather the steep cliffs of Unalga Island give a splendid radar echo. The *US Pilot* is suitably encourag-

146

ing with the remark that 'under exceptional circumstances ... in the narrowest part ... treacherous seas ... often sweep a vessel without warning ... and men have been washed overboard'. If I did miss-time slack water, Beaver Inlet to the south offers good shelter and half way through one can duck into English Bay, an excellent anchorage to which Cook's longboats had towed the *Resolution* to water and gather antiscorbutics; wild celery, angelica and sorrel.

As I came nearer to the pass it was comforting to see on the radar screen what appeared to be a fishing boat ahead of me, carefully timing his approach. Then suddenly the fog lifted, the new tide picked *Assent* up and hurried her along and a load came off my shoulders. All was now clear to Dutch Harbor and I was a day ahead of schedule to meet John Gore-Grimes and Tom Lawler. This was a meeting we had arranged by fax when *Assent* was in the Falklands seven months before. While my faithful Aries looked after the steering, I could sit and relax in the cockpit in the rather watery early morning sun and cast my mind back to the highlights of a wonderful cruise from 55°S to 55°N during which *Assent* had logged over 13,000 miles.

After our trip to the Antarctic Peninsula, Lawrence Ormerod and I flew back to England in March 1992, agreeing that he and his wife Gill would meet me for Christmas at Puerto Williams in the Beagle Channel. *Assent* had been left lying afloat alongside FIPASS, the ex-military port facility in Stanley harbour and now, in November, she was champing at the bit and eager for the next adventure. My friend Andrez Short had taken good care of her and had thoughtfully put a heater aboard for me; a necessary luxury since the southern spring had barely arrived and at the Remembrance Day parade we all stood shivering as the snow flurries whirled around us. A busy week and *Assent* was moderately shipshape but I still had to scrub her bottom and put on a couple of coats of antifouling.

Assent draws nearly 6ft and the nearest place to Stanley with a decent range of tide is at Beaver Island, 150 miles to the west. This is where the Poncets have their sheep farm and it would provide a nice excuse to cruise around West Falkland, a superb cruising area which I had been looking forward to exploring. A call to Sally confirmed that I could lie on their jetty, since Jerôme was away in *Damien II* with the BBC film crew in South Georgia and her sistership *Baltazar* was still in the mud berth where she had wintered. *Baltazar*'s skipper, Bertrand Dubois, had already been roped in to help, but she said she could do with an extra hand lamb marking. As a sheep farmer myself it sounded like a real busman's holiday!

Warren Brown (RCC) had kindly lent me a full set of charts and I had Ewen Southby-Tailyour's (RCC) excellent book, so it was with some confidence that I set off on the 19 November, beating into a moderate sou'westerly. You have to keep on the *qui vive* when sailing singlehanded in soundings so it pays to find a quiet anchorage every so often, have a snooze and stretch one's legs ashore. After a couple of pleasant stops including a visit to a Gentoo penguin colony, *Assent* was beating into a very uncomfortable head sea off Cape Meredith, the southernmost point of West Falkland, and I therefore decided to turn back into one of Ewen's secret anchorages. Under Cape Lagoon he says: '... this anchorage does not appear to exist'. It certainly did not seem very likely, as there was thick kelp all the way across the narrow entrance; but nothing ventured nothing gained and *Assent* ground her way in, sending a family of sealions diving pell-mell off the centre islet. Once I had set two anchors in the tiny space, first one sealion, then another, swam up to inspect me and soon they were all frolicking around me while two yearlings played tag just like sheepdog puppies. It must have been nearly two hours before they finally tired and I was allowed to creep into my bunk utterly bewitched and at peace with the world.

I recovered the CQR and weighed the Bruce by 0530, because I had to make Tea Island Passage, 30 miles up the coast, before the tide turned foul. It was a lovely sunny day with a light reaching breeze and I must have got it about right, since I still had 3½ knots with me through Stick-in-the-mud Passage, one of those awkward places where it can run up to 12 knots! The harbour on Beaver Island is only just around the corner, and as soon as *Assent* was at anchor I rowed ashore to a sheepdog's tumultuous welcome. I was trailed by a pet lamb, who obviously thought I was a soft touch, as I walked up past the shearing shed to the house feeling very much at home. Sally had a great haunch of roast mutton ready for supper and Bertrand and Liv came up from *Baltazar* with 2 litre cartons of excellent Chilean *Gato Negro*. Seeing the box of French wine which I had brought, Bertrand jokingly warned: "*N'approche pas à ce vin, c'est vraiment chimique!*" Bertrand has already been banned from Chilean waters for breaking the *Armada*'s strict rules. I wonder now if they will allow him home!

It was a jolly party, with the travelling teacher there as well on one of her regular visits for the two younger Poncet boys, Leiv and Diti, who are bi-lingual of course; so the talk was mostly in rapid fire French which I found pretty hard to follow. Leiv and Diti are experienced Antarctic sailors, spend-ing their holidays aboard *Damien II*; so after supper I got them to help me get *Assent* alongside the jetty at high water, ready to dry out. I awoke with a bump at 0400 to find that *Assent*'s keel had slipped into a trench dug by the keel of a bigger yacht and she was nose down and askew; this was an effective alarm clock, no damage seemed to have been done and by breakfast time she was scrubbed and antifouled on the starboard side. We had a working day rounding up sheep and marking lambs and that night carried out the same performance on the other side of the jetty.

I dragged myself away after a couple more busy days and during the next fortnight made my way back to Stanley. Cruising in the Falklands is no rest cure; the pilotage can be quite tricky and the weather unpredictable and often pretty windy — watch out for the *woolies* in some passes! There are plenty of compensations; the wildlife is fascinating, the air as clear as a bell and the welcome at isolated farmhouses in the *camp* is heartwarming. I climbed up to walk amongst nesting Rockhopper penguins, Black-browed albatross and King shags; scrambled down to look from a distance (they are easily disturbed) at Fur seals pupping on the rocks; collected fat mussels off the beach and mullet by the dozen in the creeks. Quite a holiday!

Assent was back in Stanley by 7 December, after a difficult sail in thick weather around the rugged north coast of East Falkland. Without radar it would have been prudent to stand offshore, but as usual I was pressed for time and could safely cut the corners. If I was to make my *rendezvous* with Lawrence in Ushuaia I would have to leave by the 12th, but I had time to fire off faxes in all directions from the Cable & Wireless office. Ann Fraser was to join me at Puerto Montt, Veronica at Victoria, British Columbia, and John Gore-Grimes in Alaska — it all seemed a long way off. I had one further and unpleasant chore. On our return from Antarctica the previous March, Customs had charged me another £40. I thought this was totally unreasonable, particularly for yachts on passage and only calling at Stanley for just a few days to replenish stores, and I therefore put in a strong plea to Government to have the ruling revoked. (I fear my plea has fallen on deaf ears. By contrast, in 30,000 miles I have only once been charged on entry. In Alaska, my $25 'Processing Fee' gave me a cruising permit covering a coastline equivalent to that between the Black Sea and Ireland and on to the North Cape!)

Assent was finally away at 2120 on the 13th. After the friendships I had made it was a pity to leave on a down beat; but I would be calling at Beaver on the way as I had a large packing case to deliver for Sally. The interisland

Fur seals, New Island, Falklands

coaster *Forrest* would not be calling for some time and it would in any case save her the freight. A small favour. This time I did it in one, logging 175 miles in just forty hours and after a good night's sleep was away again in superb weather, sunny and warm and with a nice easy close fetch in a south-east Force 3, backing to give a broad reach. What could be more perfect. 240 miles and forty-eight hours later I was approaching the Estrecho de le Maire with the jagged silhouette of Staten Island brooding to leeward; this was named by the Dutchman, Jacob le Maire, who sailed through his strait in the *Eendracht* in 1616 almost a hundred years after Magellan's voyage. The strait was kind to me this time and with a following breeze *Assent* was able to make against the same old 2 knot current off Cabo Buen Sucesso that had caused us so much trouble last year.

Unfortunately, the Beagle Channel had something else in store for me; the wind suddenly whipped round into the south-east and I hurriedly put in two reefs and rolled up the jib (thank heavens for roller jibs!). Motor sailing into miserably cold driving rain I made for Caleta Banner, our old friend and an excellent anchorage, having first called the *Armada* lookout on VHF *'mucho viento etc — mañana por la mañana vamos á Puerto Williams'* which seemed to keep him happy! Once I had got the hook down and was snug below it was wonderful to hear the rain still teeming down and the wind whistling in the rigging! When the sky cleared that evening the hills were covered with fresh snow down to 1000 feet.

Assent in the Beagle Channel

The morning of 20 December dawned beautifully fresh and clear. While in Caleta Banner I had been flying the Chilean courtesy flag and now, as I sailed west up the channel, I would be under Argentine regulations. Sure enough, within minutes, I was called by the Argentine lookout and hurriedly changed over the flags, whilst assuring him that I was making for Puerto Williams, which of course is in Chile. By 1500 *Assent* was moored alongside the *Club des Yates*. Formalities were completed surprisingly quickly, since the *Capitano de Puerto* already had *Assent* on file from last year, and I soon had my *zarpé* for 0800 next morning to sail to Ushuaia to pick up Laurence and Gill. I proposed to leave the negotiations for getting permission to sail north up the channels to Lawrence when we got back to Puerto Williams since my Spanish was definitely not up to it.

Approaching I wondered how I would be received, coming as I was from the Falklands, but I need not have worried. Calling the *Prefectura* on VHF (call sign: L3P — LIMA TRES PAPA) it was suggested that I go alongside the *Club Náutico* where we could lie *gratis* overnight and then make my way to the office at my convenience — all very civilised. Laurence and Gill had just flown in from Rio Gallegos and had spotted me sailing up. It was grand to see them again. Up at the *Prefectura* the bureaucracy took a little time to grind its way through the paperwork but it was all very 'correct' and then we were clear. This would be our last opportunity to get stores of any description for four or five weeks so we spent a hectic afternoon in the

Lawrence and Gill Ormerod in Patagonia

excellent *supermercado* and came away with two trolley loads of fresh veg, fruit, jolly good cheese and salamis as well as all the usual goodies. Prices seemed pretty reasonable and I was even able to use my Visa card. Beef and mutton, as well as good Chilean wine, we knew we could buy more cheaply in Puerto Williams, but precious little else. Ushuaia is something of a tourist resort with several restaurants, so that evening we treated ourselves to a *parrilla*, a real blow-out and our last chance! Before leaving we met up with some of the skippers of the French charter yachts that sensibly use this as a base, with its good facilities and communications, and were able to pick their brains about the best anchorages in the channels.

Back at Puerto Williams, we set about getting our *zarpé* to sail up the channels to Puerto Montt. This would require authorisation from Naval HQ in Valparaíso and Lawrence spent some time closeted with the *Capitano de Puerto*, Captain Miranda Williams. Basically, one is supposed to follow the main shipping route; some anchorages and passages are forbidden, some recommended and some permitted. It was the latter which we hoped to negotiate. Added to which, one is supposed to report in by radio periodically, to any lookouts manned by the Navy and to report in person to the *Capitanea* at every port you go into. *¡Qué péna!* The Chilean Navy personnel are invariably polite and friendly, but the system is overpowering.

We had hoped that Hugh Clay in *Aratapu* would meet us here for Christmas but heard that he had been delayed in Tasmania, which was a great pity. Miraculously our permit came through on Christmas morning and as I rowed the Avon around to the fuel pumps to fill some cans, the loudspeaker on the church was blasting out carols (in English — of all things!). I caused a good deal of amusement at the petrol station by joining in, but could not remember how many lords were leaping! As soon as we could, we cast off and motored away up the channel. The log reads: 'Lovely morning, hazy sun, v little wind — coffee and Christmas cake on the boat-deck'. Kanisaka (54°56'.6S 68°34'.3W), our first anchorage just behind some islands, was one recommended by Oleg in Ushuaia and was a lovely place, but obviously he has a lifting keel, for we ran firmly aground at the entrance near high water — not a very good start. When we eventually found the 'pool' we held ourselves in place with lines ashore and just took the ground at low water.

Assent carries a full cable length of 10mm Terylene rope and for the rest of our time in Patagonia we made a practice of anchoring close in with lines ashore to rocks or trees, very seldom in more than 10 metres. The winds are very unpredictable and can come howling down out of nowhere but we always slept soundly and never budged. She also carries a 20 kg Bruce which is perhaps a bit over-the-top for a Contessa 32; but none the worse for that. Unfortunately Lawrence and Gill only had four weeks and we would have to get within striking distance of Puerto Montt by 18 January, a rather tall order unless we motored a good deal.

Every day was memorable in its way. Caleta Olla; where we followed a *guanaco* trail through a forest and found beavers building their damns. Seno

Garibaldi; where we went up a fjord and anchored amongst miniature icebergs behind a small island, while the glacier at the head rumbled and crashed and we had plenty of ice for our *pisco sour*. Caleta Brecknock; a vast bowl of wind-scoured rock which reminded me of Loch Scavaig and when we climbed up *Assent* was just a tiny speck below. There were days and even pale nights of utter calm, when we motored on till dawn, and even one whole day when the wind was actually behind us. But often, we seemed to be beating with two reefs in and the jib rolled down, or the No 4 set on the inner stay, and the *ráfagas* would churn the surface of the water into flying spume. Too much of this sort of thing and we'd be looking for a snug anchorage to duck into and, with the lines ashore, batten down and listen gleefully as the frustrated wind rattled our halliards and *Assent* heeled to the gusts. Then it was time to invent a new hot toddy — one memorable one was called *Golpe de Sarmiento* but apart from large quantities of *Gato Negro* and *Pisco*, I'm not sure what went into it.

By the time we reached Puerto Edén we had logged over 700 miles and hardly seen a living soul. The people here are *mestizo* and it is doubtful if there are any pure Alacalufs left. It's not much of a place, but Gill went off to buy some fresh fish while Lawrence was checking in to the *Armada* post and I managed to get some rather suspect diesel; a splendidly primitive system of syphoning out of a 40 gallon drum using a piece of old and very dirty hose. It is as well that we have a good filter on board.

Before launching forth into the Golfo de Peñas, our first bit of open sea for a long while, we celebrated Gill's birthday with a cake (actually the remains of the Christmas cake and it even had icing). Outside it was decidedly lumpy, with squally rain showers and wonderful rainbows. The wind being fresh nor'westerly, we were close-hauled under two reefs and we rolled and unrolled the jib as the squalls went through. It is 50 miles across the Golfo de Peñas and we could just lay Surgidero Stokes, an anchorage under the lee of Peninsula Tres Montes. It was a relief to get out of the hurly-burly for a couple of hours and we anchored in 12 metres with very little swell, close in to the shore.

After a hearty breakfast, which we could not possibly have faced outside, we were anxious to press on. It is another 100 miles around Cabo Ráper and north to Bahía Anna Pink, where we could re-enter the inner channels and find an anchorage before nightfall. As we rounded Cabo Ráper at midnight we were able to ease sheets and romp away on course to clear Cabo Taitao, entering Bahía Anna Pink after lunch next day in hot sun and a following breeze. Although there are some lights, this is not a major entrance and it would be tricky in the dark.

We were now in quite different country, with the odd fishing village and a mass of islands and interesting pilotage. It was a shame to hurry, but we realised we would just make Quellón on 18 January. Quellón is on the south end of Chiloé Island, at the end of the road, and here Lawrence and Gill could get a bus to Puerto Montt and on to Bariloche and fly home. Quellón has a real frontier atmosphere, with local farmers galloping down the dusty main street on smart ponies and clad in *poncho*, *sombrero* and high leather boots and spurs. The telephone system is also somewhat 'horse and cart' but Gill managed to phone home and after being cut off a couple of times I got through to Veronica to ask Ann Fraser to join me at Castro. I was very sad to see Lawrence and Gill go, it had been fun and we vowed that next time we would take twice as long over the trip.

I had time that afternoon to sail around to Canal Queilen and into Estero Pailad (42°53′S 73°35′W). This is a delightful little creek, with small farmsteads on the hills on either side, the pastures reaching down to the water's edge where fishing boats were drawn up on the beach. A little bit of heaven that reminded me of Austria. I put down a running moor with two anchors out of the stream, and in the morning awoke to the creak of oars as a fisherman made his way out to sea, cheating the making tide close in to the bank. Not long after, in the wood just above me, I heard the 'thonk' of an axe and the quiet talk as a father and son felled a tree and then the creak of timber — perfect peace — no whining chain saws here!

Lying a few miles short of Castro is Isla Quehui with a beautiful natural harbour (according to the *Admiralty Pilot*: 'This is one of the best anchorages of Archipiélago de Chiloé'). As I had a day in hand it would be a good idea to stop off there and then go in to meet Ann. On the way north there was the wonderful sight, in the distance, of two working boats under sail. They were carrying firewood out to the islands from the mainland — for how much longer I wonder?. It was almost dark by the time I reached the entrance (the *Pilot* again: 'steer parallel with the shore at a distance of from 70 to 100 feet'). I could just make out the steep bank as I motored in and dropped anchor in the bay.

There was a rather smart modern day-sailer dried out on the beach in the morning, with somebody adjusting the rigging. As I needed some water I rowed ashore and in my best Spanish asked if I could find some *agua potable*. "Yes of course, old boy, help yourself from the tap on the side of the house" was the surprising reply! Nick Asheshov's relations live within a few miles of our farm in Somerset and I had stumbled on him by sheer chance, in rural Chile! Quehui is a delightfully unsophisticated island where everyone is mounted on ponies, including Nick and Maria del Carmen's daily who rides in every morning from one of the outlying farms, and the only wheels are solid wood on the bullock carts pulled by splendid Hereford steers. A big party was planned for the weekend, when Nick and Maria del Carmen's latest daughter, Tanya, was to be baptised in the historic old wooden church. They generously invited Ann and me to join in the fun.

Ann Fraser takes up the story:

'Willy wants you to meet him on an island' Veronica rang to say three days before my flight to Santiago. A vision of a remote rocky island in the Chilean fjords flashed before me. The contact point was more reassuring: the Hotel Unicornío Azul in Castro, Isla Chiloé.

'We're going to a christening,' Willy announced, rowing us out to *Assent*. A christening? With scarcely time for more than a quick look round Castro, a visit to the market for a poncho for Veronica, a christening present and a boozy lunch at the Unicornío Azul, we set sail through the Canal Lemuy for Quehui (pronounced *Kay-wee*), one of the many islands sheltered from Pacific rollers between Isla Chiloé and the mainland. It was here that the christening was to take place. This festive event was an introduction to a Chile very different from my image of icebergs, glacial fjords and craggy mountains. The 180 km long island of Chiloé and its archipelago has a gentler climate and topography — a little piece of England set down in the Pacific.

We arrived at Quehui after dark and anchored off the beach in front of Nick's holiday home. Ashore, we found ourselves in a Wild West time-warp with horses tethered to posts, complete with sheepskin blankets and carved wooden stirrups. Horses were the only transport on the island. 'They've just re-invented the wheel here,' said Nick later. And indeed, on the beach lay a wooden sledge drawn by oxen across the mud and sand.

The christening was held in a typically Chilote triple-towered yellow clapboard church, though a slight hiccup preceded the christening feast. The champagne (Chilean naturally) had been cooling in the sea in crates, but someone had forgotten about the tide and Nick's son had to dive for it, clad

A triple-towered Chilote church for the christening

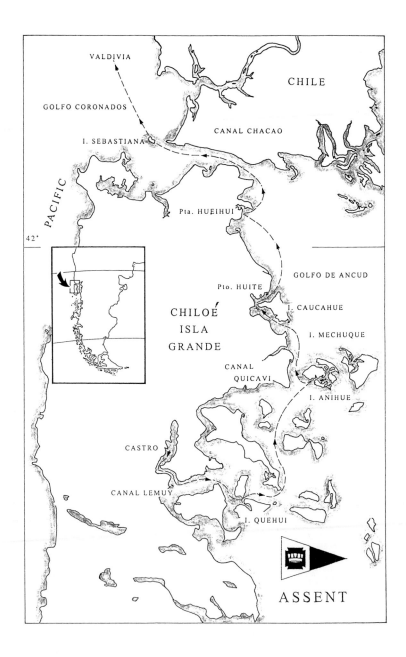

in wetsuit, mask and fins, with Willy standing by to lend a hand. The celebrations went on well into the night, with guitars and accordions accompanying the national Chilean dance, *La Cueca* — ending with Quehui's own song in which we all joined '*Adónde va la lancha? A Quehui va!*' (Where does the boat go? To Quehui!).

The next day Willy and I visited the Port Captain to get the all-important *zarpé* or clearance, the first of many frustrating encounters with hidebound bureaucracy Willy was to suffer at every port. He was asked how much fuel and water he carried, how far this would take us, to state his exact course from port to port and to report in by VHF twice daily. A little flexibility and goodwill on both sides achieved the *zarpé*.

We left Quehui with a fresh salmon in our fridge, salmon-farming for export to Japan being a growth industry in Chiloé. It was a wet and windy day with a north-easterly on the nose, and having negotiated the Paso Imelev, near Quehui, we headed north through the islands for Isla Mechuque. Tidal streams here run up to 6 knots and with wind against tide it was uncomfortable. Willy opted for a more sheltered easterly passage

Currents are strong in the Golfo de Ancud, the interior sea between Isla Grande, the main island of Chiloé, and the mainland. The tides sweep in from the Pacific from both north and south and meet in the middle, causing tide-rips and eddies and a tidal range of 7 metres. Sailing between the islands, it might have been Devon or Somerset but for the glimpse of snow-capped volcanoes in the distance. The land either side was a softly undulating patchwork of greens, browns and yellows, with crops of potatoes and wheat. Settlements clustered round the turreted clapboard churches built by the Jesuits in the 17th century, when the Mapuche and Chonos Indians, the original inhabitants, were resisting their Spanish conquerors.

The rains, fogs and gales of Chiloé's temperate climate have produced a hardy, seafaring people. The Chilotes' skill as seamen dates back to the Chonos Indians, who built canoes and rafts made of bent planks and held together with pieces of bamboo and caulked with bark. In these frail craft, they ferried the Spaniards across the notorious Chacao Channel between Chiloé and the mainland, which we were to sail later.

By early evening, as we motored slowly up a wide waterway between Mechuque and its adjacent island, Añihue, the sun was shining and the wind gentle. Heavily tree'd slopes ran down to a wooden jetty and a large house at the water's edge, roofed with Chilote-style wooden shingles.

Sadly, with flight deadlines and Willy's need to get on to Hawaii and Alaska, we had no time for gunkholing in this wonderful cruising ground. Pressing on north through the Canal Quicaví and past Isla Caucahue, we tucked ourselves in for the night behind a spit of land at Puerto Huite. '*Puerto*' on Chilean charts does not denote a port of any magnitude, merely a possible anchorage. We were using the invaluable *Atlas Hidrográfica de Chile*, which did not show the newly-developed salmon farm near the spit. We were about to creep further in when we noticed the seagulls looking curiously leggy and realised just in time they were standing on a recently silted-up sandbank.

The Indians call Chiloé 'The Place of Seagulls' — a name evoking the mystery and dominance of the sea and winds in the lives of Chilotes. Life and death is influenced by the tides. When the tide is flooding, no one can die; but when it is ebbing, the sick are at the gates of eternity.

Mythical creatures wander the shores, such as the sea-fairy, the *Pincoya*, beloved by fishermen, who dances out of the sea and brings an abundance of fish and shellfish.

The *Caleuche*, a phantom barque which sails eternally, has a crew of *brujos*, wizards or male witches who have a deformed leg. If anyone is caught looking at the ship, the witches have the power to make him go mad, so that the secret of their magic cannot be passed on. Having learned that the witches hold their covens in a cave at Quicavi, which we had passed, I was glad we hadn't anchored there for the night.

We now had to tackle the Canal de Chacao, a 12 mile channel between the top of Chiloé and the mainland, which is the exit to the Pacific. The *Admiralty Pilot* warns that the meeting of tidal streams from the Canal Chacao and Golfo de Ancud causes a line of tide-rips called Raya de Tique just before the eastern entrance to the channel. Tidal streams run at 6–9 knots over and past Roca Remolinos and another rock, causing further tide rips. There is virtually no slack water, and going out on the ebb tide of about 5 knots you meet the westerly winds and Pacific swell rolling in at the western end. It promised to be an interesting passage.

We anchored for lunch to await high water near Ponta Hueihui, just before the Raya de Tique tide-rips, then set sail. The log reads 'wind very fresh from 315°' — dead on the nose to start. *Assent* bucked and swirled her way through the tide-rips and whirlpools, often momentarily off course despite a very firm hand on the tiller and a wary eye on the rocks, as Willy gave instructions on the course to steer and pored over the chart. It got quite exciting at times.

It seemed to take for ever to get through and I began to wonder if, like the sick and dying of Chilote mythology, we too were being borne to eternity on the ebb. But at last the island of Doña Sebastiana was to starboard and we were out in the Pacific and could close reach under two reefs and furled genoa for our next destination, Valdivia, about 100 miles north.

We reached Corral, just inside the southern side of the entrance to the Rio Valdivia, 24 hours later on 28 January and anchored off this fishing port-cum-tripper spot hoping for a good dinner. We were disappointed and nearly supperless, but eventually found a small restaurant open.

Motoring up the Rio Valdivia was magic: mountains covered with pines, eucalyptus, larches, oaks and myrtles; stretches of low, rushy areas as the river widened nearing Valdivia, a few small houses dotted along the shore — and a sense of peace and tranquillity.

Willy had an introduction through Warren Brown to Tony Westcott, an

Anglo-Chilean who kept his boat, *Equinoccio II*, at the Valdivia Yacht Club. We were made welcome by the President of the yacht club, Justo Schüler, and moored up alongside *Equinoccio*. In the afternoon we explored the quayside market, stalls piled with every kind of shellfish, fruit and vegetables. Several boats were moored alongside the quay, including a big charter yacht, but it's a bit public and we were glad to be in the security of the yacht club.

Tony Westcott appeared the next day and suggested we hire a car to visit the Lake District. Willy having at length convinced the *Capitania* that both he and *Assent* had already entered Chile formally at Puerto Williams (and produced both flimsy documents) we were free to go.

Our mistake was not hiring a four-wheel drive. We reached Lago Panguipulle without incident, getting our first view of the snow-capped Choshuenco volcano, and ate dinner at the Hosteria Pulmahue in a bougainvillea filled garden overlooking the lake. After a walk up Choshuenco (during which, in trying to park out of the sun, I discovered that it moves anticlockwise in the southern hemisphere!) we thought we'd follow the unmetalled road round Lago Riñihue. In a cloud of dust we lurched and jolted for miles along a loose flint cart track, lining up planks with the wheels to cross gullies and streams and flinching at the 400 foot drop to the lake beneath us.

On our return to the yacht club we were called on by Diana Davies and Barry Gallagher, a Tasmanian girl and her English boyfriend who had sailed their 28ft steel yacht, *Gryptype Thynne*, from Hobart via Fiji and Easter Island,

Choshuenco Volcano

and who were a fund of useful information on the harbour at Easter Island.
Tony Westcott also gave us the name of the shipping agent in Easter Island
and a contact on Robinson Crusoe Island in the Juan Fernandez archipelago,
where we were bound next.

After a massive shop we set off downriver to get a repair done on the
stainless-steel tiller fitting, which had a hairline crack. We'd been told there
was a boatyard downstream that did welding, run by a German, Alex Wopper.
Alex, who speaks English fluently, came down to inspect and within no time
the job was done. Ten years ago, after doing the Mini-Transat followed by
a circumnavigation, he had come into the Rio Valdivia, liked what he saw
and set up a boatyard with his wife, Dagmar, a sailmaker. He is now building
large multihulls and has a well-equipped yard and slip, capable of doing
virtually any yacht repair, including stainless and aluminium welding.

Next morning the sun was shining and there was a brisk south-westerly
blowing. Thinking of the Pacific rollers to come and my lack of recent sea-
time, I got out the Scopoderm before we reached open water. It wasn't soon
enough. At 1700 Willy noted: 'storming along on a broad reach — quite a
hungry sea'. By 1830 the log reads: 'getting a bit too excited — 2nd reef and
rolled jib to storm size'. Later that night on watch, running under storm jib
alone in a horrible sea, I succumbed. A moment later Willy stuck his head
out of the cabin in the dark and, seeing me embracing the winch, asked what
the devil I was doing!

The rest of the 418 mile passage we stormed along in a big following sea
under trysail and poled-out jib, taking aboard the odd rogue wave, until the
morning of the 8th, when the sea became smoother and the wind slightly
less. By 1600 we could see the 3000 foot peak of Cerro El Yunque just above
the clouds, and approached Robinson Crusoe Island, still veiled in mist, in
the early evening. The mist cleared gradually, revealing granite peaks veiled
with greenish-brown scrub, burnished gold in the evening sun. We called up
Juan Fernandez Radio on Channel 16 to report our arrival in Bahía
Cumberland and anchored near a catamaran, *Fadolla*, close under the mountains in 6 metres.

Fadolla kindly brought out the Port Captain in their inflatable. With the
strong offshore breeze and no outboard, getting ashore was impossible. Pink-
footed shearwaters and dark storm petrels swooped around us as we rewarded
ourselves for the rigours survived with a stiff G & T. Williwaws howled down
at *Assent* in the night and next morning we were again ferried ashore to
complete formalities, as we were planning to leave again that night.

Robinson Crusoe or *Más a Tierra* ('the one most near the land') as it was
originally called, is an island of craggy ranges and fertile valleys, dependent
on crayfishing and increasingly, tourism, for its economy. We made a date
to sample the crayfish at the delightful cabin restaurant run by Tony Westcott's
friend Maria, aptly-named Aldea Daniel Defoe, which neatly preserves the
legend which the Chileans capitalised on in renaming the island some years
ago.

The anchorage at Robinson Crusoe Island

To work up a suitable appetite Willy determinedly strode to the top of the Alexander Selkirk Lookout, named after the real-life Robinson Crusoe who had climbed there daily for four years to survey the horizon for a ship to rescue him from his self-imposed marooning and exile, after a quarrel with his skipper. Selkirk survived by chasing and eating the goats which ran wild on the island. I enjoyed a walk up the mountain, accompanied by the gentle sh-sh'ing of wind in the pines and eucalyptus trees, with marvellous views over the bay and hedgerows filled with montbretia, hydrangeas, and purple morning glory.

Having obtained our *zarpé* from the Port Captain and promised to report twice daily by VHF (but we lost contact after the first night), we sailed that evening past the towering cliffs and ravines of the north coast. With 1600 miles ahead of us to Easter Island, we quickly got into 4-hourly watches and the regime of shared galley duties.

In contrast to the previous passage we had too little wind early on and, the wind becoming very light, we had to motor, often for hours. It got steadily warmer, and during these frustrating, sunny days we were visited two days running by tropic birds, flapping and wheeling over us with squeaky calls, a school of porpoises and a wandering albatross. Otherwise, it was a very lonely ocean.

The continued light weather forced us to decide we would have to cut out Pitcairn. With light airs and a dead run we made slow progress and it wasn't

Easter island entering Hanga Piko

until 21 February that Willy noted: 'Into SE trades at last'. Two days later we were trying to slow down to avoid arriving at Easter Island in the dark!

We anchored in the open roadstead of Hanga Roa in 20 metres. Having contacted the Port Captain, who came out to do the entry formalities, we spoke to Juan Edmunds, the shipping agent, to ask if he could arrange a pilot into Hanga Piko.

Our experiences entering Hanga Piko initially followed closely *Ardevora*'s account in last year's *Journal* entitled 'Falmouth to Tonga'. The difference was that as our pilot, Oscar, was taking us through the most alarming and surf-breaking part of the entrance, another fishing boat with a gesticulating, shouting figure aboard came up astern, and before you could say 'Juan Edmunds' he had boarded *Assent*, pushing Oscar aside.

From then on it was pandemonium. Inside the harbour, three yachts were moored on the seaward side with bows on to a buoy. While seventeen people shouted contrary instructions and Willy, to his astonishment, found the tiller snatched out of his hand by the newcomer, *Assent* was manoeuvred in a distinctly unseamanlike manner alongside a large Beneteau, with lines to the buoy and the shore. At this point the engine stopped abruptly, our self-appointed skipper having caught a rope in it.

The problem, as we learned later, was that rivalry existed between Town and Gown and we had employed a fisherman from Hanga Roa, not Hanga Piko. For future visiting boats, the mooring arrangements have improved since *Ardevora* was there. The harbour wall is complete, but only for use by the Chilean Navy and fishing boats, and stern lines are taken to fastenings on the seaward side.

We had a marvellous if all too brief time in Easter Island. We joined the crew of the Beneteau and another boat to visit many of the *moai* sites; the skipper of the Beneteau, while awaiting the return of their ailing engine from Santiago, had got involved with a Kevin Costner film about the island's history, *Rapa Nui — Navel of the World*, and showed us the reconstructed village built for the film. On our last evening we were invited to a farewell party for one of their Rapa Nui friends, Timo Atam. Timo's family owned much of the land round the harbour and his uncle, Marcello, was the Easter Island representative in the Chilean parliament, so we had a rare and treasured opportunity to meet a Rapa Nui family and their delightful children.

Departing from Hango Piko on 27 February with 1900 miles to go before reaching Fatu Hiva in the Marquesas, we crossed the Tropic of Capricorn on 3 March and had several days of black clouds, squalls and thunder and lightning and torrential rain, with which we filled buckets and washed ourselves and our clothes. Our star sights were improving, which was just as well, because just before we reached Fatu Hiva the GPS packed up and we were back to steam navigation. Secretly we were both pleased, and since the sun was very nearly overhead at noon, star and moonsights became important.

Moai in line abreast

Marquesan Ann

Fatu Hiva was reached on 17 March, where we anchored in the Baie des Vierges. There being not even a *gendarme*, entry formalities were non-existent and we were free to enjoy this beautiful and untouristy island before hurrying on to Hiva Oa and Nuku Hiva, for me to catch my flight to Tahiti.

Back to Willy Ker:

Experiences are all the more enjoyable when shared and I was sorry to see Ann go, for she had been a good companion and an able crew. Ahead was 2000 miles of empty sea to Hawaii and at least another 2000 miles on to Victoria, where Veronica was to meet me. Singlehanded sailing can be very exhilarating and I was looking forward to the trip. If all went well *Assent* should be in the Straits of Juan de Fuca by about 10 May, giving me time to sort things out, scrub her bottom and slap on another coat of antifouling, which was probably overdue after her time in the tropics.

We had been given a barrow load of delicious ripe mangoes, but I had been told that I could get limes and fresh vegetables from a garden in Baie de Anaho, on the north-east corner of Nuku Hiva. This seemed logical, as it was on the way and it proved to be a delight; books could be written of the beauties of Anaho, as RLS wrote many years ago. I set off on 26 March, with fresh lettuce, tomatoes and enormous *pamplemousse* and a splendid reaching breeze from the east. This gradually turned nasty, with squalls and rain, and I was down to bare poles for a while before it all went flat and *Assent* was left slatting in a hot and sultry calm.

Before leaving Anaho I made the mistake of climbing up through thorn scrub to get a photograph and then swimming for an hour near the coral. I should have known better, for within a day or two all the scratches went badly septic and in spite of a course of antibiotics from the first aid kit they were still giving me trouble six weeks later. It was now imperative to motor on, to break through the ITCZ and into the North East Trades. They came in with a bang on 3 April with heavy rain and a north-east Force 5 gusting 6; but *Assent* was making excellent progress, averaging 130 miles a day on the log.

The GPS had gone down shortly before the Marquesas (water in the co-ax cable, as it turned out), so I was able to enjoy myself taking sun-run-meridian altitudes which showed that we were getting the benefit of an extra 10 to 15 miles a day from the North Equatorial Current. This was good news and I should be in Honolulu around the 11th.

As dawn broke on the 10th, the 13,000 foot peak of Mauna Loa appeared above the clouds 75 miles away to the north-east looking magnificent. Just where it should be! Only 160 miles to go to Ala Wai Harbor. At the entrance there is a fuel jetty where you can call US Customs, but you need a 'quarter' to do that — fortunately I had one or two with me, given as change for dollars when I shopped at the Irish House in Moscow. Where else?

The Hawaii Yacht Club allowed me to use their excellent facilities during my stay and I was fortunate to have an introduction to Tom Kawamoto, a Met forecaster who had been riding in the High Sierras with my sister-in-law. One evening Tom took me to a Mandarin restaurant, well away from Waikiki and the normal tourist beat, and the next night to a Sushi bar, which was quite an experience. I did all my shopping close by and found all the chandlery I needed at Ala Wai Marine. Before leaving, Tom gave me a run down on the weather pattern. Received wisdom is that one should sail due north to 48°N before turning right; but Tom reckoned that with the North Pacific High where it was, I could follow the Great Circle to Cape Flattery, riding the top of the High and picking up the tail of the storms which were racing across south of the Aleutians.

Tom proved correct and I had an easy trip, logging 2200 miles in 20 days. On 17 April I noted: 'wind veering slowly, gybed — first time on port for 5000 miles!' I was getting into the westerlies, it was much colder and I was quite glad of my longjohns and pullover.

The US Coast Guard radio station (NMC) in San Francisco puts out a weather forecast four times a day for the Eastern Pacific and I listened with some trepidation as deep lows tracked across to the north, with winds up to 60 knots. I must have been lucky, as the last one of the season crossed Vancouver Island just ahead of me. I now had to keep a much better lookout as I was crossing the main shipping lanes from the Santa Barbara Channel and Portland to Japan, and I found that in the big seas my radar detector did not ping until ships were uncomfortably close.

It was a great moment when the impressive snow clad peak of Mount Olympus came up on the starboard bow, shining in the sun above the early morning mist, and Cape Flattery showed on the radar just 10 miles ahead. *Assent* rounded Race Rock with the flood at 1730 and soon was alongside the Canadian Customs jetty in Victoria Harbour. While I was waiting for Customs, I called the BC television station on VHF and got through to my old friend Terry Stamper, who had sailed with us to Greenland in '86. The young Customs officer was friendly and efficient, I was cleared in a brace of shakes and Terry and Christine were down within minutes. While Terry piloted us around to the Royal Victoria Yacht CLub, which was to be *Assent*'s home for the next two weeks, Christine drove to meet us and we were soon home. It was marvellous not to have to cook for myself; we had a superb supper, a great chat and then bath and bed. The only problem was that the bed kept on rolling and I woke up every twenty minutes to have a look around!

Veronica was due in by air on 16 May, but there was plenty to do; sails to be repaired, the GPS to be fixed etc. The RVYC could not have been more hospitable and Art Archer, the club's bos'n, obligingly craned *Assent* out in the midst of a busy spring schedule, while club members generously lent me charts and pilots for the route north. How can one thank them enough?

Our plan was to sail up the Inside Passage and then, weather permitting, across Hecate Strait to the Queen Charlotte Islands and on to Ketchikan. With Veronica aboard, we sailed north in perfect weather and even Hecate Strait belied its bad reputation with gentle breezes. This must be one of the world's finest cruising areas and I cannot better the account of *Juno II*'s cruise (*Roving Commissions* 32) including the 'one that got away', except that ours was a 30 lb Halibut and we were much too excited! All too soon, it seemed, we were alongside at the friendly little yacht club in Ketchikan, where we were welcomed with a barbecue that night.

Things have changed in Ketchikan since Veronica was there in '52, on her way to meet me up north; then it was all boardwalks, bars and bordellos, although I doubt she knew too much about the latter, being a sweet young thing and newlywed! Now the boardwalk is a tourist attraction and 'Dollie's House' is open to the public but, as the guide book says rather primly, 'only for sightseeing'. Last year 300,000 cruise ship passengers landed in Ketchikan!

Veronica now, unfortunately, had to fly home and I had arranged for Brian Newham and Jo Hardy, his girl friend, to meet me for the leg to Dutch Harbor. Brian had been Base Commander at Halley, the BAS base in Antarctica and we agreed the final details on the radio via RRS *Bransfield* while *Assent* was in Patagonia! Brian and Jo turned up on the ferry from Prince Rupert bang on time and without more ado we pressed on north. I was very keen to revisit Haines, as I had done a triangulation survey up the

Haines 'cut-off' road in BC when on attachment to the Canadian Army in 1952. The problem is that Haines is 60 miles up the Lynn Canal, a few miles short of the gold rush city of Skagway. Inevitably, the wind was blowing straight down off the glaciers and we had to plug all the way up this spectacular fjord under motor.

Haines 'City' has grown a bit over the years but still has quite a 'frontier' atmosphere. We were able to hire a car and drive across the border and up the tarmac road to the pass, where banks of snow still pressed in on either side, although I remember it as a dirt road with 10 foot drifts that had only just been cleared in early June. It is a wild and beautiful place with Brown bears as big as the fabled Kodiaks, Dall sheep and mountain goats graze precariously on the crags above and we saw a cow moose and her calf feeding in a 'slough' by the roadside, which anxiously trotted off with their characteristic high stepping gait. In '52 we had pack horses and went deep into the mountains and down to the Tatshenshini river, one of the last great wildernesses on earth. I had been shattered when I heard that they were planning a vast copper mine in my valley but we were relieved to hear that it has now been declared a Provincial Park and so is safe, we hope.

Kluane National Park in NWT lies to the north and we were making for the Parks Department office which is at Haines Junction, on the Alaska Highway. Brian is an experienced mountaineer and is planning to climb Mount Logan next summer, but he had to get permission and a 'slot'. While Brian was discussing the details with the very pleasant uniformed officer, who was right on the ball being a keen ski-mountaineer herself, I read about an expedition to establish the height using Differential GPS, confirmed at just under 20,000 feet, no mean mountain and Canada's highest. That night after a long hike we camped by Kathleen Lake surrounded by snow capped mountains, a beautiful spot, but the mosquitoes were just as ravenous as I remember them when Veronica and I stopped there for breakfast forty years ago.

After all this nostalgia we were ready to press on, but Ted Brainard (RCC) had suggested we look up his nephew John, and it was lucky we did. John and Dee have a salmon smoking business and invited us to their house for a barbecue. Getting to their house, Eagles Cliff (Bald Eagles, of course, which are almost tame), was quite an experience and entailed scrambling up 200 feet through virgin forest. By happy chance, at the party we met Tom Stimpfle from Fairbanks, who told me that his brother Jim was chairman of the Chamber of Commerce in Nome and might be able to get us visas for Russia. This was vital information, as I had heard from John Gore-Grimes that he was having great difficulty his end. The wind, naturally, had gone around into the south and leaving Haines we had another hard plug to get out, accompanied by a procession of huge cruise ships that had been up to Skagway to 'do' the 'The Trail of '98' along with the shooting of 'Soapy' Smith and 'The Cremation of Sam McGee'.

At one of our anchorages, I was out in the Avon after sounding the rather

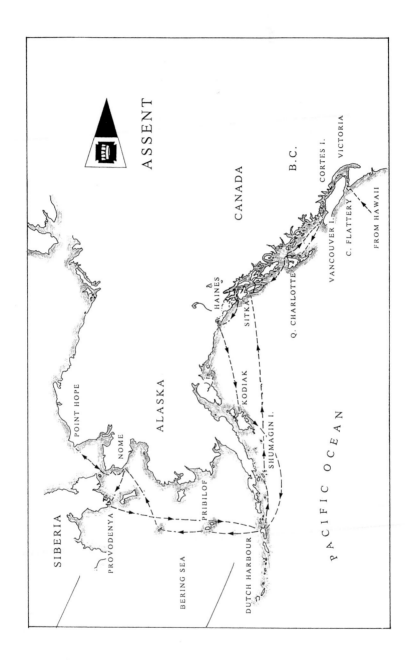

The bigger one got away ... Lynn Canal, Alaska

tricky entrance and hooked a halibut. This time I was determined not to loose him and rowed frantically for the shore; with feet on *terra firma*, he was soon landed and we thought we were unlikely to starve for a few days. At Yakutat we were given a big salmon when we went to the 'cannery' for water and, of course, as these things go, Brian caught a really nice 5 lb 'Silver', not long after. *Embarras de richesse*, without a doubt!

Cape Spencer to Kodiak is a good 500 miles and is a most spectacular passage. Looming above the clouds on the starboard hand is the great snow-clad peak of Mount Fairweather, named by Cook, and the huge glaciers of the St Elias range, sighted by Vitus Bering only thirty-seven years before, in 1741. We had mild excitement when we found ourselves being shadowed by a US Coast Guard cutter, shining immaculately white in the bright sunlight. Complete radio silence was rather unnerving, so I broke in on Ch 16 with a flippant remark about their smart turnout. This was not entirely wise, since USCG have a reputation for being pretty heavy handed, but they must have decided they were only dealing with a mildly dotty limey and not a drug-runner and after a few more pleasantries, she steamed off.

In Kodiak, we discovered that it was going to cost Brian and Jo something like $500 each to fly out of Dutch Harbor, so I suggested they leave me there and catch the ferry to Homer and get a lift on the road south. We had a couple of days in hand to enjoy the wildlife; quite the most engaging are the sea-otters which paddle around on their backs with their kits cradled in their arms, quite unafraid. They have made a great comeback since the days of the Russian fur traders and near extermination.

With another 500 miles to Dutch Harbor I would have to get cracking to meet up with John Gore-Grimes in time and was moderately lucky with the weather. After twenty-four hours beating into a fresh south-westerly which increased to Force 6 gusting 7, the wind backed and I was able to ease sheets as I rounded the Shumagins and squared away for Unalga Pass. Good old *Assent* had made it in five days.

* * *

Rounding Cape Kalekta into Unalaska Bay one is immediately struck by the sheer size of this fine natural harbour. Dutch Harbor is over to starboard, where storage tanks, cranes and fish processing plants sprawl along the shore of Amaknak Island, dominated by Mount Ballyhoo. Ahead, in complete contrast, a rather charming Russian Orthodox church stands on a low shingle bank at the head of the bay, as if to protect the village of Unalaska from the brash commercialism of 'Dutch'. There is more than mere symbolism in this, for it was the Church which tried to look after the interests of the native peoples and particularly the Aleuts when power was transfered from Russia in 1867 and the Orthodox Church is still very strong.

Using the onion spires of the church as a leading mark, sail straight in until you are nearly on the beach and then turn hard astarboard through a narrow buoyed channel. The small boat harbour is right inside and very protected; it is also conveniently close to the bank, post office, supermarket and a couple of very decent little restaurants. If you want to live it up, there is a new five star hotel owned by Unisea, the huge Japanese conglomerate, who seem to own nearly everything else as well. Dutch Harbor claims to be the busiest fishing harbour in the USA and last year, we were told, had a turnover of around $4.5 billion.

As *Assent* entered I was hailed by Jim Dickson, owner of a good looking 39ft steel cutter, who took my lines and then whisked me away for a shower and a meal in his house in Unalaska, hospitality I found typical of Alaska. He was looking after his little daughter while his wife was at a dig near Kodiak, as part of a degree course in archaeology. Next morning when I went to the airport I discovered that John Gore-Grimes and Tom Lawler had been delayed in Seattle and, being at a loose end, I was invited to join a party flying out in a Grumman Goose to a ranch the other end of Unalaska Island. The opportunity was too good to miss.

The Goose is an old war-time amphibian, still going strong and ideally suited to the job. We took off from the airfield, staggered through a pass just below the cloud base and landed in Chernofski Harbor. The technique then was to wind down the wheels and charge the beach, scattering excited sheepdogs in all directions and, at the last minute, swivel around to point

Shishaldin Volcano, 9,974ft, Alaska

back out to sea. Milt and Cora Holmes invited us all into the house for coffee, a fascinating place full of the bric-à-brac of a lifetime in the north, ivory and bone artefacts from an ancient Aleut midden, beautiful fox furs, antique guns and a Civil War sword that had belonged to Milt's grandfather, only he was not sure on which side he had fought!

I left with a warm invitation to return in *Assent* with my crew, and on the way back the clouds lifted and we had a magnificent view of the snow covered peak of Makushin Volcano. John and Tom turned up next day in fine form; we had quite a bit of shopping to do and Tim Voss, a master mariner working for Unisea, took us under his wing and ran us around town in his pick-up. As a result, John persuaded us all to join him that night at the Grand Aleutian for an excellent dinner, when Tim told us about his famous grandfather, Captain Voss, who sailed around the world singlehanded in *Tilikum*, an old 38ft Nootka war canoe rigged as a three-masted schooner, in 1905.

We were very keen to get across to Siberia if we could; the problem was to get visas. I knew that the ex-mayor of Nome, Jim Stimpfle, whose wife is Upik, had been organising exchange visits by her people to their relatives across the Bering Strait. While I put through a call to Jim, John and Tom, who is a freelance photographer and journalist, went over to Unalaska to take some pictures and get a feel for the place. They ended up in the Elbow Room, reputedly the roughest bar in the North and had a great time, returning more or less unscathed. In the mean time, Jim had told me that if we could get up to Nome, he could fix visas for us in a week. Jim Stimpfle is one of those super-enthusiastic people for whom the impossible just takes a little longer, but not much.

Nome is about 700 miles north of Unalaska Island and we wanted to stop off at the Pribilofs and St Mathew Island on the way, but we decided that the 60 mile sail around to Chernofski would be a useful shake-down and good value anyway. We eventually got away at 1630 on 13 July and motored in a flat calm around Cape Cheerful. The evening was drizzly and very mild, not at all what John expected of the Bering Sea! We were having to buck a 1.4 knot tide but a breeze filled in from the south at 0245 and we were soon cracking along close-hauled and were off Chernofski Harbor by noon.

It is a superb natural harbour with a narrow entrance and perfect shelter inside, reminding me very much of the Falklands, without a tree in sight. During the war, we were told it had been quite an important military base but there is little sign of it now, apart from a big heap of coal, which Milt mines for the house. We had caught a small halibut on the way into the harbour and we took this and a bottle of Bushmills up to the house as an offering and had a very enjoyable evening. Milt is a real old-timer with a fund of stories and told us something of the ranch. With two hip replacements he had had to cut back on the sheep from something like 5000 to just over 500, but there were still two or three thousand cattle out there somewhere.

Aleut skin boats, St. Paul Island

Our course for the Pribilofs took us close to Bogoslof Island; this is an active little volcano, which put on a good show for us with a great plume of steam. There is also quite a big colony of sealions which haul out on the black sandy beach and we caused a bit of a stir amongst the 'beach-masters' when we rounded up close offshore. We had thought of landing, but the beach was a lee shore and the soundings did not seem too reliable, so we contented ourselves with a closer look and then bore away for St Paul Island, 200 miles away to the north-west. With a fresh breeze from the east to north-east we were 'barrelling along', as John noted in the log, but as so often was the case in this area, the visibility was down to half a mile much of the time.

We were picking up the weather forecast on 4125 kHz twice a day from Kodiak and somehow it was a great comfort to hear the redoubtable Peggy Dyson. There is a slightly homespun atmosphere, with fishing boat skippers coming back for a repeat when reception is not too good — I've done it myself — and the occasional message to a wife when a vessel is behind schedule getting home. The region she covers is absolutely huge, with fourteen forecast areas, which if they were in Europe would stretch from the Aegean to the Blaskets and up to the Lofotens. Hardly surprising that the weather in your particular 'neck of the woods' does not always match up! I think I will always remember her oft repeated 'rain and faag'.

On the evening of the 16th visibility improved enough to sight St George Island away to starboard and we reduced the jib to make sure we arrived at

Northern fur seals St. Paul Island, Pribiots

St Paul Harbor in daylight. We knew there had been some new harbour works and our chart would be wildly out of date. Until quite recently, supply ships anchored off and stores were taken ashore in *bidarkas*, the Aleut skin boats, but now with two new protecting moles barges can safely lie alongside and unload and the port is being developed as the centre of a new King Crab fishery. The island also attracts groups of 'birders' who fly over from the mainland laden with tripods and telescopic lenses (in aircraft of course!)

It really is a fantastic place, something like a million Northern Fur seals, the largest herd in the world, come here to breed and the restless noise and smell near the rookeries is unbelievable. The thousands of nesting sea birds (Red-legged kittiwakes, Crested auklets and the uncommon Red-faced cormorants etc.) make a walk along the cliff edge a must, even if you are not a dedicated twitcher. There is a large Aleut community on the island and their Russian Orthodox church has a particularly fine interior. Tom went up for the Sunday morning service, which was pretty long, and after standing for the whole of it I think he felt that even his sins would all be washed away.

Thoroughly shriven, we set sail that evening on a broad reach for the uninhabited island of St Mathew, 200 miles away. The forecast next morning was for an easterly gale and fog, not exactly 'jolly boating weather' but it made for a fast passage. The sky cleared as we approached St Mathew, the stars sparkled, and in the dawn Cape Upright reared 1000 feet out of the shallow morning fog while Humpback whales spouted around us — an exhilarating scene. We found a lee, of a sort, in a shallow bay behind Cape Upright and anchored in 11 feet. With a 2 foot swell running in and the tide falling this was not too comfortable, and while John and Tom were ashore I moved *Assent* out into deeper water and naturally got plenty of stick from the oarsmen on their return. John had climbed a 1500 foot mountain and, while resting near the top, got some splendid footage on his video of an Arctic fox which came up and sniffed his boot. When I went ashore I found old caribou antlers, the relic of a herd established to provide meat-on-the-hoof for a military post during the war; without predators the population exploded and then totally collapsed. I had been told that walrus haul out here to die and had hoped to find some tusks, but had to be content with a couple of orange plastic floats. One need never buy a fender again, since regrettably there must be thousands littering the beaches amongst the drift wood all up the coast.

After this blow through we wanted to get on to Nome, 300 miles north-east past St Lawrence Island. Fortunately, the current sets north at up to 2 knots off the Yukon Delta, which would give us a helping hand, but the wind was on the nose and we had rather a tedious beat, with a lumpy sea. The wind went back into the south-south-west as we came up to Nome on 23 July, which was bad news since the roadstead would be exposed to the swells and the new mole gives little protection. Sledge Island 20 miles west of Nome offers some shelter, so we altered course to anchor there until conditions improved. If the worst came to the worst, we could sail the 120 miles north to Clarence Bay and the village of Teller, where we could probably hitch a lift along the 70 mile dirt road back to Nome.

The anchorage behind Sledge Island proved to be better than expected and we had a quiet night. In the morning the wind had eased a bit and we overheard the skipper of a tug, the *Arctic Bear*, talking on VHF to the harbourmaster in Nome; he was concerned about docking his barge at the end of the mole in these conditions. When we broke in, he helpfully suggested that we come and lie astern of the barge, as soon as he had made fast. It turned out to be quite a picnic, for having got a line to the barge I had to hold *Assent* back with the engine full astern until John could get a kedge out on the quarter with the Avon. Once we were secure, the skipper of the *Arctic Bear* ran us into town in his pick-up to show us the inner harbour and then joined us for a beer in the Bering Bar. Ed had done a trip down to the BAS base at Rothera in a supply ship, so we had a good crack about Antarctica and ice pilotage in general.

Nome's inner harbour is in the mouth of the Snake River and is very shallow with 8 feet at best, and although the tidal range is notionally only 1.6 feet the level can drop by as much as 4 feet with strong offshore winds. The entrance is over a sand bar and is dredged between training walls. Next morning there was still a 2 foot swell in the entrance and when we came in at high water there was only 6 inches under the keel (on another occasion we actually bumped). It would be easy to be trapped inside if you weren't careful.

As soon as we could, we made contact with Jim Stimpfle and he was as good as his word. Getting a visa for Russia is not difficult, so long as you have an invitation. We did not. Rather like a conjurer producing an Ace from his sleeve, Jim had one ready. We were invited to visit Provideniya, all we had to do was fill in our names and the dates. There was another form to fill in, photocopies of our passports to be made, plus three passport photos each. Jim would send them by Express Mail, together with $40 each, to the Russian Consulate in San Francisco and they should be back in just over a week. Magic!

John Bockstoce (RCC) had given us an introduction to Bonnie Hahn and her son Pat. Bonnie had been a regular crew member in *Belvedere* and was aboard her when she completed the Northwest Passage in 1988, and Pat had helped him build an *umiak* and was with him when they very nearly completed the Passage in the *umiak* in 1980. Pat and Sue live only a minute from the harbour and made us very welcome and by a happy chance had a Russian staying with them. Andrei's wife is head teacher at a junior school in Provideniya and would look after us, and we offered to take over a load of groceries, soap, blank video tapes and so forth, that are almost impossible to buy there. Sue had also arranged to fly over with her three children on a visit the following week and would join us there. Jim Stimpfle gave me letters of introduction to the Port Director and the Colonel commanding the

Border Guards — it looked as though things were falling into place. All we needed now were our visas.

Nome, of course, is famous for two things; gold and the end of the Iditarod Trail, the 1000 mile dog team race from Anchorage, which is run every year in March. Back in 1925 there was an outbreak of diphtheria in Nome and the race was first run in 1973 to commemorate the epic dog sled relay which managed to get the serum through in mid-winter. As we were told: "it's a mighty tough race — the winner in '93 finished in just over ten days but quite a few of the teams got caught in a blizzard and came in together four days later; but don't worry, there are compulsory stop-overs and vet inspections and all the rest, but it's still a mighty tough race!".

Gold fever is very catching too and ever since the turn of the century they have been mining 'placer' gold around Nome, with everything from home-made sluice boxes on the beach to gigantic dredgers, many of which lie rusting wherever they stopped work when the price slumped. There are still quite a few part-timers (and old-timers!) working the beach. One we met in the Bering Bar was Richard Wilkinson, whose family both John and Tom know well in Dublin — it's a small world! Richard had just had a good strike and was celebrating; he had been diving down 15 foot off the beach with a home-made suction dredge and sluice box mounted on a sort of pedalo. Highly dicey, one would have thought, but he had got 15 oz in a week (at $350 an oz) and the celebration was still going strong when the bar closed at 0500! A shy and very engaging man.

With a week to wait, we decided to 'improve the shining hour' by sailing as far north as we could. As part of his research into the history of whaling, John Bockstoce had spent ten seasons with a crew from Point Hope hunting Bow Head whales in *umiaks* and recommended a visit to the settlement there; but it was unlikely that we would reach the pack ice, although the edge probably lay only 200 miles or so farther north at that time.

At Jim Stimpfle's suggestion, we decided to call in to Port Clarence on the way and join his family for a barbecue. Jim's in-laws live in Teller, but most of the families were in their summer camp out on a sand spit the other side of Grantley Harbor, where they set gill nets out from the shore and catch salmon as they run up to spawn. Quite a few are put into the big deep-freezes that everyone has nowadays, the rest split and dried on racks in the age-old way. We sailed around in perfect weather, anchoring close under the spit only a stones throw from Jim's tent. Jim's wife had put together a great feed of grilled salmon, fresh from the sea, and we sat around talking into the night as the sun dipped below the northern horizon.

When we weighed just after 0600 next morning it was quite calm, but the wind filled in from the south-west as we crossed Port Clarence, a big, almost land-locked bay and the last good anchorage going north. Port Clarence and Grantley Harbor are historic places. HMS *Plover* wintered here in 1850, having previously wintered in Providence Bay (Provideniya), and it was a busy place towards the end of the century, when whalers frequently came in here to refit and water, or limped back in when damaged in the ice farther north. We had a good reaching breeze as we rounded Cape Prince of Wales and were bowling along at 7 knots — about the limit for *Assent* — and as we passed through the Bering Strait we picked up Little Diomede on radar, 12 miles on the port beam. The Arctic Circle was crossed just after midnight on 30 July, but it could have been the 31st — we were not too sure since we were on the 'Sunday-Monday line'. The log reads: 'vis poor, rather cold, dead run, lumpy sea'.

We were running dead before, as we came up to Point Hope, but we had seen nothing, even on radar, although the GPS told us it was only 7 miles ahead. Small wonder that Cook did not sight it on his way north to Icy Cape and it was not until 1821 that the Russians put it on the chart. When we did eventually see the long low spit with its cluster of buildings it looked pretty bleak and the seas were breaking all along the shore. There was absolutely no question of landing under these conditions and we reluctantly hove-to, put in a couple of reefs and set the No 4, ready for an energetic beat south. We had reached 68°21′.8N and had to be content with that.

It was Murphy's Law that, within ten hours, the wind had dropped away to nothing, but the seas of course would take a lot longer. Soon after we had reset the rolling jib the wind piped up again and the toggle at the bow fitting failed. This was the second time — after the previous failure, I really thought that I had replaced it with a strong enough fitting, but having learned our lesson we keep the inner stay set up all the time now. The jib was soon tamed and lashed down and we were back to the No 4.

The wind, fortunately, fell away to nothing as we approached the Diomedes but both islands were hidden in fog. I had picked up Big Diomede on radar at 9 miles and a little later it appeared out of the mist on the starboard bow. At the same time our radar detector bleeped, had we been observed? We were just 4 cables from the Russian border!

Little Diomede is pretty impressive, it rises straight out of the sea to 1300 feet and the tiny settlement clings to the rock rather like seabird's nests. We anchored rather insecurely $\frac{3}{4}$ cable from the cliff in 6 fathoms and I stood anchor watch while the others went ashore. Jim Stimpfle's father-in-law James Omiak, in Teller, had told us to look up his relations and John went up and met Pat and Evelyn Omiak, a splendid old couple. They also had relatives on Big Diomede, but they were all resettled by the Soviet authorities somewhere in Chukotka awhile ago. When I went ashore I was shown around by three very enthusiastic young teenagers who showed me the *umiaks* that they still use for whaling. The village quota is one 'strike' but they did not manage to land one last season. One of the boys, Vince Mogg, was a great-grandson of William Mogg, a famous whaler, and was delighted when I recognised the name. As far as we could discover we were the first sailing yacht to visit Little Diomede.

We had an easy run back to Nome, with bright warm sun, excellent visibility and with the wind in the north and very little swell no problems this time getting in. We were alongside by 1945 on 4 August. Our visas arrived back next day, but priority number one was to repair the forestay. Fortunately *Jakaranda Flower*, a big centre-board ketch, had just come in and he found an old jumbo-sized toggle amongst his spares which he let me have, and armed with this I enlisted Ramon Gandia's help. As a bush-pilot Ramon's exploits and his pecadillos were apparently legendary, but he is also a keen sailor and his was the first yacht into Provideniya when it opened up. He ran me around town looking for parts and we made up a really strong fitting in his workshop. What a wonderful man!

In the morning, Andrei came down with several cases of stuff which we had offered to take across and somehow we managed to squeeze them all down into the quarter berth and we were ready to leave. We bumped on the way out but whether it was entirely due to the fact that we were down by the stern I would not like to say. It is only about 250 miles across to the Chukchi Peninsula, but the winds were all over the place and very light, so we had to motor a good deal and paced ourselves to arrive in daylight and during working hours.

After Sir John Franklin's expedition had disappeared into the Arctic a number of expeditions were mounted by the Admiralty. One of the ships sent to the Bering Sea was HMS *Plover* (Commander TEL Moore), which left England in January 1848. The intention was that she should pass through the Bering Strait in July, but she was dreadfully slow and by mid October had only reached the Chukchi Peninsula. Moore realised that he would have to find a suitable place to winter very quickly or risk being caught in the ice offshore. Almost immediately they spotted a cleft in the hills and, sailing in, found the perfect place. Moore called the outer harbour Providence Bay and the inner bay where he wintered, Emma Harbour. Plover Bay is an anchorage behind a spit, on the starboard hand coming in to Provideniya. It is nice that these names are still remembered and, as we discovered, there is a board in Provideniya Museum with a rather quaint translation in English, which tells the story.

The approach to Provideniya is not very thrilling; rather drab barren hills, with the odd streak of grey snow, flank the entrance and the town itself can be identified by the pall of black smoke belching out of the power station chimney — no clean air act here! We had sent a message from Nome to the Port Director to warn him that we were coming and when I called up on Ch 16 I was answered by an operator who spoke some English. He sounded welcoming, which was a good start.

Andrei had shown us on the chart the best place to lie and, sure enough, there was Viktor Mukhortov, the Port Director, in a smart suit and gabardine rain coat enthusiastically waving us in to the dock. It was a warm and friendly welcome, but he had alerted the Border Guards and soon they were down, all green topped 'cheese-cutters' and deadpan faces and a couple of grey-faced men with briefcases. With Viktor hovering in the background formalities were soon completed and we even managed to elicit a few wan smiles.

Provideniya

Habits die hard, but we had played this game in Murmansk when I was aboard *Wild Goose* and found that a few cheerful smiles worked wonders. Viktor's father was a Soviet Airforce pilot, but he was in the merchant marine and, as I discovered when I went to his flat for supper, is a sailing buff with a library full of books and was over the moon when I discovered a mention of ôCCEHT in a Russian translation of an old edition of *Heavy Weather Sailing*.

Once the Border Guards had pushed off we contacted Irina, Andrei's wife, and she managed to find a friend with a 3 ton lorry (sic). We loaded up the packing cases and then we all went up to her cosy and pretty flat in one of those huge impersonal blocks that seem to be the hallmark of Soviet architecture. It is hard to describe the total dereliction of a place like Provideniya — buildings go up but are patently never maintained, roads are built but the pot-holes never filled. On our way up to the flat we climbed up a flight of concrete steps, of which two had collapsed and the gap had been filled with an old wooden pallet.

My abiding impression is of a very friendly and decent people struggling to keep their heads above water. It is a cliché that there is 'nothing in the shops'; meat is rationed, mostly from Chukchi reindeer herds, but bread is good and plentiful and there is a brewery producing quite an acceptable home-brew. We did not see very much else and we were glad that we had brought over with us a lot of fruit and fresh vegetables, as well as frozen chickens and eggs for our hosts. Irina and her friend Luba, who acted as our interpreter, put on a tremendous spread that evening with caviar and smoked salmon and it was a splendid party, with Sue Hahn and some neighbours as well, who drifted in and out.

I was keen to meet the Colonel commanding the Border Guards, and Viktor managed to arrange an informal visit to *Assent* the following morning at 1000. It was an opportunity to deliver the letter from Jim Stimpfle, thanking the Colonel for his help in organizing the exchange visits for the Upiks, and I wanted to broach the subject of cruising freely up the coast. Colonel Sergei Punogin is impressively built with a palpable air of authority, but after sampling some of our Black Bush he became quite genial. With Viktor interpreting I discovered that he had served in Afghanistan and we exchanged a few words of Pushtu, my last unit in Burma being mostly Pathans from the Northwest Frontier. It seemed a good moment and I asked him whether it would be possible, on another occasion, to sail up the coast and explore as far as Wrangel Island. "No problem — just ask me!" We parted on excellent terms and I thought to myself: 'well blow me down!' knowing the seeming impossibility of making any arrangements from outside Russia.

That night I had a very congenial supper with Viktor, talking sailing and sharing a bottle of Vodka with him, while John and Tom went to the town bar to get a bit of local colour and had a whale of an evening, finishing up by standing the crowded bar drinks all round. Their US dollars obviously went an awful long way and John got back wearing a policeman's hat. It was time we left!

Before we were allowed to leave, Luba was determined to show us the sights — the town bakery, the leather factory which tans Reindeer hides, and the brewery, where the bottling plant would only get one out of ten in a 'Health and Safety' inspection and seemed to be particularly good at crunching bottles. The high spot of the day was undoubtedly our tour of Irina's infant school. In contrast to everything else we had seen, it was spotlessly clean, colourful and imaginative. It combines the function of a school and a crèche, since most of the mums work, and every child had a neat bed in a dormitory. Most of the kids were away with their parents for the summer holidays, but the ones we saw there were absolutely full of beans.

We had to clear out with the Border Guards and the same old lot came trooping down, but this time there was a subtle change in their demeanor and there were quite a few smiles! I wonder why? When we said goodbye to all our new-found friends there was a lot of laughter and not a little sadness. We could only hope that the future will be kind to them.

Our return trip to Dutch Harbour was not without excitement. On the second day out, Friday 13 August, the forecast for our area was: 'gale — NE increasing 25 knots, becoming NW 35 to 40 knots'. At 1500 I recorded 'puffy clouds and blue sky, jolly sailing weather'; but by midnight John noted, 'big quartering seas, gusts knocking us around a bit' and at 0600, me again, 'pretty dirty morning, rain, running under two reefs'. We had already

An Indian Summer ... Klawock, Alaska

rolled up the jib and the Aries was coping well with the steering, but just after 1600 we were hit by a couple of rogue waves and I suppose I should have taken the main off her then. An hour later I was on watch, but at the chart table, when we were hit by a big one and started to pitch-pole and then broached and rolled to 90°. *Assent* bobbed up immediately but everything was very chaotic and wet. As John wrote in the log: 'If Friday the 13th don't get you, perhaps Saturday the 14th will!'

It took about forty minutes to strike the main and lash it down, after which we set the trys'l and had a much more sensible ride, with only the occasional wave breaking into the cockpit. The wind eased gradually and by 1300 on the 15th we had the main up again with two reefs and the jib half unrolled. We were back at our berth in Dutch Harbor at 2040 on 16 August having logged 700 miles in five days (allowing for crossing the date-line). Two days later, after a splendid farewell party at the Grand Aleutian, John and Tom left by air for home at 0930 in the morning, but I regret to say I did not see them off as I was still out cold in my bunk on board!

I had arranged to leave *Assent* with a friend in BC. He lives north of Vancouver in Gorge Harbour on Cortes Island, a very protected anchorage where she would be safe for the winter. With no more deadlines to make there was no point in hurrying. As I discovered, the fall is a wonderful time to cruise and I dawdled through the Shumagins, where Bering had landed, and across to Sitka. The last cruise ship had left for warmer climes and the flashy sport fishing boats, 'pukers' I've heard them called, had long since motored back down the inner passages to the 'Lower 48'. It was incredibly peaceful and after the first frost the autumn colours were superb. One early morning, in a remote anchorage, six young wolves came down to the beach and quietly inspected *Assent* before trotting back into the forest. A true Indian summer and two whole months of heaven.

RULE 2 (A) (I)

by Tim Trafford

For those whose Blue Book is not to hand, Rule 2 reads 'To associate owners of yachts, boats and canoes, used for cruising on sea, river or lake ...'; it also refers to 'other persons interested in aquatic amusements' such as FE Prothero, the Club's Rear Commodore in 1888, who was himself an intrepid canoeist.

Lying awake at night looking up at the Southern Cross, with the sound of the trade wind swell dashing itself on the reef, is perhaps one of the best memories of Caribbean sailing.

In November 1993 I was gazing up at the same constellation, but the familiar shipboard noises were replaced by a spooky silence which was only broken by the crackle of the dying embers of the camp fire. The security of the cockpit coaming was replaced by a stony desert stretching to distant moonlit mountains as strange insects made their home under my carry mat. Nonetheless sleep came easily after a day of paddling the canoe along wide open stretches of river and negotiating cascading rapids.

Having spent two weeks exploring the emptiness of Namibia it was time to take to the water. The Orange River rises in the high mountains of Lesotho and downstream it forms the border between South Africa and Namibia. Our vessels were sturdy, two-man canoes complete with two water-tight barrels for dry storage and an icebox. An interesting assortment of travellers, including Scottish, Swiss, South African and Namibians, gathered in a rush-hut in the cool of the evening to learn the art of canoeing and swap stories of adventure in the African bush. The following morning we set off in five canoes from the bordertown of Noordoewer, a rather drab riverside settlement complete with bottlestore and slaughterhouse, on a week-long 110 km paddle to the confluence with the Fish River some 100 kms from the Atlantic.

Once the trick of keeping on course had been mastered we soon fell into the easy rhythm of paddling. Fear of capsize was forgotten and the vibrance

If you would find the sea, make the river your companion...

of life supported by a river flowing through a desert surrounds you. Some 280 species of bird are found in the narrow strip of green that borders the river: most spectacular of all are the kingfishers, particularly the malachite and red bishop. These exotically coloured birds, unperturbed by the approach of a canoe, could be watched darting into the water and returning to their perch a second later with fry flashing in their beaks just like the puffins on Great Skellig.

Each morning, soon after the sun had risen over the surrounding mountains, we headed downstream. Striking camp was a question of rolling up the ground sheets, ensuring a watertight seal on the barrels and, having learnt the hard way after the first upset, making everything fast. Most progress was made in the cool of the morning while the shadows were long and the colours of the deeply incised mountains were at their richest. Coffee time was dictated by the discovery of shade provided by a large willow or thorn tree. Within a few minutes murky green river water was boiling over a fire in an enormous black kettle. By mid-day, as the temperature climbed towards the high 30°s, shade had to be found and water fights had become a mutual necessity.

The middle part of the day was spent snoozing, swimming and slowing down to nature's pace. A three foot long mole snake would glide effortlessly through the camp and on one occasion our colourful Portuguese guide requested that 'nobody move' as he had spotted a scorpion on the leg of Christiana, our large German companion. She continued her dialogue on the pitfalls of the ERM while luring the creature back to the bush.

During the first two days the river was bounded by high cliffs to the south and the Richtersveld, the southern extremity of the Namib desert, to the north. The desert climbed gradually away in a series of flat-topped escarpments that eventually melted into a shimmering mirage. We passed two 'fishermen' but they were more intent on catching 'stones' washed out of diamond-bearing pipes hundreds of miles upstream. Occasional goat grazed on bamboo shoots. Sometimes they were tended by a lone farmer, and at other times by a troop of baboons with a taste for fresh meat. Apart from the fishermen and herdsmen there was no sign of human influence and we were alone with the river, mountains and heat.

Initially the rapids were gentle affairs with navigational skills being limited to picking the deepest water. However, *Entrance Exam* — the first tricky white water — audibly announced its presence some distance upstream. The burgee (my paisley handkerchief) bravely plunged from one standing wave into another, and we emerged only to be turned upside down in calm water by a 'sleeping hippo' — a rock lurking just beneath the surface. The next few eddies revealed an assortment of sun hats, water melons and suntan lotion.

Meandering its way out of the mountains the river widened into a ribbon lake and a fair breeze allowed the bowman to set a squares'l. We reprovisioned at a farm, the only irrigation project we passed, before paddling around Divorce Bend, a featureless 10 km curve through which there was little assistance from the current. In the distance a range of mountains hovered over a liquid desert. As the day wore on they became clearer and eventually we romped through a gorge into a tranquil lagoon surrounded by towering mountains, whose shadows brought welcome relief and which radiated a soft warmth until late in the evening. We camped on the outwash fan of a dry tributary and whiled away the evening watching *klipspringers* (small antelope) and fish eagles while a joint of kudu roasted in the *braai*. That night the shooting stars were spectacular and Barry, the South African, took us on a guided tour of the heavens.

The cool of dawn lasted until the first rays of sunshine fingered their way over the barren peaks. Instantly colours became washed out, cicadas began their day-long monotone, and leggevaans, three foot long aquatic lizards, crawled onto mid-stream rocks to sun themselves. Initially I felt an intruder in the richness of river life, but after several days a curious feeling of blending into the background became apparent. *Hamerkops*, comic, brownish birds with a tuft of feathers protruding from the back of the head to balance their powerful bills, eyed us inquisitively from their dens — enclosed nests on high ledges. Ashore we found large yellow and black beetles that appeared to walk on stilts. They had developed ridiculously long legs to hold them clear of the scorching sand. Occasional Ververt monkeys scampered in the willows overhanging the river and a troop of baboons caused a hasty departure one lunchtime.

In the heat of the day dust devils danced in the desert and every now and then they ventured onto the river, whipping the surface into a circular frenzy.

On the last evening the sun set in an angry sky and fiery reds were offset by flashes of distant lightning. There was a feeling of pensiveness in the air that night and before dawn a soft refreshing rain fell out of a heavy sky. An overpowering smell of wetness on dry soil filled the air and one could almost sense the relief that the season of the short rains would bring to the desert scrub. The final rapid was conquered without trepidation and after a bedraggled morning's canoeing when even the birds did not brave the rain, we located the 4 x 4 that would return us to civilisation.

A FAMILY AFFAIR

by Tim Le Couteur

Lying on the lawn at home with two broken heel bones after a fall from the terrace above did nothing for the planning of our cruise. This had been talked of for at least five years and we knew there was only one year, 1993, when all three children could reasonably join Ginny and me; Simon aged eighteen was in his 'gap' year, Rosalind aged sixteen had passed School Certificate, the New Zealand equivalent of 'O' levels, and George aged thirteen would return for his first year at secondary school in February 1994.

Falconer, our 38ft Hallberg Rassy, had already been across the Atlantic. We had purchased her lying in Gibraltar on a three week yacht purchasing holiday a long way from our home in New Zealand. We thought she was ideal for our proposed Mediterranean, Atlantic and Caribbean cruise and for resale in Florida. I had sold my company and the year's subsequent management contract expired at the end of March 1993. A month before this I was told that the bones had mended so I exchanged my wheelchair for crutches and was fortunate to be walking without these just before we left for Gibraltar.

After ten days preparation in Gibraltar, including meeting the pallet-load of charts, pilots and other sailing equipment which we had shipped out from New Zealand, we were ready to set sail.

By making short day passages along the rather uninteresting southern Spanish coast we learnt about *Falconer*'s sailing capabilities and array of electronics. On the fourth day we rounded Cabo de Gata, Spain's south-eastern corner, and spent a night at our favourite Spanish harbour, Ensenada San Jose. From here we planned to sail north-east to the Balearics before heading south to Malta. In this way we hoped to be upwind of the prevailing northerlies which could sweep one down onto the inhospitable Algerian coast. For two more days we crept up the Spanish mainland before the northerly wind changed to the favourable south-west quarter. This enabled us to make an overnight passage to Ibiza where we spent a day exploring the 15th century citadel before continuing our journey. The first two days out from Ibiza gave us a taste of boisterous south-westerlies which *Falconer* handled better that we did. The next nineteen hours were spent hove-to 80 miles off the south-western corner of Sardinia. The wind had backed to the east and was screaming a full gale out of the mountains. The family was not impressed, in fact it would be fair to say that George was ready to pack his bags at the next port even though it meant going back to school. They were to learn that nothing in long distance cruising lasts forever and by the end of the third day we were bowling along at 6 knots with a westerly Force 4. There followed two perfect days sailing across smooth seas with fair winds; jersey's and oilskins were shed and the girls started ferreting for bikinis. I was pleased that this spell of fine weather gave us the opportunity of negotiating the 'narrows', the 85 mile passage between Cap Bon in Tunis and Sicily. I had been worried by the 2 metre Keith Reef, and names such as The Terrible Bank and Sylvia Knoll with 20 metre depths did nothing to calm me. One other worry was an engine whose fuel system was totally blocked. Happily having previously owned a yacht with a severe case of diesel 'bug' I was able to sort out the problem.

We arrived off Malta at 1900 on 30 April, and being out of ordinary hours were asked on the VHF to clear customs and immigration in Grand Harbour. The passage had taken six days thirteen hours for a distance sailed of 742 miles. We had due cause to celebrate, as did the Maltese; tonight was the start of their Labour Day holiday with a magnificent firework display. We all enjoyed our nine day stay in Malta soaking up the atmosphere of this historic, thriving and cheerful place. All the jobs that we had accumulated on *Falconer* were carried out well and we realised in retrospect that the stores and chandlery we purchased were the best in the Mediterranean. We had chosen to lie stern-to on the quay at Manoel Island rather than in the marina, a decision which enabled us to be considerably closer to the services that we needed. It also gave us a taste of Malta's dreaded north-east *gregale* — yachts lying on this quay can suffer considerable damage from the large swell entering the harbour.

We had committed the cruising 'sin' of arranging to meet friends, ambitiously nominating 20 May as the meeting date in Kas, south-west Turkey. *Falconer*'s log records that the northerly wind blew scarcely more than 5 knots for two-thirds of the 465 mile passage, during which time the motor was put to good use. Our night entry into Khania, the westernmost port of Crete, was made difficult by the dangerous boulder bank that lies across the harbour entrance. Apparently this unlit bank, which is no more than $\frac{1}{2}$ metre out of the water, is the start of a new breakwater.

Our departure from Khania was delayed by a north-easterly gale which we heard later caused considerable damage in south-western Turkey. In Khania potted trees, chairs and umbrellas went flying on the quay. Ginny and the family had a lucky escape when a chemist's sign made from glass crashed down at their feet, shattering into pieces. We were on our way again on 15 May heading for Rhodes, and had a pleasant two day sail to the island

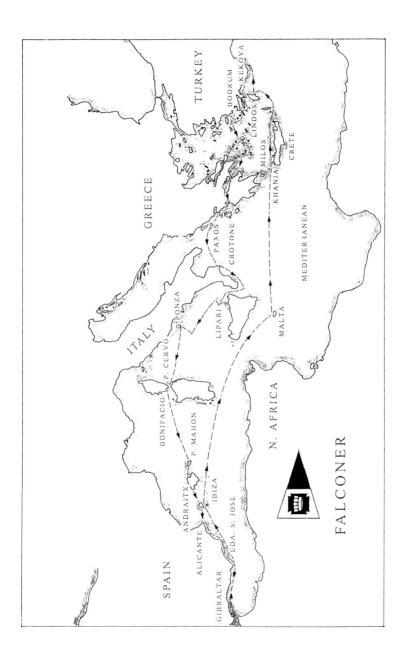

Simon Le Couteur

Knights of St. John Castle Rhodes

choosing the quiet anchorage of Lindos, 20 miles south of the main harbour, Mandraki. Ginny and the family caught the bus to Rhodes the next day. It being Monday the shops were open but unfortunately the restored Knights of St John Castle was closed. We learnt later that this is the norm with Greek national monuments, as is the practice of making no charge on Sunday. Outside the tourist hours of 1000 to 1600 the anchorage at Lindos was perfect tranquility and we enjoyed our first swim in the Mediterranean. Much as we hated to leave, there were only two days before our Turkish rendezvous. An overnight passage on the night of 18 May brought us to the most south-eastern Greek island, Kastellorizon. Stern-to on the quay between the two main restaurants, we were pleased to find ourselves close to *Morning Star* with Dick and Sheila Trafford (RCC) on board. They left shortly after, making room on the quay for a succession of Turkish charter yachts. We watched with amusement the antics of the rival restaurateurs beckoning these new arrivals. It is not surprising; as we were told afterwards that each yacht could spend more than US $250 on their crayfish lunch.

The following morning we motored the four miles across to Kas harbour on the Turkish mainland; entry procedures were lengthy but courteously carried out. We had entered a different world of *bazaars*, street vendors and *mosques*. If there was ever any doubt the *mullah*'s call to worship five times a day including 0400 emphasised the difference between east and west. We were fascinated by it.

During our three week 'holiday' in Turkey we cruised between Kekova Island in the east to Bodrum in the south-west. The wind was almost non-existent for most of this time but distances were generally short so motoring was not too much of a hardship. We were joined by Rosemary and Peter Wakeman in Kas, by Robert and Jenny Loosley in Fethiye and by my mother Daphne Cresswell (RCC) and Noel Bond-Williams (RCC) in Bodrum. We had been told to get to Turkey before it all changed and certainly this advice is sound. Everywhere we saw the burgeoning tourist industry despoiling the coastline and natural harbours.

Having said this, south-west Turkey must be one of the best cruising areas in the world with an abundance of safe, clean natural harbours and the historical legacy of Lycia and Caria. I would order better wind conditions but, this apart, a cruise in these waters in spring or autumn would be hard to beat. In most of the popular anchorages, particularly round Fethiye Bay, one would find a crude temporary restaurant camped on the shore. It served food at almost the same price as one could buy it in the shops and cook on board, so the temptation to eat out was great, particularly when barter came into it. George, our chief negotiator, would outboard round the bay comparing prices, discussing menus and the number of pieces of meat on each *kebab*. As an inducement to return with his party of seven he was often treated to a free coke! From an antiquities point of view our highlight was two days spent in the ancient and rather dangerous harbour of Knidos. Robert Loosley, an antiquarian by vocation, made the whole site come alive for us, complete with its famed Aphrodite (without her nightie!). From a cruising point of view I can think of nothing more pleasant than a week flopping around the many anchorages of Fethiye Bay. Marmaris with its smart German-owned marina, complete with Turkish carpets in the showers, had the best shopping and *baazar*. To show you how large it is Simon had the misfortune to lock our bicycle in a side-street of the *baazar* and was then unable to find it again. It says a lot for Turkish honesty that a very desirable Bickerton bicycle was still chained to its lamp post when he found it some two hours later. Kas offered the best choice of carpets; from here *Falconer*'s aft cabin was embellished by a small *kilum*. At Marmaris also we met Dena and Arthur Blackburn (RCC) on board their Hallberg Rassy 35 *Fuzette of Gorey*. Dena had sailed Firefly dinghies against my father at West Kirby Sailing Club so this was a particularly good meeting.

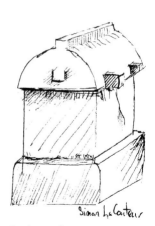

Simon le Caiteur

Lycian tomb

Finally Kekova Island which offered some of the most varied anchorages and least spoilt villages ashore.

It would not be fair to pass this area without a brief description of two incidents where *Falconer* and our cruise could have come to grief. Both incidents related to anchoring. The first was in Tomb Bay, Fethiye, where the depths in the bay force one to tie stern-to the shore. We believe the yacht alongside us disturbed our anchor, but in any event we woke to find 30 knots blowing from a clear sky and *Falconer* lying side-on close to the rocks. With the bow anchor not gripping disaster was averted by passing a line to a neighbour also clawing their way off the lee shore. We spent the rest of the night at anchor in 25 metres keeping anchor watch. The second occasion was at Knidos. We knew the holding was dubious but the quay was full, the weather seemed settled and a dive to inspect the anchor showed it well dug in. Simon, Rosalind and George were on board whilst Ginny and I sampled the delights of the restaurant ashore with Robert and Jenny Loosley. Unbeknown to us the wind had again sprung up out of nowhere and one large gust dislodged most of the yachts lying in the anchorage, including *Falconer*. Seeing navigation lights suddenly appear in the anchorage we guessed something was wrong. By the time I had jumped into the dinghy and rowed out Simon and his able crew had just motored clear of the old boulder breakwater and re-anchored. This was another night that we kept anchor watch. It served to remind us of the tenuous nature of cruising even when in apparently perfect cruising grounds. For the rest of our cruise through the Mediterranean our trusty 45lb CQR was as firm as a rock.

The close proximity of Greece when cruising these waters tempts one to duck into an occasional Greek island for a change of cooking. We had a 'steering problem' when passing the island of Simi which took the night to repair! Despite our enjoyment of Turkey this brief sortie into Greece during our cruise north to Bodrum gave a taste for things Greek. We therefore

The ubiquitous Aegean pellican

eagerly anticipated our arrival in Kos for the start of the Greek section of our cruise. This stop was made special by Noel Bond-Williams taking us to his favourite restaurant, with fond memories of his last cruise in these waters twenty-five years ago. Moreover we were celebrating my forty-eighth birthday and the last time I had cruised with Noel I was seventeen!

Our next stop was Vlikathia Cove on Kalimnos Island where sadly Noel and Daphne had to leave us. Noel's blood pressure was playing up and we were heading away from good medical facilities.

I was lucky to find a young Greek charter skipper in Kos and we spent a leisurely hour or two drinking beer whilst he marked our charts for the Cyclades. From this evolved an ambitious three week cruise which first took us to the northern Dodecasese, Patmos, Lipso and Arki. We met unsettled weather for the week spent in this charming group and found the very sheltered anchorage at Patmos welcome. The monastery ashore was one of our cruise highlights. The two days with *Falconer* tied alongside the new quay

Patmos

at Arki whilst the northerlies blew Force 6–7 gave a wonderful insight into a totally unspoilt community. Arki also gave us our only New Zealand-style barbecue of the Mediterranean cruise, on a little beach by the harbour entrance.

Finally the strong northerlies abated giving us the required slant for the 70 mile passage to Mikonos. One night of 'flesh pots' was enough and very early in the morning we motored across to the Delos/Rhinia passage with its windy reputation. Because of the calm we were able to enjoy a magical day wandering round the ancient site of Delos, swimming in beautiful, sandy Fourni Bay where *Falconer* was anchored.

From Delos we headed south hoping to get to Santorini. Unfortunately this was not to be as the settled spell of weather changed. After brief stops at Paros, Antiparos and Milos, none of which particularly impressed us, we made for the beautiful anchorage of Vathi on the island of Siphnos. We were lucky to be in such a charming, sheltered spot because the north-west wind blew very hard for three days and we were happy here whilst we waited for it to abate. Finally we sailed north to another highlight, Serephons, with its much photographed 'chora' perched high on the hill overlooking the harbour.

There is no doubt that cruising the Mediterranean gives one practice at the various methods of anchoring. By now I had a smooth team working for me, which was just as well at our next stop, Hydra. Two months earlier I would have taken one look and turned away. Yachts were tied stern-to all round the quay with latecomers two and three deep. This was our first stop in the Home Group islands and the best one by far. Hydra's perfect little harbour, mules rather than cars, high quality of shops and beautiful mansions give the place a very special feel. Poros, our next stop and mail drop, was rather an anticlimax by contrast. It did however give Ginny and the family the opportunity of catching the ferry to Piraeus for a day at the Acropolis and the National Museum, not to mention McDonald's and the Volvo agent for spare parts.

The next part of our Greek cruise was the Ionian and I had reconciled myself to the expense of the Corinth Canal rather than sail round the Peloponnese. The cost for *Falconer*'s 11.6 metres was approximately £110; despite this we thoroughly enjoyed our transit which was made in company with two other yachts. One of these turned out to be our saviour when the teleflex gear cable broke just before the canal entrance. Ginny operated the gears by hand for the transit and this 'friend in need' offered his spare cable which I fitted at the next anchorage.

In many ways we were glad to have calms for the Gulfs of Corinth and Patra since both these places act as natural wind funnels. We were a little bored however with three days of motoring though it took us to Galaxidi for a day at Delphi and the following night at the tiny harbour gem of Navpktos where Ted and Mary Lyne (RCC) on board *Caravela of Exe* joined us for after dinner coffee.

Three weeks for the Ionian were scarcely enough for this fabulous natural

cruising ground. As a consequence we omitted Corfu in the north and Zakinthos in the south. Our circuit was planned to give Simon windsurfing in Vasiliki, George time with his Australian cruising friend in Fiskardho and Rosalind time to recover from her third bout of tonsillitis. More importantly *Falconer* was booked in with Lefkas Yacht Services. This mini refit proved to be really worthwhile as we were able to solve several pressing problems with the charging system, refrigerator, wheel lock, anchor windlass and leaking fuel gauge.

Highlights of the Ionian for us were Kioni harbour where Ginny fell in love with one of the harbour-side houses. It was here that we had the pleasure of meeting Janet Sanso (RCC) in her 21ft *Ojala* which we towed to Nidri for engine repairs. Assos, on Cephalonia, we were lucky to visit during a settled period of weather and loved it. Also on Cephalonia, Fiskardho would have our vote as the most picturesque harbour and having fought for our place on the very crowded quay we enjoyed having our cockpit amid the restaurants. Finally our last Ionian harbour, Gaios on the island of Paxos, was a happy stop for our last Greek meal ashore. One thing that is not so good about this cruising paradise is rats! Having visited many harbours in different parts of the world we had never experienced this cruising menace until now. We managed to get rats on board from two Ionian quays. Pera Pigadhi on Iphaki, from which the cruising guide said all rats had been exterminated, and also at Levkas.

Ginny and Tim, centre, with l to r: Simon, George and Rosalind

The 'holiday' had ended, it was 25 July and we had booked *Falconer* for a much needed haul-out on 2 September in Gibraltar. It was time for serious passage making again. The first part of the journey was overnight to Crotone, our first Italian port. Simon left the ship here bound for an assignation in Vienna to meet friends who has been tutoring in English schools. Down to a crew of four we made our way across the Bay of Squalls in a flat calm to the new, unfinished yacht harbour of Rocella Ionica. The following day started in a calm and ended in a Force 5–6 beat as we rounded Capo del Armi at the entrance to the Straits of Messina. That night was spent with the wind screaming in the rigging in the noisiest, dirtiest harbour of our cruise, Reggio de Calabria. Our passage through the Straits in the morning was enlivened by chasing whirlpools and seeing those amazing swordfish boats with their high steering positions and bowsprits. We lost the wind on the western side of Messina and motored out to Lipari, our first stop in the Eolian islands. It was 29 July and three days from the official start of the Italian summer holiday. We were unprepared for the numbers of yachts, launches and rubber boats that pressed upon the two possible mooring quays. This was our first experience with the berthing masters called *ormegiattori* who charged £8 for tending our lines. Lipari town was worth it and being opera lovers we decided to stay another night to watch a proper Italian opera played in the open air amphitheatre within the old citadel. With the moon reflecting on the harbour below the animated crowd waited eagerly as the first aria came from offstage. Strange, no more music, only dialogue. We had mistakenly come to see the original play of *Cavalleiria Rusticana!*

The Eolian islands are famed for their volcanoes, Vulcano and the world's oldest lighthouse, Stromboli. We had explored Vulcano that day and to get the best effect of Stromboli we motored around it by night before continuing on our 300 mile passage to northern Sardinia.

The Tyrrhenia Sea is known for its calms in late summer. We met a millpond so another forced passage under engine was required, but this one was not to be. Two days out, after a brief spell at drifting under sail, the starter motor decided that this was the moment to jam. No amount of persuasion could get it going again. So with 120 miles to Porto Cervo, our Sardinian destination, we altered course for the Isle of Ponza 65 miles to the north-east. This was a lucky choice since a beam wind of 5 knots sprung up shortly afterwards, giving us 3 knots under cruising 'chute. The light wind held fitfully through the night to that by morning we were seven miles from land and inched our way close into the bay of the island's harbour before the wind died. By tying the Avon alongside we managed to outboard the remaining two miles. Fifty or more Italian yachts lay at anchor in the bay where we thankfully came to rest. By 1100 we were left alone in the middle of the bay by the exodus of 'beautiful' people to the beach, speeding out at full throttle churning the water white. Our luck held and we found a mechanic on this little island who was able to fix the problem. Two days later we were on our way again.

After all the drama we were grateful for an uneventful overnight passage to Porto Cervo even though we were back to motoring stolidly through the calm. Ponza had been a fascinating stop with its soft white chalk cliffs carved into stairways and houses. Porto Cervo on the other hand was rather disappointing. The beautiful marina was only half full, most of it with large day launches. We lay at anchor outside the marina with the other 'proper' yachts for no charge. For the next two days as we negotiated the Straits of Bonifacio the calms were replaced by Force 6 westerlies, another of nature's wind funnels. One night at La Maddalena marina berthed at right-angles to the prevailing wind cost £15 with no facilities. This was the most expensive stop of the Mediterranean cruise but like so many places the town ashore made up for it. The summer sales were on and the 50 percent off at Benetton was too good for Rosalind to miss. There is no doubt that the Corsican harbour of Bonifacio is one of the most dramatic in the western Mediterranean. For our brief stay of one night we clung tenuously to an unofficial stern-to berth by the boatyard opposite the citadel.

By the end of our first day at sea on passage to Port Mahon we were down to storm rig and feeling very ill as we rode out a full *mistral*, happily not the three day variety. Our approach to Port Mahon later that night coincided with a reduction in the wind. We really appreciated the tranquility of Mahon, probably the best sheltered natural harbour of the Balearics. During our three nights there we were pleased to meet *Norfolk Quetzal*, the Laurent Giles

Donella class classic, with David and Susan Garrett (RCC) on board. Next we sailed down the southern shore of Minorca with its dramatic *calas* indenting the 40 metre cliffs. Tourism has finally caught up with Minorca and many of these beaches have been ruined. Cala Santa Galdana for instance was described by Keith Robinson (RCC) in his book *Islands of Blue Water*. He says the bay had pigs rooting on the beach and fishermen drying their nets in the caves; thirty years later this beautiful spot has a fifteen storey hotel right on the beach and pedalos carrying topless tourists! The weather was far from settled and we had our first rain since Crete three months earlier whilst lying in Galdana. Our final Minorcan port was the old capital, Ciudadela, another picturesque but crowded harbour.

Having only limited time and not particularly liking marinas we decided with David and Susan Garrett's help to cruise Majorca's less popular west coast. After the pretty overnight anchorage of Formentor we sailed past the dramatic high cliffs to Soller, the only harbour on the west coast. Ginny, Rosalind and George spent the following day travelling across the island to Palma on the early 19th century tram and train system. In this way we avoided taking *Falconer* to the capital and its crowded harbour. Five nights in Andraitx, our next stop, the very attractive yachting harbour on Majorca's south-west corner, were spent on another small refit for *Falconer*. Keith and Barbara Robinson (RCC), who live in this charming village, had kindly acted as our *poste restante*. This meant that George and Rosalind had quite a pile of marked work waiting for them from the Correspondence School. Ginny met up with an old school friend with an apartment at San Telmo where she and the family enjoyed three lazy days on the beach. Finally Simon returned after his month's hike round Europe bringing with him David Martin and Robert Apierdo who joined us for a week.

Although we called at Ibiza on our eastward journey we stayed to the north of this previous track for another five days. Two of these were spent on the northern shore of Ibiza before making the 60 mile crossing to the closest port on the Spanish mainland, Moraira. Then south to Alicante where another Donella class caught our eye, *Carola of Lymington* with Hamish and Murielle Hunter (RCC) on board. They joined us for coffee that evening. After a day storm-bound in Torrevieja and finally rounding Cabo de Palos we completed our circuit of the Mediterranean crossing our eastward track.

The Rock

It had taken four months ten days, during which time we had covered 4170 miles.

The weather was very unsettled for the final five days hopping along the Spanish coast. The easterly *levanter* made most of the marinas near Gibraltar untenable but we made good use of the fair wind to get *Falconer* back on 31 August for her scheduled haul-out prior to sailing the Atlantic. We had visited two continents, and anchored in 101 harbours and bays on thirty-seven islands.

Tim and Ginny Le Couteur and their three children continued their cruise via Porto Santo, Madeira, the Canaries and Cape Verde islands across the Atlantic to Barbados.

THE NORDIC FRINGE

by John and Sue Sharp

(The cruise for which the Claymore Cup was awarded.)

On 5 August 1993 *Ocean Grace* was anchored in Brusundet sound (60°37'.7N 4°49'.5E) dressed overall and heading nowhere. This annual procedure was now in its third year and represented the commanding influence of the youngest crew member Tristan on his birthday which, as is customary, dawned bright and sunny. The saloon was similarly bright having been copiously festooned by Carolyn and Philip with balloons (which were to remain inflated for a good month) and flags of the nations (meticulously coloured up on previous cruises). There followed a rush of presents that mysteriously appeared from hidden locker spaces to confirm the occasion over a prolonged breakfast. We then went ashore to scrounge for blueberries prior to establishing camp for the purpose of smoking the previous days catch of mackerel and brewing coffee. It would have been difficult to find a more idyllic and isolated anchorage. After a rather extended birthday lunch, the afternoon's activities turned to testing new fishing gear and windsurfing lessons in the gentle breeze. Tea and cake followed with a slight lull prior to a barbecue over a fire of driftwood collected from around the rocky shores by dinghy. Birthday celebrations in grand cruising style.

The cruise had originally begun on 28 July when we shipped *Ocean Grace*, our 43ft Holman & Pye cutter, from our winter berth at Hauge Marine Services, Sotra, which had been recommended at the end of the previous season by the Bergen Sailing Club. Being well sheltered in the lee of the hills forming the north/south island of Sotra, it had proved to be an excellent berth afloat. The trip from Jersey to Sotra was a prolonged one, and there followed a day of stowing and fitting out in readiness for the fjords whilst model yacht racing was the highlight for the junior crew division. Later that day after a pleasant sail in the warmth of a gentle evening breeze we picked up a mooring off the beautifully situated Bergen Sailing Club, dined aboard and turned in.

Dressed overall for Tristan's birthday

By 1045 the following day, all spruced up after a visit to the BSC showers, we slipped our mooring and headed south against a cool southerly Force 3. Two hours later with the wind dying we resorted to screw propulsion and headed east across Bjornafjord, destination Hardangerfjord. Snow was sighted on the distant mountains and the sea bottom was recorded at well over 400m in parts, one of the many remarkable contrasts of the Norwegian west coast. By mid afternoon we were into the narrow steep sided Lukksund and after entering the main fjord were able to make sail again at a suitably leisurely pace. This allowed fishing (one of the major pastimes of both Philip and Tristan) to commence in earnest and efforts were suitably rewarded by a 'huge' cod weighing in at 3 lb, length 51 cm. Spurred on by this initial success (which if it had continued could have easily sparked off another cod war) we proceeded slowly up to Kalvasund, a delightful little sound offering a more or less completely protected anchorage opposite Rosendal. The children explored the present day Viking exhibition with the friendly owner and returned aboard with presents of local postcards.

Unfortunately our shakedown sail had revealed two problems. Firstly during relaunching after antifouling, the crane had provided a liberal coating of black grease on the upper backstay and topping lift that had now dispersed itself onto the mainsail. Secondly the diesel injectors which had been removed and refitted by the yard were not properly seated. To solve the former problem Tristan, ever keen to be aloft, had rigged up the bosun's chair (cradle) at the foot of the mast prior to breakfast. By the time we had finished breakfast the impatient chair had already ascended the mast and the halyard had made an equal but more muddled descent inside the mast. After a morning of derigging, cleaning and rerigging, black had been transformed to a fawny tinge and under this guise we proceeded to Rosendal to try and rectify the second problem.

The afternoon was spent visiting the Rosendal Barony, a former Danish manor house founded in 1677, which once controlled over 600 farms along the Norwegian west coast and still possesses many contemporary furnishings as well as an 'English' styled rose garden. On our return march, the heavens unexpectedly opened and both crew and boat were thoroughly rinsed, all hatches having been inadvertently left open. (Fjord lesson No 1).

Having procured specialist tools in Rosendal the leaky engine was tackled but not finished before a vicious wind and accompanying sea had sprung up and pinned us against the exposed pier. (Fjord lesson No 2). We departed with difficulty but unscathed and returned to our anchorage of the previous night to enjoy another fine and sheltered evening.

After the trials and tribulations of sorting out the boat, the Skipper resolved to make an early start (cruise time) and by 0830 on Saturday we had weighed anchor (unbreakfasted) en route for Maurangsfjord, Sundal and the Folgefonni glacier. Sundal, even in the overcast fjord weather, is an extremely attractive landing with its white painted buildings and dramatic valley back-drop infilled with the Bondhusbreen glacier. We managed to moor alongside a small but rather permanent German yacht and took an anchor our forward in case it should blow (see lesson No 2).

By 1200 we were all ashore, sailing boots having given way to climbing boots, but oilskins still to hand. The normal practice for leisurely cruising people is, as recommended by RCC FPI, to walk up to the glacial lake and inspect the lower glacial offshoot at a respectable elevation. We decided that it would be of greater interest to see the main glacier firsthand, and so after an easy walk up the valley we turned off and commenced the long uphill climb along a track first pioneered by Kaiser Wilhelm to take visitors on horseback (poor horses) to see the sights. One of the great benefits of the Norwegian rainfall is the lush and varied vegetation that clings to the valley side slopes and the impressive waterfalls that descend them. Fortunately the rain does not occur all the time and this day was one of the pleasant exceptions. We eventually climbed up through the tree line, over waterfalls and past summer farms before beginning a longish hike up rock-strewn slopes to the glacier itself. The main aim at this stage was actually to make contact with the snow that had seemed so distant yesterday. By 1615 we had reached the hut on the edge of the glacier and paused thankfully for oranges and biscuits prior to a limited inspection of the glacier itself at an altitude of some 1400m (4700ft) above boat level. In the eagerness of the descent, the junior members of the crew (to the envy of the Skipper) careered down on anorak sledges stopping just short of the icy lakes at the foot of the snowfields. On the way down we were rewarded with wonderful views of the mountains with their heavily glaciated morphology and tumbling waterfalls. Far down below lay the magnificent turquoise glacial lake and in the extreme distance with the aid of binoculars our mast could be seen rising above the buildings of Sundal.

Sunday 1 August was not an encouraging start to the month and as if to restore the law of averages with the sunshine of yesterday, it poured. By lunchtime an 'upfjord' breeze had sprung up from the west where we were now heading. Undaunted we made all sail and tacked from shore to shore. Within the space of a shortish lunchtime, the wind had increased to Force 5–6 south-westerly and so with a reefed main and a change to a No 2 jib we passed the afternoon en route to Lukksund. With all sail once again set we ran out of wind in the narrows under the Lukksund bridge and so motored the short distance round to Gripnesvaag, via a delightful entrance into a relatively unspoilt cove.

Supper that evening was interrupted by the arrival of Magnus who grows fruit. He brought us a large bag of tomatoes, extremely welcome in Norway where fresh vegetables are anything but plentiful. By 2230 the children plus Skipper had taken to the water again with Magnus for a late-night shark fishing trip. We first laid very deep (500m) baited lines attached to floats and then went fishing for whiting (later gutted and filleted in an unrecordably short time by Magnus). The so-called shark fishing actually produced a green eyed specimen from the deep with an ugly countenance and we were pleased to see it returned, hopefully to its sea-bottom existence. Nevertheless it was an enjoyable and unusual diversion to the days norm of sailing to windward.

Considering the lateness of the previous night's activities, to be underway at 1030 was not too bad. We sailed west along the south side of Bjornafjord via the attractive Godoysund area to visit the islands of the Hundvako group and some of the small harbours en route. Spoilt for choice in terms of pine and heather covered rocky islets, we finally settled on a minute anchorage off Lamboy where the catch of the night before and three fish just landed were consumed (duly cooked!). The waters in the shallows were almost turquoise but any other comparison with the tropics would have been ridiculous. After a sortie in the dinghy we weighed anchor and wound our way northwards through the islands to Hjellestad for provisions. Although a convenient location it has little to offer scenically, so we returned to the Bergen Sailing Club.

After an early start we headed north to Bergen and having passed under the impressive new Askoy suspenslon bridge (in company with the odd cruise liner) we made our way into the attractive and historic old harbour, now reserved largely for smaller craft. The Tall Ships having left (and the Norwegian summer almost over) we had plenty of choice for berthing and settled for the central pier at the eastern end of the Vagan (Torgutstikkeren)

Fjaerland, near the Jostedal glacier

away from the road. Although noisy (by our standards) it is nonetheless an agreeable harbour. Our time in Bergen involved a trip up the funicular railway for a worthwhile overlook of the city, a walk down through the woods and gardens (recommended) and then a walk (not recommended) to the aquarium which is excellent. Feeding time at the 'zoo' for the seals and penguins at 1800 hours rounded off the day prior to a pizza overlooking the harbour.

The following day saw the Skipper (mechanic) up early, armed with newly acquired spares and more expensive tools, with his head in the engine putting to rights the wrongs of winter. By 1100 we were ashore for a tour of the Bryggen (wharf) area, starting at the archaeological museum where the earliest settlements are preserved. The remaining Bryggen wooden warehouses (approximately half were destroyed by fire in the 1950s) are an impressive piece of seafaring and trading history and are now a World Heritage site.

Being moored by the fishmarket, lunch was an easily accomplished affair and at the same time we stocked up on 'wild' salmon for supper. By 1645 with the engine back in its box we left Bergen and sailed north up the Hjelteford under dullish skies and a south-westerly Force 3 breeze knowing we still had many hours of daylight to our advantage. Once north of Sotra the islands form a chain known as Oygarden. Although by nature rather windswept and living under the shadow of the North Atlantic, they have a pleasing rocky form with abundant heather and are dissected by sounds and inlets. After a considerable discussion between the Skipper and Tristan on possible birthday sites, Brusundet had been chosen on the basis of shelter, interest, remoteness and a strong FPI recommendation. After an excellent baked salmon en route (never to be equalled in freshness and taste) we handed sails at 2040 and motored into the inlet in the gathering dusk. This inlet, which leads through to Nautreset on the west coast, becomes exceedingly narrow in the form of a canal prior to opening out into an idyllic pool where we dropped anchor.

After the ritual lay-day of 5 August, the 6th dawned bright and sunny, rather typical of the drier coastal islands. Once the fisherboys had retrieved various baited lines (for which the famous salmon had taken a dismal interest) we hoisted the main and chugged northwards a short distance to have a look at Hjelme (an FPI highly recommended anchorage and well worth the detour) and for a walk ashore to inspect the fishermen's huts and church. By late morning we were heading north again under full sail close hauled with a north-westerly Force 2. Fedje seemed like an interesting island with a snug harbour on the northern side so we went in for lunch to devour the spoils of the smokery from the day before. The harbour is a bit overcome with fishing and a suitable souvenir of tinned herring exported only to the USA was purchased. From Fedje we had a pleasant sail north and westwards dodging through the seaward islands of Kjellingoy.

Sognefjord was to be the second fjord of our cruise and the one in which we expected to spend the most time. Our main destination was Fjaerland, the nearest port of call to the Jostedal glacier, the biggest living glacier in Europe. We dropped anchor off Rutledal, a beautiful anchorage inside a rare fjord island ready for an early start the following day, for provisioning.

By 0820 the following morning we were alongside in Leirvik and surveyed the not very attractive scene until 0900 when the shops opened. We spent the morning motor-sailing east with occasional deviations to either shore for inspections. Depths noted (but not measured) at 1300m were just about the same as the height of the surrounding mountains. By 1300 we had some wind to sail and having set the genoa we consumed yet more mackerel for lunch. We detoured into Ortnevik, a pleasant looking anchorage, and sailed out in company with a Norse sailing vessel fashioned after a 16th century craft and apparently out on a maiden voyage with the boatbuilder and his family.

We pottered into Vik with its rather plain seafront and tarry quay (a not uncommon feature as many of them belong to the highways departments). The plan was to visit the Stave Church of Hopperstad, originally built by the Vikings in 1130 and under more or less constant but faithful restoration since the 1880s when it was rescued from demolition. The Stave Churches are an incredible testimony to the shipbuilders' art turned to building structures and are highlighted by the braced mast construction as well as the longevity of pine as a building material. With stone a foreign material, they fashioned circular Roman arches out of wood and decorated them with intricate carvings. The main structure of the churches was, however, very closely related to shipbuilding methods with extensive use of grown knees being common. We invested in a book describing all the Norwegian Stave churches (*Stave Churches in Norway* by Gunnot Bugge, Drayer 1983) and vowed to see more. Lack of interest in Vik harbour led us on to Balestrand on the north side of the fjord which was a fashionable tourist destination dating from the late 1800s. At that time it appeared commonplace to build and rebuild hotels at two or three yearly intervals as a result of which, by the early 1900s, the largest wooden structure in Norway had been created. At the same time, the English church (in the fashion of a Stave Church) was erected. By 1910 Balestrand had become the holiday retreat for Kaiser Wilhelm and in 1913 he deposited two very large statues (gifts to the Norwegian people) on either shore where they remain to this day.

With the mountains now all around us and many of them topped in snow, we proceeded the following day under power in a Force 0 wind to Fjaerland and by 1330 were tied up at the attractive quay with our bow facing towards the glacier. The seniors and Philip made a foray up the mountain south of Fjaerland alongside a cascading waterfall. Some 500m above fjord level, now a deep grey-green vision below us, we broke out of the woodland and into a summer pasture area which provided a great picking of blueberries. Duly pleased with this excursion we dined at the Hotel Mundal, another imposing piece of woodwork dating from the turn of the century and a haunt of the early glaciologists. The children on this occasion decided that the ferry kiosk menu was more to their liking (and the food without doubt was definitely faster).

The following morning we visited the impressive Norsk Bremuseum at the head of the fjord and enjoyed a 3-D cinemagraphic view of the Jostedal glacier above through the eyes of five lenses attached to a helicopter. A remarkable film well worth seeing. After some time studying glaciers in theory we set off on foot from sea level at 1130 hours to experience them in practice. By 1300 we were climbing steadily and an hour later we were enveloped in thick driving mist. We eventually spotted the Flatbrehytta (mountain hut) below us and stumbled into another world of fully provisioned mountain living, from the cold swirling mist a thousand metres above the fjord. Miraculously our luck held and just before 1600 the mist cleared and the sun appeared affording views of the glacier and fjord alike. We walked up to and around the rim of the glacier inspecting and photographing the deeply crevassed blue ice from the safety of the adjacent moraine. By 1630 we were back at the hut to collect our packs in preparation for the steep rocky descent via a different route. Overall the excursion up and down took some five hours, good going for the pre-teenage crew (not to mention the Skipper!). Thereafter followed a further $2\frac{1}{2}$ hour walk back to *Ocean Grace*. The day was completed by an evening cruise under power to Balestrand ready for an early start.

At 0545 on 10 August we were underway motoring into a minimal head wind bound for Flam and the morning train up to Vatnahalsen Lake at the head of the valley. A spectacular valley with abundant waterfalls but rather too many cruise ship patrons and their bossy shepherds for our liking. On the way up the train (an ex-Stockholm suburban model) broke down causing chaos with the morning timetable and the strict routine of the cruise ships. We departed Flam for Gudvangen via Undredal. The Stave Church here is extremely small, in fact Norway's smallest at 5.3m by 3.8m. Although much rebuilt it is worth a visit together with the remote and largely unspoilt village. We were lucky to find the church open (as it is generally locked) as without doubt the interior woodwork and painted panelling is its primary attraction.

We entered Naeroyfjorden having read some impressive reports in the FPI. The narrow, twisting fjord with attractive landings and occasional anchorages turned out to be one of the prettiest and most spectacular fjords we visited (in spite of the pouring rain). Gudvangen is not a brilliant night stop, even less so in the incessant rain, but at least we were greeted with the rare sight of another yacht (Swedish).

The last major port of call in Sognefjord was the inlet at Kaupanger where we visited the newly opened maritime and fishing museum. This was well worth a detour, if only to see the photographs of Bergen at the turn of the century and learn of the extensive summer trade from the fjord to the capital, all under sail. We then anchored across the bay to visit yet another impressive Stave Church with its long rows of free-standing masts supporting a lofty nave. Ecclesiastical studies were followed by a plentiful harvesting of wild raspberries. Contrary to the new Norwegian Pilot there is no diesel in Kaupanger! At 1500 we weighed anchor and after an $1\frac{1}{2}$ hours of motor sailing were greeted with a fresh head wind and set sail for Fresvik. Although definitely after hours, the girl at the post office summoned the supermarket owner and fuel was gladly provided — also gladly received! We then beat down the fjord for a couple of hours in a freshening breeze causing us finally to reef. Just before Balestrand where we put in for a third night (almost unheard of during a Sharp cruise) the wind suddenly died and once again we were blessed with a quiet night.

Thursday was something of a lay day and after a morning of washing and maintenance we sailed round to the next anchorage westwards inside Kramsoy Island for a junior windsurfing session and an adult church visit. We found a friendly local guide dog but otherwise the island appeared deserted and the church locked. The time had come to leave the fjords so we headed (or rather pottered) west against a light head wind and contemplated rural fjord living. The isolation of some of the farms is extreme and, with no road access, a small quay and boathouse are essential links with the outside world. We spent the evening at Bjordal, an attractive inlet on the southern side of the fjord and enjoyed a pleasant sunny walk ashore rewarded by more raspberries.

Friday the 13th was in hindsight a poor day to contemplate a crossing to Shetland with strong westerly winds in the offing for the North Sea. Instead we decided to explore the outer islands and headed northwards towards Afjorden with the weather brightening all the time. The scenery to the north is extremely impressive with precipitous granitic islands stretching as far as the eye can see. We passed through a number of intricate channels bordered by heather covered, low-lying rocky islets before reaching our destination of Buskoy for an afternoon stop and minor replenishment of stores. It was in this idyllic backwater that we learned of the Shetland Bus from one of the 'drivers'. (The Bus was the name given to small boats that supplied allied and resistance operations in Norway and elsewhere from bases in the Shetlands.) He also told us of the ill-fated torpedo boat operation from one of the inlets of the adjacent islands — the crew had been shot after being captured. This kind gentleman then went off to collect his present day boat and took the children fishing around the island before coming aboard for 'English tea'. On hearing we were heading for the Shetlands he suggested packing his suitcase and revisit the islands that had sheltered him during the war and left him with many happy memories. We headed slightly south for the night to Hardbakke, a small regional centre well sheltered off a narrow sound. Berthing alongside as usual was no problem.

The idea of departing for the Shetlands the following day was formulated on the evening of the 13th, with a forecast for North and South Utsire giving southerly Force 4–5 occasionally 6, which was confirmed the following morning. This seemed like a fair wind and a chance to make the passage before the wind veered west. The deck log that morning was brief due to much activity on deck. By 0930 we left the sound and headed west with the genoa and an increasing number of reefs in the main. By 0945 we had the working jib up and were reaching westwards at well over 8 knots. Because of the very uneven submarine topography we expected rather confused and possibly breaking seas until we were clear of the offlying shoals and shallows and into more uniform depths. We did not, however, expect the Force 6–7 gusting 8 that we encountered which made life very unpleasant indeed, particularly when rogue waves came aboard, attempting to fill our deep and generous cockpit. Discretion prevailed and after an hour's rough and tumble we headed back to our snug refuge in the islands. We surfed in under big quartering seas and regained the land in record time. The fishing boats still tied up in Hardbakke nodded their approval at our return and advised us that the gale would continue for the rest of the day — sound and correct advice.

By Sunday morning the fishermen were preparing to go to sea after a heavy night aboard (where does alcohol come from in Norway ?!) Taking the south-westerly Force 3–4 and the fishermen's actions as good omens we decided to make an inspection of the sea state of the Norwegian coastal margins once again whilst we still had half a chance of avoiding a head wind to Shetland. The wind having moderated to a steady southerly Force 4 and the seas now being somewhat tamed we headed out south of west under full sail and were clear of the outer shoals by 1015.

We sailed in the company of two fulmars (soon to be named Bill and Ben) that circled ever closer as we headed westwards. We made good progress in spite of the incessant rain until later that afternoon when the rain stopped and the wind died. To repay us for our southerly heading, anticipating a gentle shift to the west, the wind now came up from the north-west at Force 3–4 and we tacked to suit. By 2000 hours the wind dropped off and we motor-sailed on towards the ever brightening oil rigs through a sloppy confused sea with its residual southerly swell.

The bonanza of oil rigs, with the Alwyn and Ninian oil fields to port and Brent and Cormorant to starboard, was passed during the hours of darkness. With up-to-date charts we found no difficulty in identifying individual rigs except for those that seemed to pass in the night, which turned out to be two huge exploration rigs under tow which were most exciting to witness. To add to the display there was good competition from the stars and the Northern Lights. It was a bright but quiet night except for the odd hour or so that the engine was brought into play. The morning saw us close-hauled with the engine on and off until we were hit by a series of squalls in opposing directions. Land appeared out of the murk at 1115, a welcome sight especially for the children. By noon the day had brightened once again as we sailed close-hauled, accompanied by quite a few dolphins and porpoises. Bill and Ben (unless they had changed shift in the night) were still on station circling around and showed no interest in passing offerings of bread, preferring instead to remain aloft.

By the time we closed the north western shores of Shetland the weather had fined considerably and we tacked into Balta Sound, green and welcoming, and dropped anchor off the pierhead at 1800 gaining an extra hour in the process! The Balta Sound Hotel up from the pier turned out to be a most welcoming and hospitable haven with showers (in aid of the Lifeboat), an excellent menu (copious chips for the children) and a bar serving draught Guinness. The Mate recalls having nearly fallen asleep at the table which means she undoubtedly did.

Balta village with its extensive general store could replenish most things. The community appeared friendly and open, a spirit we were to subsequently experience throughout the islands. Wiser with the knowledge of island sailing from Christopher Thornhill's excellent cruise log (*Roving Commissions* No 33) and topped up with information from the friendly shipping / harbour office, we decided to circumnavigate the northern skerries and the Isle of Unst to experience marine life first-hand.

We sailed in a leisurely fashion northwards and rounded the impressively situated Muckle Flugga lighthouse off Unst (the most northerly habitation in the British Isles). The islets and the northern tip of Unst, all rocky and steep-to and often precipitous form a huge sanctuary for gannets, fulmars and puffins. After tacking through the crowded skies and waters, witnessing the often aggressive antics of the great skuas ('bonxie' being the local name), we finally received a suitable christening over the genoa and tacked southwestwards for Blue Mull Sound. The north Unst scenery with its major bird sanctuary was certainly some of the most memorable on our whole trip, even if it was from time to time partly shrouded in mist.

We had a pleasant evening sail tacking south to Mid Yell with the mate in the galley and the afterdeck crew hauling mackerel in one after another. Approaching Mid Yell we were hailed by friendly local fishermen and given two huge ling to add to our more than ample day's catch. (An excellent fish pie to follow!) In return we offered them some mackerel but they said they used it for bait!

The following day after a brief excursion to Yell for stores (other than fish) we headed south in the face (predictably) of a fresh southerly breeze, tacking inshore to inspect the seal topped island fringes and the various 'Nesses'and Stacks that form the coastal promontories.

By 1630, off the northern approaches of Lerwick, we were met by the sight of what looked like a convoy of World War II supply ships at anchor. As we wove through the fleet of some thirty ships, many of them in an extremely sad state of decay, we realised that this was the former Russian factory fleet now displaying ensigns of the new independent states. The conditions on board the 'Klondikers' (as they are known) did not bear close inspection and the waters, a sort of reddy brown with fish offal, both smelt and looked quite uninviting. We passed on rather thankfully into Lerwick Sound, the top part of which is primarily dedicated to oil supply services. Alongside also was a particularly sad looking 'Klondiker' which we learnt later had been rescued the previous winter after breaking adrift in a gale and without sufficient power to make harbour. Apparently the crew were still aboard, penniless and reliant totally on local charity.

We entered the small boat harbour at 1800 passing the majestic Norwegian STS *Statsraad Lehmkuhl* against an ebb of numerous sailing dinghies making a last minute dash for the starting line for the first race of the annual interisland regatta (Lerwick 'Cowes' week). The frenzy of dinghy racing erupted at periodic intervals. The following morning we were lucky enough to be able to look over the *Statsraad Lehmkuhl*, fresh from her Class win in the Tall Ships Race before she left for what promised to be a triumphant welcome in her home port of Bergen. Lerwick proved to be a good place for provisioning and the chart agents in particular were extremely helpful in arranging a chart delivery from Aberdeen for early the following day.

Friday saw us galebound so we watched the spectacular regatta starts of over-canvassed dinghies, often to be followed by numerous capsizes and rigging failures. We were also fortunate to run into one of the Coastguard helicopter pilots from whom we sought information on the new harbour at Fair Isle which was opened in July 1993 and which we planned to visit. Our inquiries at Lerwick had revealed little about the actual plans except that a new breakwater had been built affording extra protection and allowing the ferry to lie afloat instead of being hauled out as was the practice in the past. Tony Brewster, the pilot concerned, promised an inspection the following day as part of a routine exercise and a report back involving a *rendezvous* at sea between Noss and Mousa.

Having finally battened down the fo'c'sle for the night the senior crew members paid a last visit to the Lerwick Boating Club, still awash with regatta sailors, and collected LBC Great North Sea certificates for the junior members (in case they forget the experience).

Saturday 21 August was a mixture of showers and sunshine with a northerly Force 5–6 gusting 7. We left at 1200 and reached around the south side of Bressay. We dropped anchor twice before holding in the small bay on the west side of Noss, which we had planned to explore on foot. Vicious squalls called for a change in plan and after a quick lunch we weighed anchor and left on a marine excursion instead. The geology, caves and cliffs of Feadda Ness and Noss Head (180m high) are quite spectacular and well worth a visit. The gannets appeared to think so too.

After a close inshore inspection we freed away southwards for the island of Mousa. South of Bard Head and according to plan, we were called up by the Coastguard Sea King which we then spotted approaching fast from the south. The report on Fair Isle was favourable and we were then requested to sail close-hauled on the port tack for an aerial transfer. With great precision and skill, the imposing Sea King, complete with night radar bulges, hovered over us as a canister was lowered into the cockpit containing the *Saturday Independent* — what a delivery! After much photography, waving and exchange of greetings, the great bird flew off only to reappear unexpectedly in an

Ocean Grace *photographed from a Shetlands Coastguard helicopter by Kieran Murray*

exciting and fast low-level flypast. Such craft and crew that perform heroic feats of rescue under appalling weather and visibility conditions are a great testament to human invention and ability. We felt duly honoured by such an impressive display.

We passed down the west side of Mousa to inspect the Broch, one of the best surviving examples of its kind and built in the period between the 1st century BC and the 3rd AD. The round broch tower some 15 metres in diameter at its base and rising 13 metres in height is perfectly constructed in dry stone masonry and thought to be more of less complete. Little in detail seems to be known about the origins of these towers, but with their thick walls containing internal passages they are quite unique structures. We finally sought shelter in Hos Wick Bay after an exciting day's sailing.

By 1300 the following day we were off Fair Isle in heavy overfalls but could see beyond to 'flatter' waters off North Haven. With a new breakwater in evidence linking the stack off Bu Ness to the shore, we made our way in under the lee of the cliffs. Seals were there to greet us as we abruptly rounded up and tied up at the new pier ahead of the *Good Shepherd*, the island's sea link. Otehwise nothing stirred. Although not devoid of swell, the berth was tenable and after a quick lunch we made a brief tour of the adjacent cliffs and inspected the rather turbulent entrance through which we had recently arrived. The 1400 shipping forecast informed us that the wind was due to veer to the north Force 7 and sadly we decided that even with the new protective measures, such winds could lead to rough and even dangerous conditions for a vessel of our size. The strong winds and rough seas also seemed to rule out South Harbour as an anchorage. We thus left Fair Isle and headed out into the rough seas once again, bound for Sanday in the Orkneys. Even the fleeting impressions that we gained of Fair Isle, including a pleasant reach down the east coast, were enticing and we vowed to return on some fairer future occasion.

From Fair Isle the intrepid Sharp family sailed to Orkney and westwards round Cape Wrath.

NORTH AGAIN

by David and Judy Lomax

Kristiansand to Haugesund, by David Lomax

Our eldest, Jane, who lives aboard a converted whaler in Oslo, is understandably biased about her adopted land. "You can't go back to England without exploring the coast of Norway," she said. "It's the most beautiful cruising ground in the world and no-one knows about it." So we decided to collect *Cloudwalker* from Kristiansand and head north. And as the country has so much coastline we planned to winter the boat in Tromsø, leaving the option of another expedition in '94.

In mid July I stepped aboard in Kristiansand marina, where I was joined by Malcolm Fuller and his son Tom, who were to help me as far as Stavanger. I knew Malcolm would be good company: he had recited Hillaire Belloc amongst pack-ice in Greenland. Tom, an engineering student from Aberdeen University, had only dinghy experience but was keen, congenial and good at repairs.

Our first day took us rock dodging through the leads to the west. Jokes were difficult off Lindesnes — the Naze — with the wind on the nose, but Malcolm and Tom did their best. We were reefed down well before reaching the secluded anchorage in Skarvoya, where we celebrated in a strange grey overcast evening with Scotch, mackerel and Rachmaninov 3. There was no sign of the 'sheep with bells' mentioned in the FPI pilot.

In the next few days we made good progress in spite of irritating head winds and calms. Rekefjord was disappointing because of the vast unsightly quarries on either side of its entrance. Nesvåg, a few miles to the west, was a delightful spot, followed by a long motor through a sloppy sea to Sirevåg. An extraordinary gun emplacement on the rocks overlooking this harbour was spotted by eagle-eyed Tom, who led us to it over vast boulders. The defensive position had, we learned later, been built, like many others along the coast, by thousands of Serbian and Russian POW's. Now there were only ghosts and a panoramic view of the approaches. Down below workmen were blowing up boulders to make way for more holiday cottages.

From Sirevåg we beat northwards for 30 miles to Tananger, passing distant Tall Ship entries who weren't doing much better in the lumpy conditions. Next day, in more settled weather, we were able to explore Utstein Kloster and its restored monastery before reaching the spectacular harbour at Skudeneshamn with its old clap-board houses and street market. From there it was only an eight hour crossing to that most exotic forecasting legend, Utsire. The familiar name turned out to be a small island, not unlike a few places in the Hebrides, with a resident population of 220 and a network of fields and brightly coloured farmhouses. We moored in the southern harbour, then walked a mile to examine the forbidding but probably equally safe harbour on the north side. There were Kiwi fruit imported from New Zealand in the shop. According to locals fish catches in Utsire are so poor that the famous Sild factory has to buy its raw material from as far away as Canada.

In the next few days we explored harbours nearby, caught as much cod and saithe as we could eat and eventually tied up in Haugesund next to one of the vast catamarans which ply so speedily along the inner coastal routes. Malcolm and Tom left on a south-bound ferry, and were replaced by Judy and her sister Sally, who had caught another on its way north from Stavanger.

Haugesund to Tromsø, by Judy Lomax

By mid-morning after an early start we were ghosting along on a gentle reach. Whenever David thought of putting out a mackerel line, the wind freshened and we reached a short-lived 5 or 6 knots. Astern, row after row of hills and rocks formed a softly silhouetted backcloth as we wove our way between islands of smoothly folded grey rock mottled with tinges of fuzzy green-brown. Sheep bells were the only sound.

The superb cruising ground south of Bergen presented us with some complex rock dodging. A rounded fat grey sumo wrestler of a mountain glared down on us as we goose-winged gently between Selbjørn and Huftarøy, and then broad-reached at 4 to 5 knots across the Kasfjord and into Bergen Sailing Club's marina at Kvitspollen. There we were visited by one of our fellow Vikings from the 1991 'Vinland Revisited' expedition.

Next morning we motored under a bridge too new to be on our chart, then turned to port away from Bergen, which cowered beneath lowering cliffs, rounded hills darkened by conifers, and threatening black clouds. The sun came out, a breeze came up, and a warm lazy afternoon beat was marred only by the sudden collapse of the CD player at a critical moment in *Aida*'s second act.

Sally was on the tiller as we felt our way in Uttoska Våg, following the FPI's instructions into the second of three pools. Alarmed at two rocks awash to port in the middle pool, David took the helm. "That'll make sure there aren't any more," Sally commented. After scrambling over boulders set in a

Mortsund, an hour before midnight

bog richly carpeted with wild flowers and heathers to the top of a granite hill, we looked down on *Cloudwalker* and across islands banked in purple ranks against the sunset. We read in the cockpit until midnight.

Snow glistened on the mountains inland as we negotiated what David termed 'interesting wiggles' between rocks and islands and across the mouths of the Fense- and Sogne- Fjords. A blue and white spinnaker pursued us on a spectacular run north between smoothly folded and lumped rock on Ytre Sula to port and Ranøy to starboard. Sheep grazed optimistically on minute green patches. The spinnaker veered of after chasing us through a fiddly series of stakes and rocks past Inderøy, Olderøy and Olderkalv on one side, Lågøy, Lågøråhl and Fóróy on the other. The *øy* — islands — were as confusing on as off the chart, and made it essential to keep a close navigational lookout, even with the help of little Norse marker towers with hand-like direction pointers showing which side to pass what. Many of these *varde* have been in position since Viking days.

Ignoring what looked like a snug little anchorage on Inderøy, we were drawn inexorably through more rocky complexities towards the brooding strength of Alden, a 480ft mountain island nicknamed '*den norske hesten*' — 'the Norwegian horse' — and notorious for its sudden squalls. David caught a small truant mackerel as we jilled slowly towards the horse, which looked to us more like a crouching lion.

Not trusting Alden for a night at anchor, we continued towards snow covered mountains to a pontoon mooring in Hórland. By the time Sally and I had walked up and up and up a long straight road between meadows of wild flowers, the view we had hoped for of the other side of Atløya was invisible in torrential rain; so we squelched happily back down to interrupt David's peaceful vigil on board.

Norwegian weather takes no notice of the rule 'rain before seven, fine by eleven'. Well reefed and oilskinned, we set out nevertheless before midday for a fast tight sail. The reputedly Mediterranean-style Svanøya — Swan Island — was obscured by downwind spumes of cloud. Cats-and-dogs rain flattened the sea. Florø, a pleasant but unexciting little town with a supermarket, showers, washing machine and tumble dryer, provided an overnight pontoon berth for the Norse equivalent of £2.

The approach to the dreaded 15 mile offshore passage round Stattlandet took us running and broad-reaching between spectacular cliffs. Minute hamlets clung to bright green patches of grass between rocks and beneath noisy waterfalls and occasional patches of snow. The Statt was a merciful anticlimax, but the lollopy seas even in such a flat calm bore witness to how unpleasant it must be in less clement circumstances. The air had a sharp northern bite. David re-established his reputation as the clan's hunter by catching three cod while we motored gently to Bringsingshaug.

There were more Vikings to be visited, way up-fjord. 'Take the second on the right, then first right, then we're onto the road map,' David instructed Sally as we motored inland in cold glittery sun. The wind barely reached a measurable force that day.

The further inland we motored, the softer but even steeper the scenery became. Snow glittered on mountain peaks, sometimes above coniferous slopes with fertile lighter green clearings around scattered houses, sometimes with valiant greenery clinging to the rock surface of near-vertical cliffs dropping hundreds of feet to the water's edge. From Straumshamn, which translates as Current Harbour — because of a fast flowing narrow rock-strewn river under a low bridge — we were taken by our Viking friends to the valley from which their family name was taken. For hundreds of years, the Bjørkedals of Bjørkedal have farmed in the summer, and have built and repaired Viking style boats in the winter.

We interrupted our 20 mile return down fjord to shop in the small town of Volda, which lacked only a *vinmonopol*. These state liquor stores, the only legal outlet for alcohol, are few and far between. We were again unable to replenish our liquid supplies in Ulsteinvik, which we reached through the intricacies of 'the Green Corridor', our progress alternately impeded and enlivened by the rapid switches from too little to too much wind and its complete disregard for the direction in which we wished to proceed. The lack of alcohol on sale was made up for by the hospitality ashore of another neo-Viking. Our ears were assailed by a million squawks next day when we followed his detailed instructions about the approach to the bird cliffs of Runde.

Picturesque Geiranger

There are some things which must be done once, if the opportunity arises. We did Geiranger. Although the picturesque village at the head of the fjord is daily besieged by cruise ships, we did not regret the 60 mile detour past the grandeur of its Seven Sisters waterfalls and the improbability of the farms perched on almost sheer cliffs with no visible way of reaching them either from above or below. But because of the fjord's great depth and steepness there are few stopping places.

On Sally's last day, the sun came out and many of her clothes came off. Visibility was crisp, the sea a vivid blue-green, the mountains with their snow caps clear, and the sunset still red well after 2200.

Then, for the first time for several years, David and I were alone on *Cloudwalker*; she seemed just right for two. There were several more Vikings to be visited at Håholmen, an island so tiny it was marked on a large scale chart only with an H. To reach it, we sailed for a day and a half between mountain-islands and rocky intricacies marked with a forest of perches and *varde*.

In Kristiansund we bumped into yet another neo-Viking. Then we were really on our own. Our first anchorage was so quiet that we could hear fish mouthing in the soft evening light. It became less quiet during the night, with an unpleasant lollopy swell which tugged and jerked at the anchor. Not long after dawn we set out on an exhilarating wild wet sail, with the log's propeller leaving the water at seven knots in squalls. By mid-afternoon we were exhausted and decided to run for cover. *Cloudwalker* swung wildly round her anchor in the gusts.

Although the wind had moderated by morning, after a few hours heavy continuous rain blown unkindly into our faces by a north-north-east Force 4 in the shadow of the Koppavan mountains sent us scuttling towards Stokksund. Three men in a minute rowing boat continued to catch cod with true Norse nonchalance while we followed signs to a mini marina hidden behind a new causeway and approached past a trawler graveyard and skeletal fish drying racks. Because of the rain, the chart was below; and in any case we had become used to everything hittable being marked as a hazard. Fortunately the only damage from the rock we touched at 3 knots was to our pride.

Our attempt to reach Rørvik ahead of a forecast storm involved some of the trickiest navigation so far. The menacing shoreline held secrets of trolls and battles between giants and gods, and the sea itself hid a long and spiteful reef which made a 20 mile sortie into open sea a necessity. By the time we were outside the reef, the wind had risen from north-west Force 4 to 5 to 6 to 7.

"How does she feel?" David asked me. "She's having fun, and so am I," I replied as we roared along at speeds which varied erratically from 5 to 10 knots with huge following seas under a dazzling blue sky.

My euphoria vanished with the sun. The waves and wind continued to rise, the clouds glowered more and more ominously ahead, and *Cloudwalker* became difficult to control. When she broached in a particularly vicious squall she came up almost before we had realised she was down, so quickly that nothing got wet, except the charts onto which a container of orange juice hurled itself. Everything else movable met on the cabin floor. It was a useful object lesson in always being prepared for the worst at sea. We carried on under triple-reefed main and jibless, and charged at 7 knots under the bridge into Rørvik in a full gale with heavy rain and atrocious visibility.

Somehow our reassuring phone calls home became garbled. David told his father that we had suffered 'a near knock down', and I told my mother I was wet because it was raining hard. They spoke to each other, and our offspring were then informed that we had survived a capsize.

Myths and monsters belong naturally in the barren grandeur and beauty of west Norway. We sailed as close as possible to Torghatten mountain, an archetypal troll, hunched, huge and brooding, with a bulbous nose and a single all-seeing eye through which the wind blows and the light shines. For several days the peaks of the Seven Sisters — five single, one pair of twins — looked down on us from constantly changing angles. They were watching when we anchored at Alstahaug beside a sagging row of wooden boathouses on stilts, and again when we made our way cautiously into the enclosed pool in the middle of the idyllic little island of Hjartø, where a sea eagle had made its untidy great nest in a tree. Soft fruit grew wild beside the ruins of an abandoned settlement which only a generation ago had been home for a self-sufficient population of sixty; in its heyday it had supported two hundred. Jumbled boulders marked the sites of Viking graves overlooking the water. The sun on Hjartø, and the exertion of a couple of miles of energetic rock scrambling exploration, very nearly persuaded me to swim; but then the sun dropped and the wind rose, and after another seven hours of alternate motoring and sailing at 7 knots in the rain we were happy to anchor in the shelter of Tomma's thumb. A solitary puffin which had forgotten to leave the land supervised our entry, against the background music of sheep bells and waterfalls.

"I could get addicted to sailing in Norway," I told David at the start of our second week alone. It treated us to yet more stimulating but well guided navigation through rugged scenery, with wildly fluctuating weather, all in the relative shelter of the inner leads. But even these can become rough. The blinding stinging rain and angry seas thrown into our faces by our next gale — on the nose, of course — sent us scuttling back the way we had come looking for shelter, and then kept us up all night after a dramatic nocturnal dash to re-anchor. By dawn there were still occasional wild gusts and intermittent rain.

To guarantee being in Bodø in time to meet our thirteen year old daughter Emily and her friend Amity without attempting the inner leads by night or embarking on an offshore passage in bad weather, we relied more than we would have liked on the engine. Sod's law that wind is a current of air coming from the direction in which a sailor wishes to proceed was in the ascendance, and there was no time for a detour to Svartisen, the second largest glacier in Europe; but we could both see it and feel the extra chill it created in the air. I was on the tiller as we crossed the Arctic Circle, at 6 knots with a wind which allowed us to tack between Gjerø and Renga and across a sound towards Rødø, a tiny harbour nestling under the red mountain which gave it its name.

The air felt truly arctic as we motor-sailed the last 43 miles to Bodø. An eagle made an abortive swoop for a fish, missed, swooped again and rose with its booty clutched in its talons. Another did an ungainly butterfly stroke with its wings to the nearest rock rather than drop a heavy catch; it is apparently not unknown for them to be pulled under the water and drowned rather than let go. Following the eagles' example, we drifted for our supper in 17 metres, and within a few minutes had two cod.

We tied up behind *British Steel Challenge* on a visitor's pontoon in Bodø, a functional rather than a stimulating town, with some excellent but expensive restaurants, a modern shopping centre and *vinmonopol*, and a have-it-washed-for-you launderette in a bleak little suburban industrial estate. David phoned Jane to make sure that Emily and Amity had arrived safely in Oslo, and to say that we were within walking distance of the airport.

"You may be able to walk there, but you certainly won't be able to walk back," she warned.

We used the car we hired to fetch them and their 63 kilos of luggage to

Cloud Walker *and her admirers in the Lofotens*

take the advice written in red on our borrowed chart, and drove to Saltstraum. After picnicking on fresh prawns on the rocks above the raging swirling maelstrom, we set out for the 50 mile crossing to Reine in the Lofoten.

"How far do you think it looks?" I asked Emily and Amity as we sailed towards a brilliant sunset and a dragon's back of peaks. One guessed six miles, the other seven. They thought I must be pulling their legs when I told them the hills which looked so near were mountains 46 miles away.

When we eventually resurfaced after our night crossing, Reine in the sun was a vividly picturesque introduction to the Lofoten, with its brilliant blue lagoon, brightly coloured box-like houses — most of which seemed to be let to tourists — and old wooden church, in which there were several 'No Smoking' signs alongside advertisements for bibles to be sent to the Ukraine. As a reward for arriving safely we treated ourselves to an evening meal in a fish restaurant run by a Dane who had lived for twenty years in Sussex.

In the next week we averaged two shore visits a day, all the time marvelling at the scenery, frequently frustrated by the rapid changes of wind strength and direction, and never warm enough for sunbathing. The Norwegian summer had officially been over for a fortnight; so had the northern heatwave.

We have left *Cloudwalker* in sight of the Harbour Master's window. The harbour is ice-free, and Tromsø itself is a delightful little city. Its chief Customs Officer, a keen sailor, thinks that more people should know about the wonderful sailing available in north-west Norway. He is right.

ON THE ROOF OF THE WORLD

by Peter Ingram (Cadet)

Peter Ingram had been sailing aboard Aratapu *with Hugh Clay from Punta Arenas to Puerto Montt where he left to explore other parts of South America. We join him on the shores of the lake still worshipped by the descendants of the Incas as the birthplace of the Sun.*

My interest in Lake Titicaca had been awakened whilst reading Tristan Jones' *The Incredible Voyage*. The islands he had written about are scattered in the southern part of the lake, 110 miles long and 40 miles wide. It is regarded as the highest navigable body of water in the world, straddling the Peru-Bolivian border. On 5 June, having finally managed to persuade a gullible shopkeeper to change a $50 travellers cheque, I quickly gathered my things together and caught the local bus to the fishing village of Huatajata on the eastern shore of the southern part of the lake.

This was probably the best place from which to reach the islands and it was also the base of the Bolivian Yacht Club. The village was merely a collection of crumbling farmhouses gathered along the shore, pigs and goats gently grazing outside, with the crisp white yacht club at one end. The yacht club seemed deserted apart from two savage Dobermans which made me thankful for the high barbed-wire topped walls and chainlink fences which surrounded it. The small harbour, hacked out of the reeds in front of the clubhouse, contained a number of motorboats and one fairly new GRP yacht of about 30ft, padlocked to the quay by a huge chain round the foot of the mast.

The islands I wanted to see most were Suriqui, where not only the lug rigged wooden fishing boats used on the lake are built but also the Aymara builders of the local reed boats live, and the uninhabited island of Quebraya where Tristan Jones had found numerous previously undiscovered pre-Inca tombs. Here I found another problem, as I had only a small map which showed the positions of the islands but not the names, and every person I

Lug rigged fishing boat

asked had a completely different idea of the names of the various islands. Wandering along the shore towards the next village, I found a house with a man building a traditional *totora* reed balsa craft outside. I mentioned that I was looking for a boat to get out to the islands in, and he immediately revealed from under a huge pile of spare reeds a bright yellow Mirror sailing dinghy. The rig and sails were hiding in the back of a barn in excellent condition and within a couple of minutes a price of $3 and my cigarettes had been agreed for the hire of the boat for two days.

After a night disturbed by wild dogs howling at the full moon I took my sleeping bag, hammock, food and a few other useful things in my rucksack and set off to meet the owner at his house. The dinghy was rigged and in the water by 0730 and I set out into the calm waters of the lake, the mountains forming outrageous mirages in the clear blue sky. The thin clean air high in the Andes gives incredible visibility. From the low perspective of a boat, and only able to see the tops of nearby mountains because the bases are below you, it is a rather weird sensation. The wind soon increased and I sailed close-hauled towards one of the larger islands. Playing with the sheets and marvelling at the scenery I was enjoying the realisation that I was sailing on the roof of the world. In the afternoon as I was approaching the island a fleet of about thirty fishing boats came running down from the Straits of Tiquina, heading for the village on the south side of the island. They made quite a sight with their large single brightly dyed sails swung right out. I too must have looked somewhat strange to them, as some came alongside to find out who I was. I planned to camp out that night, so I made for a small bay which I could see on the eastern shore and which appeared fairly deserted, though as I drew nearer I noticed a small hut and a few cleared areas by the shore. I dropped the sails smartly in the bay and poled the boat in through the reeds and pulled her clear of the water.

Two children of about seven or eight appeared as I unrigged her and stood watching me in absolute silence as if I was completely insane, nodding quietly to anything I tried to say. I took my bag and found a suitable spot to sling my hammock between two trees about twenty yards up the steep shore. As I set myself up various other people came to see what was going on. These were Aymara people, different from the Quechua Indians who inhabit the mainland, and most of them only spoke Aymara which made conservation very hard work. It also became a constant struggle to keep hold of my things which seemed rapidly to be disappearing into peoples pockets, and I was warned not to leave my bag out because it would be stolen. The Aymara were regarded as the most evil, bloodthirsty tribe in the Inca empire and made up the major part of their army (though they were still slaughtered by Pizarro in 1532), and in his book Tristan Jones notes of his dealings with the Aymara that 'although they were in the main a highly intelligent people, for the most part this intelligence was employed in doing evil'. I can readily believe this, but it did not become a major problem and eventually I was left alone. I rigged the mainsail over the hammock as a tent and with my bag

Reed boats

tied down by my feet I had a very comfortable night, though at 12,500 feet above sea level and with a clear sky it got pretty cold.

I made a start at about 0630 after a cup of tea boiled in a corned beef can on a small fire and headed out with a northerly wind blowing about Force 4–5. I had been told the night before that I was on Isla Supicachi and that Suriqui was the next island to the south so I set a course to the small village on it which I had seen the previous day. It was extremely enjoyable sailing on a dead run with the sails pulling hard and the short choppy waves making quite a spray. I reached the village after about three hours, running down the narrow channel through the reeds under jib alone. A group of fishermen greeted me and showed me proudly round their village which consisted of four bare, unfinished, reinforced-concrete buildings owned and deserted by the Bolivian customs authority and a few small huts with fishing nets hung around outside. When I asked where their boats were built they pointed to the next island to the south which they said was called Suriqui and that this was the island of Supicachi! I did not think it was sensible to go further downwind as it was showing no signs of decreasing and I should not have been able to beat all the way back up to Huatajata before nightfall. I stayed for some lunch and then set off to the mainland to deliver the dinghy back to its owner. It was a beam reach and fast sailing all the way home and I was moored up to the small jetty I had started from by 1600, just as a light drizzle began.

TRAIN HARD FOR AN EASY WAR

by Hamish and Ewen Southby-Tailyour

Ewen: Black Velvet is based on the standard sloop-rigged hull onto which I drew a sail plan which looked aesthetically right and balanced. When the 'experts' translated this into working drawings it was pleasing to find that my centre of effort, horizontally, was only 2 inches out and, as planned, was 2ft 6in lower than on the bermudan rig. My sail area came out at 300 square foot greater on a length, from boom clew to cranse iron, of 42ft. To balance this we added nearly a ton of lead to the keel, placing this in solid shaped blocks. This ensured an even lower centre of gravity when compared with the shot and resin mix of the standard hull. We hoped to produce a rig that would keep going in a blow. After 4000 miles I think I can say we have achieved that aim — but, with the weight at all four corners she doesn't like short seas and light airs — and I don't blame her!

Hamish (at age nineteen) was probably the youngest ever co-skipper to have completed the Round Britain Race and certainly the youngest RCC member to have entered: at fifty-one I was probably getting too old for the arduous mix of outlandish weather which would keep us awake twenty-four hours a day only to be replaced every 500 miles or so by equally arduous parties for forty-eight hours. However, as I had entered for every race since 1966, and with Hamish eligible to compete for the first time, this was not the year to opt out. My only concern was that a beautiful father-son relationship could be ended just when it was beginning to take fruit. I needn't have worried in the slightest and found his companionship superb and his ability, especially in heavy weather, quite remarkable. I could not have wished for a better co-skipper — but then I would say that!

Hamish: I didn't think father would be able to take the pace and would become scratchy and difficult (especially ashore!) but it was great fun sailing with him as a twosome and I learnt a great deal about conservation of energy — and that I don't like everything cooked in red wine and garlic!

Both: After various 'sea trials' we picked up Black Velvet from Lymington

Black Velvet, *35ft LOA*

in June and sailed straight off for the 300 mile qualifying passage with exactly the time required left to satisfy the scrutineers — there was no leeway for bad weather or damage. With seventeen halyards and over 800 yards of rope on a yacht just 27ft on the waterline we had a great deal of knowledge to digest, and to pretend that we did not have teething troubles would be false. Although initially not designed to carry *Black Velvet* in a blow, the jib stood up to all we asked of it (on a Wykeham-Martin system it has to be all out or all in — we kept it all out up to gale force), only reefing the stays'l, depending on conditions.

The start on 4 June was a rather quiet affair in light airs. The only other fully RCC-crewed yacht was *Roc* with Desmond and Kitty Hampton, who were also competing for the newly instituted Hasler Trophy (for the first 'family' entry home in a monohull under 46ft); Mervyn Wheatley sailed in *Independent Freedom* and Mary Falk in *Q2*.

Unusually, we had to complete a circumnavigation of Plymouth Breakwater and back round Melampus buoy in the middle of the Sound before laying a course for the Eddystone and Cork. This was good for the spectators, sponsors and media but tiresome for gaff-rigged boats in light airs and so by the time we made our second exit from Plymouth Sound we were well and truly last. Others, more 'racy' than us, had set their spinnakers round the back of the Breakwater but unfurling our huge squares'l was not practical for a one mile leg: we sat in the cockpit and discussed life with our supporters' motorboat — with the windy-up gramophone it was all rather civilised.

The passage to Cork was (almost) uneventful and, crossing the line last, we motored quickly to the Royal Cornwall Yacht Club where we were met on the pontoon with a champagne welcome from the race sponsors (Teeside Development Corporation) and the RWYC race officials — including Mark Heseltine (RCC).

Throughout the compulsory forty-eight hour stopover we watched the barometer dive and the wind settle in from the south-west at a steady Force 6. When Blondie Hasler 'invented' the race in 1966 he calculated that two full days would be right for recovery — little realising, perhaps, that hospitality from fellow competitors and local yacht clubs would mean that we now go to sea to get the rest. Indeed with *Black Velvet*'s watchkeeping system, devised for the 1970 race, we get all the sleep we need — and more. It is based on the principle that we should be on watch together for an hour at breakfast to discuss the day ahead and previous night, lunchtime for companionship's sake, and three hours in the evening for cooking supper, carrying out the non-essential chores that need two people and for, well, a thoroughly earned drink or two. Day watches are five hours each, night watches three; the system changes every day and the person who has two of the three night watches has all afternoon 'in' before as well as all morning afterwards. It really does work and is wonderfully flexible. It also means that Hamish has three 'slots' a day when he can play his bagpipes when we are both on watch and not when 'father' is trying to kip!

Having sailed on cue — and last — we turned westwards into a rising sea from the north-west — just off the bow which was nearly good news, but it was not to last.

Hamish: It was clear that we were not making much progress and with a further foul tide and winds, plus damage to the jib (without which we would not go to windward at all) father gave the race office in Barra a call to say that already we were very far behind schedule. They told us that *Illyria* had put into Baltimore, a place we had earmarked as an excellent place to sit out bad weather.

Ewen: But this piece of news was welcome for *Illyria* was crewed by the other nineteen year old in the race — the lovely co-skipper of the Cooksey's daughter and father team. She had even stayed with us before the start while her parents had the boat to themselves. We turned back for Baltimore (!) and were off the entrance at 1300.

Sadly, for I was looking forward to a yarn with David, and Hamish would have liked very much to have seen Leanda again, they were not there having sailed for home just a few hours earlier. The wind was strong in the harbour where we jilled around rather inexpertly handing sails and squaring away for only the second anchorage we had made in the boat's life.

Both: A superb meal, hot showers, drying heaters for our sodden clothes (all facilities on board) and a lengthy spell on the end of the bowsprit for

Hamish saw us ready to sail as soon as the wind either moderated or shifted a couple of points: any direction would have done — providing it let us round the Fastnet.

At dawn the wind dropped and, although the direction had not altered, we sailed into a beautiful morning, eventually rounding the Rock in time for a wind shift to the north-west.

As we were still not going anywhere very fast we decided to get well away from the land so headed due west into the Atlantic.

Hamish: We were suddenly alerted by a fisherman shouting for help over the VHF. No Mayday calls, just a very Irish description of his situation. Could anyone help? Cork Radio answered immediately. I called back saying that we were well offshore, but upwind, and could run back, helped by the engine, and perhaps be with the problem within the hour. Yes, they said, and we set about undoing three hours of very hard windward sailing. With about a mile to go, the Irish Navy suddenly appeared in the form of a patrol craft, sending in their rubber dinghy to pass a line. The day had been saved. We were thanked for our help and released, but we were now inshore and downwind — oh well!

The west coast of Ireland was not good with light or contrary winds, poor visibility and confusing weather forecasting from the BBC. Many forecasts running gave totally different descriptions of what was actually happening in Valencia. In the end it was best not to listen to them as there was not much we could do about it anyway.

Both: Having been forced back towards the coast we tacked in and out of the bays — the stunning scenery making up for the frustration of slow northerly progress. At one stage, with a strong north-setting tide we had to motor 'in a panic' to avoid being swept onto the Bull (eventually admitted to the race office and accepted as part of the problem of having to attend the Mayday).

Hamish: Navigation was 'visual' off the south-west corner of Ireland but across Galway Bay with no sight of sun, stars or moon, dead reckoning seemed to be perfectly adequate — indeed Inishtearaght was the last solid object we saw until the entrance to Barra Sound — the next time I would use the sextant was in the North Sea. Barra Head was seen, on radar, at only two miles due to wave clutter and low rain clouds, so I was quite pleased with our landfall.

We entered Castle Bay, Barra, at about 0300 where a helpful Dutch entrant lit up a spare buoy for us in the dawn light just as father was clearing away the massive fisherman's anchor to cope with the notoriously poor holding ground and thick kelp. After that it was nonstop repairs and watering ship by many trips inshore with small water cans.

The trouble with an arrival at 0300 is that the start is at 0200 to make the line on time. For some reason now forgotten, and certainly not recorded in the log, we started the next leg at 0403. Perhaps father can remember why!

Ewen: No I can't! ... and we started what was to be one of the most uncomfortable sections of the next leg into a southerly near-gale with finely driven mist masking everything beyond a quarter of a mile. As we rounded Barra Head — unseen, even on the radar — at what we hoped was a safe two miles, the wind veered to the west leaving us with a close (a very close) beat towards St Kilda. Rounding St Kilda has always — to me — been the high point of the race and despite passing it twice before, and having landed in Village Bay for a long walk, this was the first time I could see the highest peaks. They really are magnificent and dramatic.

Although the wind veered again — on cue — we were able to make our rhumb-line course (for Muckle Flugga) with more ease than usual, but with an unpredictable weather system on its way we decided that we should try and keep some north in our track and so headed 'offshore' again. I think it paid off for we were to overtake at least one yacht on this stage of the leg — only to lose our place on the run down to Lerwick in calms and light breezes from the south having been swept by strong tidal eddies round the northern most tip of the British Isles at 0920 on 20 July.

Hamish: We finished at 0340 (again) but this time it was my birthday and a reception committee came onboard with the ingredients for *Black Velvet*, even before we had docked in the southern harbour. As birthdays go it was among the best and lasted the full forty-eight hours. We had arrived in good order and with no repairs to make and just water to top-up were able to relax — and father wasn't arrested this time.

Playing the Skye cradle song on the foredeck

The race committee gave us four hours advantage as a result of our attempts off Mizzen Head allowing us to sail at the saner hour of 2340. Before that we had finished my birthday in the Lerwick Boating Club in great style and so while father took the helm we motored slowly past the clubhouse under full sail in the half light while I played the Skye cradle song on the foredeck. With all our newly-made friends on the club balcony it was a lovely sending off.

Ewen: ... spoiled by heading into a flat calm off the start line where we lost all our time-advantage, and more, as three yachts ghosted past us over the next few hours. However, as I am not a racing person, I was not too fussed but I think Hamish felt a little despondent. I think he should tell the next part of this tale ..

Hamish: All was reasonably well and normal: the wind picked up from the south-east forcing us inshore further than we wanted to make our destination of Hartlepool — the home of the race sponsors. I managed to obtain a few sun sights but nothing else. Towards the end of the leg we were forced further offshore than we wanted and so started our approach to the coast from about sixty miles east of the Farne Islands. The navigation lights off the coast around Hartlepool tend to be masked by the shore lights so much that even at a few miles offshore we could identify nothing at all for a sweep around the bows of about 150°, which wasn't very encouraging. The radar was not much use either and so with the echo sounder on and the lead-line ready we had no alternative but to forge onwards keeping a good look-out. Father was on watch and I know he was anxious for some form of identification, but there were none that made any sense.

At the change of watches in the early morning of 26 July he announced that he could see the leading light for Hartlepool and had borne away for it over the previous hour or so. 'Excellent news,' he said, as he had been a bit worried. He then turned in, happy. But I wasn't so happy, and with the aid of a stopwatch identified the 'Hartlepool' light as the entrance to Whitby, about twenty-five miles further down the coast — and downwind. I woke him. The thought of a twenty-five mile beat to windward into a Force 5 did not appeal to him and he decided, there and then, to give up the race and head on home: we nearly had our first and only row. I argued that we owed it to our sponsors to make the effort, and anyway, I wanted to complete the course. He relented and we swung north-west along the coast to arrive in the lock gates in time for yet another champagne greeting, and, more usefully, a huge breakfast laid on in the race office beneath a banner proclaiming 'Welcome to Ewen Whitby-Tailyour'! It was the start of an excellent stay which even father was glad he had not missed.

Ewen: I will cast a veil over that and, indeed, most of the next, and final, leg save for two incidents. Under the new rules whereby Hartlepool had replaced Lowestoft as the final port of call, this last leg was now the longest, and it is, as always, undertaken when boats and crews are at their most tired:

it also involves all the worst shipping and tidal problems of the whole enterprise.

We sailed at 0925 on 28 July. At 1805 I was below at the chart table naked but for a sarong. Hamish was sitting in the companion hatch keeping a look-out ahead and, occasionally, astern. The weather was quiet, the visibility excellent, we were about five miles south-east of Flamborough Head and there were no ships in sight. We had just finished listening to the forecast when a bump and voices alongside had us both on deck in seconds. The inshore lifeboat was keeping pace with us while the coxswain shouted across that the coastguard on the Head had reported us as being unmanned and steering an erratic course. I was unamused to think that we had been inadvertently the reason for a launch; the crew were equally unhappy at being called out on a false alarm. As a member of the RNLI Boat Committee I found the whole thing rather embarrassing and offered them a whisky but they sped away without looking back — I didn't blame them.

Off Lowestoft we hit bad weather, poor visibility, a foul tide, contrary winds and oil rigs not marked on my charts with morale, at least mine, taking a dip. It was not helped a little later by an incident which scared me more than any other I have experienced at sea in a yacht. A few miles north of the Outer Gabbard lightvessel, in the early, and very dark, hours of 29 July I noticed a fully-lit passenger ferry approaching from the port quarter. We had about 2 knots of steerage way while the ferry, bound, I reckoned, for Harwich, was probably steaming at 18. I judged she would pass close, but clear, down our port side and so kept *Black Velvet* on a steady course. It quickly became obvious that she had not seen us and was heading closer than I thought safe with still no sign of an alteration in course or speed. I debated turning to starboard to make it easier for her but that was the direction she should have altered to. I called her on the VHF — no answer. I produced the massive searchlight borrowed from the farm. There was now little escape. With 2 knots I could not turn to port and get clear, and anyway that was where she was heading — just. I could not turn to starboard because that was where she should be going. At one cable, and with her steaming lights now directly in line, I felt helpless. Luckily the engine keys were still in the ignition from the dogwatch charging and so I was able to slam the thing into full-ahead with full port rudder. We shot under her bows. She had not altered course one jot and with the full 2.5 million candle power (so the instructions say) blazing into her bridge and causing no stir there was no doubt that she had not seen, nor heard, us at all.

We were thrown violently in the wash: Hamish appeared. I had completely forgotten to shout to him. We called the ship for the umpteenth time and eventually a languid and very English voice answered. 'Yes, he had seen a yacht close to starboard.' I asked him what was on his funnel and he told me. It was the correct ship and I gave him a very hard time about keeping a seamanlike look-out, visually and on radar, but I was dismissed as being a panicky yachtsman. Having told him I was unimpressed and frightened by his appalling manners I was about to switch off when a British tanker captain came up asking for my working channel. I gave it to him whereupon he apologized on behalf of the British Merchant Navy for my treatment and then proceeded to tell me that he had seen our radar echo disappear into the echo of the offending ship. He had already assumed the worst and was about to send a Mayday call when he was 'thrilled' to hear that we had escaped. So were we! After a few pleasantries, we went our respective ways with him wishing us *bon voyage*. I have analysed this often enough but am still not sure what else I could, or should, have done.

By contrast the passage across the Thames Estuary and through the Dover Straits was a peaceful and happy affair; we even took a detour close into Deal beach to pour a tot of whisky over the spot where my father's ashes had been scattered. Earlier, we had done the same thing for my mother off Rame Head at the other end of the Channel.

A very nasty, and totally unforecast, blow off Beachy Head forced us into Brighton where we sat out a further six hours of Force 8 and foul tide. This turned out to be an excellent decision for not only did we dry out but we actually caught up two places against others who had hove-to (or who had been just bashing themselves to windward for no geographical gain).

Hamish: Sailing shortly after midnight we headed south-west to get into clear air; another tactic that paid off for we had a beautiful, if close, beat down channel while others suffered a frustrating time dodging tides and fickle contrary winds in the bays. Finally, for we had not enjoyed much of the actual sailing, it was with some relief that at 1602 on 2 August we finished the 1993 Round Britain race having sailed almost exactly 2400 miles. But just to show that there was no ill feeling, the wind freed as we approached to a mile short of the finish line off the Royal Western Yacht Club and for that last mile we screamed along at an amazing (for us) 6.5 knots. In fact the wind did have the last laugh, for 50 yards short it shifted and we were forced to gybe for the first time in the race. Friends were watching from the club balcony as we made a complete mess of the whole evolution, but then, as we were obliged to explain, we had had no practice. Finishing 35th out of fifty-four starters, we were pleased with *Black Velvet*'s performance, especially as she was the only gaff-rigged entrant.

Two days later we sailed on a family holiday for the coast of France: a short and unremarkable cruise except for our involvement in yet another Mayday.

Both: At about 2230 one night south of St Peter Port a crew member drew our attention to a red glow over the horizon. We called St Peter Port harbour control who told us to get off Channel 16 and call on their working channel. We explained that we thought we might have a 'Pan' call and wanted to check if there was anything operating in the area. As we were speaking, two red rockets lit up the western horizon, and we headed towards them, at the same time transmitting a Mayday relay. St Peter Port asked for a range and bearing which took us a moment to establish and deduce for we were on dead reckoning, however we estimated the casualty's position to be about five miles south of Les Hanois light. The lifeboat was launched and we were told to continue westwards.

Luckily we possess a pair of night vision goggles (by courtesy of a South American dictator) and these and the farm's lamp were brought on deck. Another yacht had copied the Mayday and after half an hour she came up with a small French yacht about where we had estimated her to be. The news was bad. The husband (and skipper) had fallen off the stern leaving a wife and two tiny children in a small yacht with no sails set (the wife had undone every rope in sight) rolling wildy in the short sea and a cool easterly wind. The family could not sail, nor did they know how to operate the engine, nor the radio (although we never knew whether or not they possessed one) and the husband had only been wearing a buoyancy aid.

Using our 'magic' binoculars we were able to find two life-belts in the water from which we could establish a datum point for drift. The other yacht stayed alongside the Frenchman as a calming influence, for the family were beside themselves with grief. Indeed none of us gave out much hope for success at that time but we had reckoned without the arrival of a search aircraft fitted with a thermal imaging device. By this time the French skipper had been in the water for over two hours and while the lifeboat put a crewman onboard the casualty with a radio, we continued our search upwind of the lifebelts.

Then, quite suddenly, the aircraft announced that it had a possible contact half a mile to the east of our position and we set off at full speed into the short seas, with night vision goggles and searchlight in the bows. Luckily the lifeboat had by then finished transferring its crewman and at 25 knots was able to overtake us. A few minutes later a voice announced that they had recovered 'a man' from the water. We all held our breaths as the lifeboatman onboard the French yacht asked if he was alive or not. "Wait. I'll check the answer with the coxswain, out!'

Then: "Please tell the wife that her husband is alive but we'll take him straight ashore." The wife was clearly overjoyed but so, too, were the crews of two yachts, one aircraft and the St Peter Port lifeboat.

VIA THE WESTERN FRINGE

by John Wiltshier

Friday 25 June saw the start of our cruise south from Ardfern Yacht Harbour, just north of the Crinan Canal, where we had been so well looked after during the winter by David Wilkie and his team. The crew was Alison and me plus David and Eileen Cassidy for the first week. Destination south-west Ireland via the west coast. Having had a major shop in Oban we stored ship in driving rain and then motor-sailed, still in driving rain, to Crinan where some friends came aboard for dinner.

Sunday 27 June was a real Scottish cruising day — bright sunshine, Force 3–4, sheets just cracked as we sailed in three hours from Crinan to Craighouse, Isle of Jura, for lunch. We then sailed gently through the uninhabited Ardmore Islands on the south-east corner of Islay. The passage requires concentration but, with the benefit of Martin Lawrence's sailing directions, it is not difficult. There were hundreds of seals and a wide variety of birds. We tied up to the pier at Port Ellen and watered ship before picking up an H&I Development Board buoy in the bay for the night.

Away at 0615 after a roly night despite there being only a light breeze from the south-east. We sailed at an average of 7 knots, occasionally calling on the engine to keep up boat speed especially in the swell running inside the island of Inistrahull with its prominent lighthouse. We sailed up Lough Swilly and picked up a mooring off Rathmullen in mid-afternoon. A lovely sandy beach was a surprise but made an excellent dinghy landing 40 yards from the boat. A 71 mile day ended with an excellent dinner at Rathmullen House with skiing friends whom we have kept in contact with but had not seen for twenty years.

We woke to rain in the morning which dictated a leisurely start and some shopping in the very friendly local shops. Away at 1400 — still raining and no wind but with visibility down to 100 feet vertically as we motored down the Lough. The conditions were ideal for radar practice and as a light breeze came up we set sail as we entered Lough Mulroy and picked up a buoy among the fishermen in Fanny Bay. This provided excellent shelter but the cloud was still at 100 feet and the mist even lower. A good dinner on board with the coal stove alight and no inclination to visit the shore from any of the crew.

Wednesday 30 June. A bright day with the wind nor'nor'west Force 5. The coast is a dramatic, treeless landscape with Horn Head a really impressive headland, but Bloody Foreland is flat and inconspicuous decrying its name. We sailed inside Tory Island but did not fancy its landing stage and anchorage in the swell that was then running. David was at the helm when I called "Tack fast" having just spotted the first of many illegal fishing nets. We sailed around the end which was marked by an open boat 18ft long with three sheepish looking lads aboard. The net must have been more than a mile long and we met many more in the next few days and kept a closer lookout.

As we sailed inside Aran Island it was nice at last to lose the swell. The pilotage was interesting as we approached the fishing harbour of Burtonport where some of the entrance channels are only 80 feet wide. Warm rocky grass-covered islets and sunlit sandy bays were a delight after the rugged nature of the north coast. We tied up alongside a trawler in this most friendly port at 1440. David made arrangements to visit a dentist in the morning and we bought salmon, both smoked and fresh. The evening was lovely as we anchored back between the islands just clear of the entrance channel to the north of Duck Island and then walked ashore.

Thursday 1 July. Back to Burtonport for the dentist plus stores. The weather was on the change by that evening and we had 80 miles to go to Broadhaven, the nearest reasonable anchorage. The 0600 forecast on Friday was for Force 6–7 on the nose. With David's tooth still troublesome (good

Anchorage between Dutch Island and Inishcoo… 'as safe as in God's pocket'

excuse), we concluded that we were on holiday and hired a car for the afternoon to enjoy the countryside. Even worse conditions on Saturday but the friendliness of all the locals plus the welcome from Freeway, a mongrel dog who acts as if he owns the place, made our enforced stay most enjoyable.

Sunday 4 July. The 0600 forecast gave nor'west Force 5–6 and a chance of a close fetch rather than a beat. David and Eileen left as planned for Dublin and home to his own dentist. By 0800 Alison and I sailed under genoa (five rolls) and mizzen out into the swell to find a considerable sea running. Even in Force 5 the seas were breaking on a 5 fathom shoal. This is lots of water to us East Coast sailormen and reinforced the fact that this is not a coast to close in rough onshore weather. In some trepidation we sailed clear on the route advised by the Burtonport harbourmaster which was not the obvious one to choose from the chart, and with the wind mostly Force 5–6 we were able to lay our course with occasional help from our 88 hp Yanmar diesel which is very smooth and quiet.

There was some rain at times but the barometer rose steadily and this was a comfort bearing in mind the inhospitable, bleak coastline with not another boat to be seen all day. Eighty-one miles on the log as we dropped our 55 lb Delta (Simpson Lawrence improved CQR type) close to the lifeboat off Broadhaven. This bay is 10 miles short of Eagle Island which is the northwest corner of Ireland. We were glad to be in and the roast lamb was on the table within fifteen minutes. Well done Alison. This had been our first long trip on our own, in adverse conditions, and we were thankful for such a comfortable boat.

Up anchor at 0730 with the weather grey but dry as we beat out of Broadhaven Bay. In the ever present swell we were thankful to be able to

The harbour at Inishbofin

ease sheets round Eagle Island at last — it had been our destination for five days. We then had a lovely sail with a flat sea inside all the Inishea Islands, past the 2000 foot Achill Head and into Inishbofin on a lovely evening. Alison's log says 'sunshine adds enchantment' and we both thought the anchorage was high on our list of favourite places — Cromwell's fort at the entrance, excellent shelter inside and easy access in any weather. An early dinner at Days Hotel ended an excellent day's cruising.

Tuesday 6 July. Up anchor and sailed out at 7.8 knots with just No 2 genoa and mizzen. The first yachts we had seen under sail since Scotland were met off Slyne Head. As the wind dropped we motor-sailed to get to Inishmore, one of the Aran Islands, in time for a visit ashore. Fifty miles by 1415 when we anchored just clear of the lifeboat. A 20ft rubber duck with six wet-suited customs officers aboard visited us to find out whether we had seen any other vessels. Two days later they succeeded in a major drugs haul.

We travelled by horse and trap to the Dun Aengus prehistoric fort and walked back. A lovely afternoon. However we felt that Inishmore did not have the same magic as Inishbofin. I am sure others will view them differently.

An early start at 0630 hoping for a slant on the longish leg to Dingle. With the wind westerly Force 3, *Moonbeam* was happy at 7 knots with the sheets just started. By mid morning we were headed and had to tack to weather Loop Head off the entrance to the Shannon. A lumpy sea on top of a swell and drizzle made the going hard work still hard on the wind. We motored to help us save time around the seaward end of yet another fishing net. Then with the 300 foot cliffs to the north of Sybil Point quite close enough, Alison suddenly bore away straight for them. A small fishing boat was cheerfully but positively waving us towards the shore. The net they were guarding was very hard to see in those conditions. We spotted an orange buoy much closer to the cliffs than I liked but still the fishermen waved us inshore. Alison looked at the chart and said that at least the coast appeared clean. Finally about 200 yards offshore they waved us around the inside buoy. 200 yards off a shingle beach is quite a long way but 200 yards off a 300 foot high cliff is too darn close for the likes of us after a long day in that swell.

The tide was running against us as we eased sheets around the headland and sailed inside the Blasket Islands and the uneven bottom showed what a rough place this passage would be in bad conditions. At 2030 we moored in Dingle's new marina. After 102 miles we were glad to arrive and were made most welcome.

Moonbeam was sailed back to Falmouth by friends and then completed her cruise up channel by easy stages to Ramsgate.

CHICKEN-LEGGED TO THE OUTER HEBRIDES

by Michael Bolton

Sally and Steve wanted to see the Outer Hebrides and the Skipper wanted to avoid beating to spare his back; so with a moderate south-westerly, the start was up the Sound of Mull. By Lismore it was dinner time: cold rosbif and the trimmings, with strawberries and cream to follow. A meal not to be rushed, so half the genoa was rolled away for comfort. By chance, the colour of the plates matched the oilskins, Mike red, Sally yellow and Steve green and it was decided to stick to these for the voyage, then we would know who was who for second helpings. Dinner over, Loch Aline became our anchorage for the night.

Tacking out of the loch next morning against wind and tide, a motoring motorsailer tried to overtake us to leeward, failed, reversed and went round our stern. An angry face poked out of the wheelhouse. "What a display of seamanship!" he retorted as he slammed the door. It was sad to realise that, to him, good seamanship entailed using the engine to beat wind and tide.

Outside the loch, the wind fell away and clouds covered the sun. As *Revel*, our Rival 34, revolved in small circles we remembered a titbit from the CCC Journal: 'When the sails are simply hingin'; press the button, start the ingin!' But we didn't. We enjoyed the peace and Steve, to whom most things on board were new, had his first opportunity to start his official duties. He entered in the log 'On the roof of the boat there is a funny blue plate which apparently is a solar panel. It was switched on but evidently not working as we had no sun at all'.

Steve was also properly introduced to other things like winch handles (replacements if thrown overboard £80 each) and the fresh water system (use as much as you like provided *you* carry it aboard. *Revel*'s tank is filled when she is launched and topped up by cans for the rest of the season). Gradually a breeze filled in to help the tide take us out of the sound to Canna, where our anchor was cast among others in time for dinner.

They wanted to go to the Hebrides, so *they* were roused at 0700 to a hum

The Navigator and the Logwriter

in the rigging and sounds of pattering rain. Mutterings from the Logwriter about 'this Fascist regime' but we sailed after a forecast of fresh nor'westerlies. North of Canna it was distinctly unpleasant and shortly the log read: 'Daddy's back didn't fancy a F5–6 dump/plonk/dump session on a beat, neither did Steve's tummy and neither did I, so we turned tail to the wind and hoofed it back to Canna'.

Knowing Canna's reputation for thick weed, we exchanged the usual Bruce for the bigger one and re-anchored. It blew harder and Iain and Jean Nicolson of *Jasmine* (CCC), who had wisely decided not to sail, came aboard for coffee. A large bareboat charter ketch also returned and anchored ahead of us. She dragged immediately and spent the rest of the morning re-anchoring, the routine being to throw everything over in a heap and go full astern before the anchor had a chance to take hold, but eventually it did when the wind eased.

It was still raining and blowing in the morning but a moderation was forecast. And it was Sally's birthday, so the Outer Isles and a place for a celebratory dinner were a must. Once out of Canna Harbour it was as bouncy as before but the wind had backed allowing a course to be laid for Loch Maddy. There was even some sun as the wind died in the entrance to the loch and at last the engine went on to get the crew there in time for dinner. But there was disappointment in store at the hotel. Showers were £3.50 each and the only one had a queue of five for it! Also, the dining room was fully booked and a bar meal wasn't really the thing for a birthday. But then a party of twelve cancelled and the manager was only too pleased to retrieve us from the bar. Good food and wine and huge portions, so all hands slept well that night.

The Birthday Girl still wanted her shower but not at £3.50! The Youth Hostel said we could have them free — with cold water. But the new Outdoor Centre obliged at £1.50. Clean and shining we sailed for Loch Grosebay. The Logwriter recorded that *Revel* ran chicken-legged out of the loch. Ah yes — goose winged.

Steve was down below at sea for the first time and he celebrated by producing excellent cheese/apple sandwiches. We munched and minched along dodging lobster pots.

That crack in the rocks in Loch Grosebay which is Scadabay showed up and this is where it *is* seamanlike to use the engine. Inside was *Scaraben* (CCC), with the Editor of the *Sailing Directions* Dempster McLure and Margaret, and we were soon joined by *Hanky Panky* (CCC) with the Reeves on board. All except Margaret (recovering from a broken ankle), came aboard *Revel* for conviviality.

Dinner was to include cheesecake. The Navigator was cook and she instructed the Logwriter to prepare a ginger biscuit base for it. "Crush the biscuits first ..." 'How do I crush them?' 'Oh — put them in a plastic bag and sit on them!" He did but they didn't and the Skipper had to dig out the large engineer's hammer and the fish cleaning board.

Wednesday's activity started with a thorough clean ship — where does all the fluff come from? How the day continued is recorded by the Logwriter:

'Scadabay is inhabited by MacLeods — always has been — always will be. Among the many are Alastair and Flora Ann who are weavers of great renown and skill. Between them they turn sheep into Harris Tweed for jackets, woollen socks, jumpers and the like and are thoroughly entertaining. The explanation of how the machinery worked was superb. Then, after an exhilarating walk round Loch Plocrapool, we were invited in for a *strupak* (a cup of tea and a little something to eat). There were scones and rockcakes and fruitcake and lemon curd and syrup to boot (both please, but don't worry about the bread, said Pooh, not wishing to appear greedy)'.

The skipper bought Sally a pair of thick socks for her birthday. They were far too long but Flora Ann shortened them incredibly quickly. The *strupak* made lunch unnecessary and we had a fast sunny sail with interesting pilotage for the Navigator to Scalpay North Harbour.

Thursday had to be something special for Steve as he had his ferry to catch from Tarbert next day. It was. The Logwriter entered 'As we sailed out of Scalpay there was a loud squark (sic) from the Navigator when she thought that the echo sounder had gone from fifteen feet to two: "ReadyaboutleeohDaddy!!!" As we tacked in a big hurry she was informed that the switch was no longer at feet but fathoms and what was all the fuss about.

The Navigator recovered later in the day to write: 'Blobby bobbly clouds

Revel *and puffins in the Shiant Isles*

on Skye and huggy hat clouds on the Shiant Isles and why don't we go there? We did. Lots of puffins zooming around at an altitude of two feet — fat little fuselages and purposeful faces. Masses of fulmar petrels. Spent twenty-five minutes anchoring to find that the anchorage *isn't*. The wind hollers through the gap between the islands and there are boulders below. We dragged (bumpily over the boulders) and re-anchored in the corner by the natural arch — a fine sandy bottom in 5 fathoms on which the anchor can be seen. Rowed under the arch which has two roof pillars in it and kittiwakes nesting noisily above. The puffins were very friendly and made little 'gulump' noises as they sat for their portraits.'

Shiant was certainly good business for film sellers what with the natural arch, and tame seabirds. It had been a good day and Sally celebrated on the trip to Tarbert by producing a tuna spaghetti (real, none of your tinned stuff) creation with special sauce, with crispy stuff and fruity mush and chocolate goo to follow.

Tarbert was not actually our anchorage because the ferry terminal takes up most of the space; we anchored in Bagh Diraclett next door. Careful pilotage was needed because of strings of sunken rocks. As the ferry left at 0715 we thought we'd better time the walk over the hill to the terminal. Just as well we did.

On Thursday, the alarm roused all hands at 0515. Breakfast over we left *Revel* in teeming rain to squelch over the hill and deposit Steve on board his big ship. The shops wouldn't open until 0900, which gave time for baths and coffee in the motel. About to board the dinghy back in the *bagh*, we noticed huge mussels on the rocks and collected some; they were the best ever, large and delicious! Some had sizable pearls (which later replaced those missing in a brooch). And the *ceilidh* that night was fun — songs, accordions, fiddles, Highland Dancing and two sketches, all perhaps a bit too much in the Gaelic for the visitors. It ended at 2200, leaving time for everyone to get well oiled in the pub for the dance starting at 2330.

Saturday evening the ferry was to bring Patsy and we filled the time with a walk to the Laxadale Lochs. The ferry was late but there was no mistaking the red oilskinned figure waving from the deck. *Revel*'s Mate had arrived.

In the morning outside the loch both sails were set and reefed for a beat south in low visibility. Not pleasant, so Loch Stockinish selected as the next anchorage. But it was pleasant down below with the heating on, tucking in to the Navigator's cooking. Patsy wrote in the log next day. 'The charm of remote lochs definitely diminishes in proportion to falling temperature and rising windspeed. Add cloud down to sea level and stair-rod rain and you see why we are still sitting, full of breakfast wondering 'What next?''.

Scrabble was next until the visibility improved but the wind then fell to nothing. A mixture of motoring and ghosting in light variables took us to Loch Partain. The wee shop was closed but kindly opened specially for us.

The following day found us at Castlebay where we took a close look at *Britannia*, a large Boston fishing boat ketch, anchored off. She was beautifully kept and very obviously now a yacht. The skipper, Ross, invited us aboard for a look round. Up to 1960 she had continued fishing and was then converted for skippered charters. The gear was massive. We were then invited aboard *Ron Glas*, a junk rigged schooner, by Jock MacLeod (RCC) and there spent a convivial hour or so discussing other junk rig yachts. Jock had been Blondie Haslar's partner in junk rig yacht design, of which *Jester* was the most well known. His mate Ruari Hilary was a character. He had recently hired Kinloch Castle in Rhum for a large and formal dress family party.

Wednesday brought a moderate fair wind for crossing the Sea of the Hebrides chicken-legged. It rained the whole way, which allowed an opportunity to try a garb recommended for helmsmen by Kenn Stewart — a cycling cape. It was good; no condensation and warm hands. But when the wind increased to Force 5, it became a perfect pest.

Once through Gunna Sound, the visibility closed in to a cable or two and after an hour the end of Bac Beag appeared suddenly ahead. There was a strong tide sweeping north and we had to gybe to get a safe offing. Bendoran gave the best shelter from the increasing north-west wind and the anchor went down between the moorings and the pier.

The forecast for Thursday was of winds from the south later, so there was time for an expedition in bright sunshine to Camas Tuadh to see the youth camp established in the old fishermen's cottages. Sally had been a youth leader there years ago and she wanted to see if it had changed. The leaders welcomed us and showed off various improvements. It was a brilliant picture of greens and browns, greys of the cottages and the contrast of bright orange salmon nets poled out to dry. The youngsters were all busy and happy.

Well reefed in a fresh north-westerly, *Revel* beat round to the Sound of Iona and, paying close attention to the *Sailing Directions* for it was low water springs and there was very little water over the banks, we passed through and chicken-legged for home, dining off a tasty soya chunk fry up off the Garvellachs. Overall it had been a great cruise with a plentiful variety of weather, scenery and fun.

BLUE SKY, BLUE SEAS, BLUE ENSIGN

by Ian Taggart

The last weekend in September is known to us in Glasgow as the Autumn Holiday Weekend and Eileen and I decided to make our vacation cruise a Royal event.

On board *Venture*, our 29ft 6in Albert Strange yawl the peaceful night of windless calm gently slipped into day when darkness passed into a glowing

Venture — *Aux. Bermudan yawl, 29ft 6in LOA, built in 1970*

orange-yellow light. Oh boy it was nippy taking off the cockpit tent, hoisting the blue Ensign and the red and white burgee with its Maltese cross. We slipped the dinghy to the moorings since the Avon was aboard and quite sufficient for us both.

Breakfast underway of porridge, Lorne sausage (the flat sliced local type) and egg followed by toast, butter and marmalade with plenty of hot coffee.

At 0900 we were in the Dorus Mor. The whirlpools were placid even though it had been flooding for $2\frac{1}{2}$ hours. No doubt the fact that the wind was with the stream gave a flattening effect to the normally turbulent gate.

It was becoming warm now as the sun ascended and as we progressed toward Cuan Sound. With the north end of Shuna Island abeam we hoisted the main having completed all the morning's housework and enabled the skipper to be smartly shaved. The CCC Cleit Rock perch was observed to be needing a fresh lick of paint as it was almost invisible against the browning background of Luing. Cuan Sound was soon cleared.

The narrow passage between Easdale on Seil Island and Easdale Island was taken as a short cut and soon we were freely sailing again on a broad reach towards Bach Island and Kerrera's western shores. The engine was shut down while we took coffee and Tunnocks and gently explored the three lovely bays of this island's exposed shore.

The Oban-Craignure and Oban-Barra ferries each crossed our track as we approached Lismore on our port beam. The vista of the numerous Argyll mountains — Ben Cruachan's twin peaks, Bidean nam Bian, the Aonach Eagach ridge and Ben Nevis was breathtaking (to say the least) in the clear crisp September atmosphere.

We took up a mooring off Isle of Eriska just inside the narrow and shoal entrance of Loch Creran, leaving the mizzen on to keep us head to wind in the tide eddy anchorage.

Ashore we met the local hotel owner, the Rev Robin Buchanan Smith, a former Commodore of the Royal Highland Yacht Club. On the island Robin is laird, conservationist, farmer, naturalist, historian and there are many other facets to his remarkable character. We enquired about dinner and were most enthusiastically welcomed and informed that venison was being carved that very evening and we were offered baths forbye.

The venison was most greatly enjoyed after an excellent starter of chowder. The fresh fruit salad laced not lightly with Grand Marnier was served by Natalie, an experienced young French waitress who trained in L'Hotel Escribe in Paris. We viewed this hotel the following weekend and seeing its extreme splendour, passed by!

The highlight of the mealtime was in fact an interruption between courses to see three young badgers out for the evening from their nearby sett to take prepared food from the lounge bar patio door at 2130 as darkness had descended. This was a first for both of us and truly fascinating to see these nocturnal animals in the flesh.

The mizzen was left on all night and again as light came over the Loch

Three badgers out for an evening meal

Creran mountains an hour ahead of the sun we were up and away. We navigated round the top end of Lismore to Port Ramsay where we had breakfast at anchor. The morning was warm, the skies were blue and the high barometer was steady as a rock.

At 1000 we lifted the pick and on clearing this tricky entrance hoisted the sails to make across the Lynn of Morven to Loch Choire, a lovely 1½ mile long loch reaching into the Morven Argour landmass. Much fish farm activity was present in this loch but in no way did it restrict navigation or yachting interests. At noon we turned at the top of the navigable area to come out again through the lovely pink and light grey flecked headland entrance and turned south to make for Torosay Castle at the north-east corner of the Isle of Mull.

In Torosay Bay we anchored in 3 fathoms and went ashore to view the house and fine gardens which were the home of a former North Devon MP. Later we took the narrow gauge railway to Craignure. This well operated attraction is complementary to the tourist facilities and interests of this pleasant corner of Mull.

In the evening we left for Puilladobhrain, sailing to pass between Bach Island and Kerrera and onwards down the now risen moon's reflection to the Seil Island anchorage. As we neared the entrance we took off all sail and merely kept the engine running slowly seeking the 40 gallon drum headmark with searchlight. Only seven other yachts were in, giving us plenty of room to anchor in 3 fathoms.

After a lazy start next morning we prepared mark maintenance gear and rowed off in warm and calm conditions. The orange drum mark was only that colour because of rust. As we had only white paint we had to change its colour and next day reported to CCC and RHYC, with a notice to yachtsmen issued to the local Scottish yachting periodical. On leaving, the fresh white paint stood out superior to the former decayed rust effect.

On dipping the fuel oil tank we found the level to be so low as to be at risk of an engine stoppage so we planned to go to Croabh Haven. However as there was absolutely no sailing wind and we needed to catch two tidal gates, Eileen had the bright idea to call in at Easdale since the tide was high and would allow ample depth at the quarry haven entrance. Jim McLean kindly took us over in his Avon to Easdale Harbour where ferryman Plunkett gave us 5 gallons of diesel. He refused payment but was sent a bottle of wine via Jim who received one for himself also.

Much relieved we set course for Fladda Sound and Dorus Mor and on up to Ardfern, where we had some supper before stowing sails and preparing to moor the ship.

Truly an excellent weekend's cruise making to places neither of us had been before. The weather was the principal factor in enabling us to fulfill all we did without rain weather gear or rough weather practice. Eileen, in her third year of cruising, is now fully confident and greatly skilled.

A FUNNY THING HAPPENED ON THE WAY

TO THE OPERA

by Jill and Tony Vasey

It was pure coincidence that we had booked for the opera at Drottningholm on 21 July, exactly one year after our adventures visiting Savonlinna last year, but it took more than coincidence to get us there on time.

We left Helsinki, where we had laid up *Shiant* for the winter, at the beginning of June but we had one or two calls to make before Drottningholm. The perennial Baltic problem of gas was rearing its head again. Last year in Tallin we had stuffed every bottle we had full of chicken methane but that was fast running out. Our new *Baltic Sea* guide told us that there was propane to be had in Riga, and since that was only 250 miles upwind it seemed worth a try. So off we went for a sparkling sail that was well worth it in its own right, but with the lure of propane it was doubly enjoyable. There wasn't any! They had never heard of it; not in this city of millions could they produce it, but they were very nice.

The wind had, of course, turned northerly, and the Gulf of Riga is shallow and fresh so we had a lumpy beat back up through the famous Moon Sound and east to Tallin. As we entered the harbour our chicken farmer friend was just sailing out and waved cheerfully, misunderstanding my frantic gesticulations as a friendly greeting. That evening, when I was disconsolately strolling the waterfront calculating how to make 2.5 kgs of propane last three months, he steamed in again and with hardly a word carried off our gas bottles. He was back within the hour regretting that he could not fill the big cylinders but assured me that he had stamped it down well in the four small ones.

Martin Lawrence (RCC) had succeeded in filling his cylinders at Mariehamn-East Harbour last year and that was only a couple of hundred miles away, and anyway was not far off the route to Drottningholm. It poured with rain but the fresh norther just allowed us to stitch our way up through the archipelago, dodging the islands and taking risky short cuts to avoid a

Shiant *in search of gas*

tack. I have a deeply held philosophy that if it is foul weather, go to sea. If you stay in harbour you fret below thinking that it is sure to be better out there, but if you brave it and make a good passage you feel doubly virtuous. We were feeling very virtuous when by mid-afternoon we had made 50 miles in seven hours, all in blinding rain and cold as charity. The passage was getting very narrow and there was a marked absence of sailing boats which we explained by lack of bottle, but when the fishermen had to raise their rods to let us pass we became distinctly suspicious. The answer wasn't long in coming. I had just negotiated a punt when round the corner was a bridge, not a high bridge, not even an opening bridge, but a low plank bridge that I am sure we could have demolished had we had the guts to ram it. We let sheets fly to get some way off, then luffed hard into the shallows and just got her head through when she slowed in the mud, but before we had time to panic we were off again on a wild reach in the opposite direction. The chart said 'Fixed Bridge 3m' very clearly, but our pace had been so hectic we hadn't had time to read such detail. Twenty miles and three hours later we let go the anchor the other side of the bridge, still in pouring rain; but we did feel virtuous.

Mariehamn didn't have any gas. We lugged a cylinder miles across the town to the East Harbour but they hadn't heard of it, so we left it with the West marina office where they promised to enquire in the morning. Friends arrived that night and we were anxious to show them the joys of island hopping, so when dawn broke clear we slipped quietly out to sea for three days' idyllic pottering through the Åland archipelago. At Turku we knew it was possible, we actually knew someone who had done the thing, but when we went into the lazarette for the bottles there was only one; the other big one was still in Mariehamn-West marina office.

We met a chap on a bicycle with a trailer so we temporarily traded him one of our Bickertons on faith and set course north with our one empty rattling along behind. We had only a latitude and longitude given by the Kelletts (CCA), but we knew them to be accurate folk so followed our lodestone with the aid of a map of southern Finland. Ten miles and £13 later we were back at the boat and calculated that, with economy, we could last the summer; and then our problems began.

Our batteries were getting old, but the horrendous Scandinavian price of replacements had so far deterred me until I was seduced by some American deep-charge batteries on offer at the biggest chandlers in Finland and so had two delivered to the marina. Thus, heavy with batteries and light with gas, we put to sea for a loop around the Gulf of Bothnia. Our friends left us on the Swedish mainland but we still had ten days to get to the opera, so when we got forecast of a soldiers wind for Mariehamn we reached briskly the 50 miles across the Åland Sea. They had that day sent our gas bottle by ship to Turku to be replenished by the very fellow who had filled our other at such great expense. We took the return half of the soldiers wind back to Sweden, now painfully aware that one of our new batteries wasn't taking a charge so would have to be replaced.

Kind man takes battery

In Stockholm we phoned the Turku chandler who would, on production of a certificate from an electrician, exchange the faulty battery, but it would have to go back to him since he was the sole agent in the whole of Scandinavia. The only way to get it back was on the daily ferry berthed across the harbour from our marina. The shortest way was by dinghy, but that took us to a high steel wall with a slippery ladder under the bows of a 50,000 ton ship. When Jill was woman-hauling the heavy battery up the wall whilst I steadied it from below in the heaving dinghy she stopped to remark that it was a hell of a way for an ancient Brit to earn her OAP. We emerged to find we had broken into the bonded area and had to get out of it lugging our suspicious package on a shopping trolley. The ferry folk were very nice but they couldn't take such dangerous cargo unaccompanied, so we did the whole harbour wall charade in reverse and set about arranging a courier.

The day of the opera dawned absolutely foul, lashing rain and half a gale, but we did want to explore the old town before leaving. We bravely cycled into the city and snapped the lock through the iron railing of a smart café. Suddenly I had a premonition — we had forgotten the key — and there wasn't a housebreaker in sight. We hailed a cab and demanded to be taken to the nearest hardware shop, but we might as well have asked for a chandler in this medieval quarter. An hour later we were back with a bag of tools purchased at the other side of town (we declined the offer of burglars' masks) and set to work. The sun had come out so a few braves were sitting outside the café; there was a noticeable lull in their conversation as Jill held the wrench whilst I sawed the chain. We had just got them free when we heard a police siren. A Bickerton doesn't make a very good get-away vehicle on 15th century cobbles! There was now just five hours to go before the opera.

Drottningholm is the home of the royal family, where the theatre was built beside the palace in 1750 by the opera loving Gustav III. Not only did he write operas but he also acted. Unfortunately, in a too realistic assassination scene in 1792 they shot him, and so dampened was the royal enthusiasm for opera that they closed the theatre and it remained sealed until 1921 when it was rediscovered perfectly preserved with all its properties and incredible machinery still intact. Now it is used to stage a few 18th century operas each year, the only concession to modernity being electric imitation candles each of one candle power. It becomes fully booked at the start of the season and we were admonished to be in our places by 7.30 pm, after which our seats would be sold.

It was now 3.30 and we had ten miles, three opening bridges and one lock to negotiate, apart from finding somewhere to park *Shiant* outside the theatre. We charged into the waterway with the engine smoking on maximum revs knowing that the bridges would not open during rush hour, but no one seemed to know exactly when that was. It turned out to be from 4 pm and we arrived at the last bridge at five minutes past. I could see the bridge operator in his cabin so radioed him on the hand-held whilst waving from below, but he regretted that it was more than his job was worth to open during rush hour. I pleaded, explaining that we had sailed all the way from England to go to the opera and that we must be there on time otherwise our seats would be sold. He had a heart of stone but at least promised that he would open promptly at 6.30. There was no way we could cover the seven miles, anchor and get to the theatre in an hour. So near and yet so far!

We were in office country and by the time we had found a mooring most were closed. As far as a public telephones went it was a desert, so full of hope we rang a door bell. The charming young man who answered sympathised with our predicament and immediately volunteered his telephone. The answerphone told us that the theatre would open at 7 pm so we recorded a promise that we would be there, if late, and on no account were they to sell our tickets. Then the young man suggested a fax so we repeated our promise, heavily underlined, saying we had sailed virtually non-stop from England and that it was imperative for international relations that our tickets were kept for us. At 6.30 we were hovering under the bridge and, good as his word, he opened promptly. There was only a light breeze but with full sail and full engine we made seven knots, me steering whilst Jill laid out our opera togs. When the palace came in sight there was no sign of the promised marina — indeed, there wasn't anything except a magnificent stately home with a tranquil pool in front. We threw out the anchor, bent on our long frocks and dinghied ashore to arrive panting at the theatre door at ten minutes to eight. In the melée of folk waiting to buy cancellations the sweet young thing at the desk recognised us as the crazy Brits and waved our fax together with the tickets. I was all for kissing her, but Jill restrained me saying we had caused enough of a scene already.

I don't remember the name of the opera but we did enjoy the sailing.

Pause for reflection

ALONG TWO WEST COASTS

by Jeffrey O'Riordan

At times *Adrigole*'s first season in home waters seemed to be more an exercise in crew changing than in seamanship. In the space of three weeks we managed no less than six different combinations. This was no mean feat as some areas of the west coast appear to be slightly less accessible than Tibet. However, even those who had to travel by Shanks' pony across the pot-holed roads of Ireland had no complaints. For it is no cliché that the West Coasts of Scotland and Ireland offer some of the best cruising grounds in Europe.

Our first, and easiest, crew change took place in Arisaig. Our son, Dermot, had sailed *Adrigole* there from Dublin. Arisaig is a splendid place to leave a boat. There are strong moorings there laid by the yard, who keep a careful watch on things, although it would be unwise to lie to anchor because the holding is poor in places. A great advantage of Arisaig from a Southerner's perspective is that a very civilised northern equivalent of the Orient Express travels overnight that way from Euston. One arrives in the early morning at Fort William. After provisioning at Safeways, it is a short but beautiful train ride to Arisaig. There is then only a short walk down the hill to the harbour.

We were greeted by Cait who had been staying on the boat with a couple of friends. By mid afternoon we were ready to cast off. Rather embarrassingly we ran aground on a sand bank shortly afterwards. We had been told to keep on a straight course between the buoys, and I still maintain we had. However, the only damage sustained was to Cait's friends' nerves. As novices, they took some convincing that this was not the norm aboard *Adrigole*. The next (scheduled) stop was Armadale where we moored to a solid Highland and Islands visitors mooring buoy. With eight people on board one problem was the presence of twenty-eight pairs of shoes or boots, one for each foot of waterline. The plethora of footwear was not enough to mar the atmosphere. We saw two rainbows at the same time and listened to the bagpipes played on the shore.

Next morning we motored over to Mallaig to put Kay and Sergei ashore.

Heading north inside Skye up the Sound of Sleat, we put into Loch Hourne to have lunch and wait for the tide as half a dozen seals lay on nearby rocks taking little notice of us. The pilot says the loch is best seen 'on a dark day with the clouds streaming off high mountains'. They were certainly streaming at high speed, and a pretty impressive sight it was.

With the turn of the tide we went on up to Kyle Rhea. Earlier in the year we had had to keep away from this part because the fishermen had imposed a blockade to protest against the building of a bridge over to Skye. We were hoping to get shelter in Broadford Bay but the wind seemed to accelerate down the hills and there was no future staying there. Instead we turned tail and went to Plockton. As we did so a worrying finding was made. The compass had a deviation up to 15° or thereabouts: there had never been any deviation aboard before. Fortunately the spare compass that had travelled about 20,000 miles in various lockers was alright and rose to the occasion when mounted in the prime position in front of the helm. A number of the navigation buoys shown on our charts were not present on the way into Plockton: not sure when they were removed.

We did not have time to go further up the coast so returned through the Kyle of Loch Ailsh to Ornsay on Skye. Apparently it used to a be a major fishing harbour but now has just a few cruising boats at anchor when it is crowded. There is a nice art gallery near the pier. The water on the pier however is not so nice — those approaching the tap from the sea need to be careful because they will not spot the notice about $\frac{1}{4}$ mile up the road that says the water is contaminated and the supply is being improved.

Brackenbury suggests that, whilst in Scotland, the skipper should be ready to change plans if the weather deteriorates. I was beginning to wonder whether the same applied if the weather improved suddenly. There were others aboard of a less optimistic persuasion. Cait believed that Scottish weather was an 'Escher staircase', appearing to be going continuously down. In the event the weather did improve, allowing us to stop for lunch in the harbour on the south-east corner of Eigg. There we met Christopher Russell (RCC) on his father-in-law's boat with his family.

From Eigg it was a short trip to North Loch Moidart. It is good to get there at low water, at least because then the dangers are visible. Later when we met Christopher Russell again he said they had gone to South Loch Moidart because they thought it had the simpler entrance — each one to their own poison. North Loch Moidart was deserted and very lovely. The girls took a dinghy round to the south harbour and on the island were surprised to meet some very friendly pigs. Next morning the only problem was getting up the anchor — it had bitten deeply into the glutinous mud, so the holding can be rated as excellent!

We rounded Ardnamurchan Point in a glassy calm — no need that day to stand off for a couple of miles as we made for Tobermory. That used to be training ground for the naval training school during the war run by a fierce admiral. We heard of his throwing his hat on the deck and asking what anyone would do if it really was an unexploded shell. An Able Seaman responded by throwing the hat overboard! The Admiral's reaction was not good news,

From Tobermory we had a splendid sail to Oban. Unfortunately, it was time for crew change three as Cait had to leave us to begin to look for gainful employment. Will Le Quesne who had just left school took her place. For a few days before the crew change, Phil had been feeling unwell with a fever. There were four doctors on board: me, the physician, Jonathan, the psychiatrist plus two visitors (Will's parents), a neurologist and a surgeon. Medical opinion had it that a dose of antibiotics might be of some help. So after a quick trip to the chemist, we left Oban.

The Garvellach Islands sounded nice but we tried both anchorages and found no shelter from the southerly wind in either of them and so had to carry on. The Gulf of Corryvreckan looked pretty inhospitable but things improved as we anchored on the north side of the entrance to West Loch Tarbet on Jura. From there we had a pretty good view of the Atlantic but little shelter. Fortunately it was not needed.

However by then it was clear that Philly was not getting better and we had to make plans to get her ashore. Not much use trying *Pan Pan Medico* with two doctors on board — they would have laughed at us. We decided to leave at dawn and try Port Askaig on Islay. The tide was just right — just as well because it runs up to 5 or 6 knots through the sound. Luckily we chose Islay and not the neighbouring Jura which has a very small population. On Islay there is a splendid hospital at Bowmore and Phil was admitted there. Everyone was incredibly kind to us and even found a car hire to help us get round the island. We headed down in the evening to Port Ellen and were able to lie alongside a fishing boat. The Highland and Island buoys out in the bay seem rather exposed — apparently they were meant to be further in, but careful survey showed hazards. Next morning Phil was a lot better but still not well enough to go on sailing so Sal and Natasha left us to stay with her. That left Jonathan, Will and I to go to Ireland.

We left Port Ellen on 16 August for Ireland. We had lost some time and our chief navigator. However, we had met Arthur Orr in Port Askaig. He had just produced the ICC's new edition of the *Sailing Directions to the South and West Coasts of Ireland* with lots of fine coloured pictures. So, armed with his good advice as to where to go on the West Coast of Ireland and a splendid north-west wind on a bright sunny day things were looking up. Originally we thought of going to Portrush but conditions were so good that we bore away for Loch Swilly. By the time we got to Inishtrahull the formidable tide was against us but we slowly got the better of it. There is one anchorage, described by Arthur Orr as 'stony', on the north side of Inishtrahull. We could see the mast of one boat in it — that meant the harbour was full! Passing Malin Head was an anticlimax — it had always sounded so impressive on weather forecasts but it's really not a great headland.

As we made for Loch Swilly we enjoyed the lobsters we had bought on the quay at Port Ellen. There were no vegetarians onboard now so our gluttony was not rebuked. It was dark by the time we anchored but the Loch is lit so entry was not difficult. Tory Island for lunch was our next destination. Opinions seem to vary about this north-west outpost of Ireland. Jonathan and Will went ashore and thought it was decaying. Staying aboard *Adrigole* at anchor I agreed but others seem to have liked it.

At the turn of the tide we sailed down to Aranmore Island. For the first time this year I had an uneasy feeling that I did not have the right chart — though we had about 180 on board for the season. Many of the Irish charts were old — the oldest was one bought for 4/6d and had *Moonraker*'s name on it. Their lordships of the Admiralty have confused things by retaining old numbers but changing the area covered so you may think you are alright but will find there is a gap. It was for such a gap that we were headed. The *Directions* into Aranmore however were good and we anchored in the right place as dusk was falling.

The next day was to be a rest day — trying to communicate with Sal —which was not easy from a coinbox on a remote island. The news was good. She had got Philly home to London by plane and train and the patient was recovering. Sal was setting off on an epic journey via Knock, by plane and buses to rejoin us (crew change number five if you are keeping tabs). By the next morning we had been reunited on the quay. We should have gone

Juno II *and* Adrigole *in St. MacDara's Sound*

up to Burton Port to meet her on the mainland but I was not certain about the channel into the harbour so we had waited at Aranmore. The community there is still very isolated. The only shop on the island sold a book telling of a disaster that occurred in the late 30s. Apparently then the islanders used to go to Scotland to earn money potato picking or 'tatty hocking' as it was called. Returning by boat in November a number were drowned.

Even with Sal to reinforce the crew, crossing Donegal Bay was pretty miserable with a nasty sea and a southerly wind. Radar did a good job showing up the slit that is the entrance to Broadhaven, where we anchored by Ballyglass Pier at 0330. Four hours later it was time, we thought, to be off again to get the south going tide. Off Eagle Island, south of Erris Head, however we still seemed to have the tide against us for ages. The inside passage from Annagh Head to Achill Head was a bit hair raising. It required identification of a selection of breakers but since there were breakers everywhere that was not too easy. Sal and Jonathan enjoy that kind of sailing. Will disparagingly referred to them as the 'half moon navigators' — apparently a reference to their deteriorating eyesight. He similarly wrote me off as 'sitting in my playpen' — the navigator's table with its electronic aids. Once we were through the narrow channel we found that only the lower half of the Cliffs of Achill were visible, the upper regions being in the clouds. Reaching Inishboffin we anchored close to *Juno II*, sailed by the Commodore and the ex-librarian and made a plan to meet in Cashel.

By this time Sal was reliving her youth — she was brought up in

Sal in front of St. MacDara's

Connemara. The butcher in Roundstone remembered her family, the Berridges. Going into Cashel we lost face and had to do a U-turn to reassess our position — rather embarrassing with the Commodore already anchored in comfort there. The 'half moonies' excuse was that with the sun low in the sky in the evening it was difficult to spot a pair of ruined cottages that are critical for navigation in those parts. After a brief tangle with a shrimp pot we had a splendid supper at anchor, partly on *Adrigole* and partly on *Juno II*.

On the Sunday morning we sailed together to St MacDara's island. The minute chapel has had its roof restored after a few centuries without it. Tradition has it that sailors dipped their sails to MacDara but the reason is not clear. One version says it was out of respect for the saint while another says it was out of fear since he cast spells over those that did not acknowledge him. Anyhow it is still a magical island.

By contrast Aran Island has become overwhelmed by tourism. There are fast ferries going into Kilronan very frequently. We stopped there for a few hours before setting off at dusk with a northerly wind to Dingle. The passage was pretty uncomfortable until Jonathan and Will got the jib out goosewinged in the night. We had a fast trip and were rewarded by having the tide right with us as we sailed through Blasket Sound. The Islands were as majestic as ever, though desolate with so many abandoned houses.

As we entered Dingle we were greeted by Fungie the dolphin. He has been there about 8 years and had made a few millions for the town by attracting tourists. Over the last few years Dingle has changed enormously. Not so long ago there was a store that stocked a few cabbages, some carrots, plenty of sheep dip and lots of firelighters. Now the shops are excellent and the restaurants first class. Jonathan left us there and so did Will, who signed on to sail back to England on *Juno II*. The great news though was that Philly was better and she came back on board with her grandmother, Cicely Berridge (the final crew change). Our cruise finished with some splendid day sailing from Dingle. We sailed out to the Blaskets, where we anchored so that Phil and Sal could go ashore for a walk on Inishvickillane, and to Ventry Harbour. The weather was perfect for a change. Fungie added to the fun. Once he jumped right out of the water and on another occasion rose just behind us with Philly at the helm. The splash caught her unawares.

It was in Dingle that our ever changing crew left *Adrigole*. Of the original company of eight only three remained. Later, Dermot with another crew sailed her back to Cork in September. So the only member of team to complete the full circumnavigation of Ireland via some of the Highlands and Islands this season was *Adrigole* herself. Some boats have all the luck.

YER MOORING'S A LOBSTER POT

by Rex Williams

We had definitely reached Ireland; thirty-two hours from the Longships, close hauled to the northwest wind and wondering where *Shemay*'s landfall would be. Kinsale we hoped but Dunmore East it was, and glad we were to be there on the evening of 30 July. The berths in the harbour were crowded and inspection of the mooring area outside next morning led to a vacant buoy which, in an east wind, would have been rather close to the north pierhead. However, the west wind blew, our need was only until the rising sun cleared some of the inside berths, the standard riser buoy had a standard pick-up buoy and with it we secured for breakfast. About an hour later the magic words came to us from the pierhead, a concerned motherly voice floating on the wind, 'yer mooring's a lobster pot'.

Back in the harbour we spent a lazy day watering and sketching to be fit for an early start to the west. However, the 0623 forecast of south-west increasing Force 6 or 7 suddenly turned our thoughts to the advantages of river boating. We had missed the River Suir on earlier Irish cruises and the last of the ebb at noon found us far from the sea off Duncannon Fort and all was peace as we approached the junction of the Suir and Barrow at Cheek Point nearly two hours later. There we considered a row of well spaced yellow crosses on posts extending north from Cheek Point to the channel buoy in mid-river. Fortunately the tide had not quite covered the groyne on which the posts stood and the way round was obvious. About $1\frac{1}{2}$ cables further west appeared the markings of another groin and the space between provided an enticing anchorage off the Cheek Paint Inn. Three hours later on the flood there came round the point a large Irish yacht heading at speed to pass between the yellow crosses straight towards *Shemay*. Happily my frantic shouting and waving to the north averted a certain wreck.

Ashore for a fine supper at the Cheekpoint Inn I learnt from an ex-salmon netter that the groynes, designed to scour the channel, were only four months

Waterford

old. He added that they should have red lights, they have ruined the local netting and the pilot has towed one vessel off!

Next morning, after heaving the anchors out of same splendid mud, we carried on past the Bingledies to Waterford fourteen miles from the sea. On the huge pontoons under Reginald the Dane's Tower, was an island of peace surrounded by a bustling city and an active container port. It was 2 August in a fascinating place up a beautiful river and there were just two other yachts in sight. Family and friends came for curry on board on the following evening before we sailed for Kinsale in the morning.

We could do without the machine before lunch and had an hour of spinnaker before tea when, off Capel Island, the west wind set in. Off Ballycotten Island the sight of a salmon boat allowed us easily to avoid the net, but only Liz's sharp eye saved us from the next; 150 yards or so of cut away net, the grey headrope floats less than fifty yards ahead. At 2130 we passed between the Big and Little Sovereigns to reach the western anchorage in Oyster Haven with the last of the light.

On Sunday 8 August we began the eight hour motor beat round the Old Head of Kinsale to Glandore. A slightly modernised Glandore with many more moored boats and yachts now, including three Dragons, and a busy dinghy scene in the small drying harbour. There were half a dozen visiting yachts at anchor, only one of which was dragging its single anchor as the early morning forecaster was chanting 'south-west veering west Force 5–6'. How brave they are to sleep soundly on a single anchor in such a place.

Some years ago, anchored across the Bay off Union Hall for a south-westerly gale, a similar yacht was towed back to our anchorage by a local fisherman who had seen it at first light just before it dragged onto the east shore beyond the Dangers.

Middle son was delivered from Lismore by car at noon and, after a run ashore to the Glandore Inn that night, we motored away in a flat calm at 0800. A family of seals, lounging on the rocks of Eve Island, blinked at us as we passed close by on the way to Rabbit Island, there to avoid another salmon net before anchoring off Castletownsend to see if anything had changed. Evidently not so, after coffee and reminiscence we sailed away to the rising west wind and made Baltimore Bay for lunch. The telephone from Sherkin Island informed us that granddaughter Hannah would be pleased to dine with us on the following evening so we duly anchored off the Baltimore fish quay and trooped ashore to Declan MacCartney's Inn. There, in a bay window on the first floor with a magnificent view across the bay, we passed a delightful evening with excellent food and wine.

There followed four days of calm weather in which we pottered past Lettuce Point and Spanish Island to Hare Island. Then, avoiding Two Women's Rocks, to Schull and on to Crookhaven for supper at the O'Sullivan's. The remarkable weather enticed us to North Harbour on Clear Island where we berthed on the south-east side of the main pier ahead of the ferry in 9 feet. From there to the Ilen River to anchor for the night off a tiny cove facing Ringarogy Island; the log records 'a night so quiet the tick of the small electric clock was heard for the first time'.

We put Shrimp ashore in Baltimore, said goodbye to Hannah and motored

North Harbour, Clear Island

away at 1100, south-east for the Longships — to reach Glandore six hours later!

> Before the 'shipping' in Ireland
> We are treated to speeches in Erse
> But the Beeb gives us the Archers
> Which is often a great deal worst

And after the Archers the man had said Variable becoming south-east Force 3 or 4 which sent us straight to wait for a shift at that obvious strategic point dead downwind of the windward mark, the Glandore Inn. The next day was flat calm so, there being no diesel in Glandore, we motored over to Union Hall and found a new (to us) hazard. On a line running east and parallel to the shore, from a point just beyond and to the east of the end of Union Hall Quay, there stretched, two feet below the surface, over a cable length of polypropylene connecting moored buoyant prawn pots; a system which keeps the pots just clear of the bottom and marked only by a very small buoy at each end. We had arrived at low water deliberately with the aim of anchoring close inshore but, though I'd stopped the engine in time, the rope was between fin and skeg and lightly holding us on what would be the track of inbound fishermen when the tide made. Fortunately our anti-driftnet, equipment a 12 foot sweep with a V cut in the blade end, was available to push the rope down and away from the hull and then to scull clear — smug you look, said herself.

And all to no avail — or nearly so, we were still in Ireland. Ashore with the big fuel can I found that the nearest diesel point was in Leap some three miles away. As I trudged back to the dinghy a voice hailed from the quay 'my daughter will drive you to Leap', and laughing away my feeble protestations about diesel cans in cars, she did, and told me something of her part in the thriving Irish Dragon scene.

We went back to Glandore for a day of calm, mist and drizzle and then on Wednesday 18 August we set off into the mist. The wind never exceeded Force 1 from the south-west, but motor-sailing at good speed we anchored off Coverack thirty-six hours out. There was enough west wind in the morning to sail clear of the Coverack pot markers but it didn't last and eight hours of engine later we reached the Yealm, fifty-seven hours out from that other world.

FALMOUTH TO FALKLANDS

by The Rev Bob Shepton

The expedition that never was — or so it seemed initially. After a great send-off from the Royal Cornwall Yacht Club on 15 September with family, friends and a good crowd of kind supporters on the pontoon to bid us farewell, including our Commodore and Rear Commodore (we were greatly honoured), and our old friend and Patron Bishop Mike giving us an encouraging word before blessing the expedition, the crew, *Dodo's Delight* and most other things, we took our departure with boats following — and sailed to the Helford River!

The discerning may have noticed a pole sticking up astern with nothing atop it. The problem was a wind-generator, and a part for its repair which had not yet arrived, so we had to skulk in there till it did. But the next evening we were able to sail out on the tide and down past the Lizard to the open sea. A beat across the Channel and a hard beat on the wind all the way across Biscay then allowed us to pick up the Portuguese trades south of Finisterre, which bowled us along with a following wind all the way down to Porto Santo, the northern isle of the Madeiran group. From Porto Santo with its three mile long golden sandy beach and clear water, a leisurely sail through the night took us to Funchal which by comparison we found a bit of a dump! But we did meet up with Tim and Ginny Le Couteur and family in *Falconer* there for the first time, and we had an interesting diversion (though that is not really the way to look at it), spending three days in the mountains of Madeira forming one of two search parties looking for a missing British yachtsman who had gone walking in the hills. We did not find him.

Putting out of Funchal in the face of a bad forecast ('these locals must be fair weather sailors') it proved worse than anticipated and we lay to bare poles for three hours to let the storm pass. The chief problem had been water pouring down one of the dorade ventilator shafts, else we would not have stopped, of course! Then we were running before with poled-out twin headsails, down to Santa Cruz de la Palma. This was a big commercial

Dodo's Delight *leaving Falmouth*   *Photo: Anne Hammick*

harbour but charming town. They spoke Spanish rather than the dreadedly difficult Portuguese, and the officials looked at us as if wondering why we had bothered to check in at all. This was our sort of place. A brief break to water, bunker and victual, and we were zig-zagging downwind through the night past Gomera and Hierro, picking up easterly trades the next morning. These should not have been there, but we were glad that they were, as they bowled us along at a great rate towards the Cape Verde islands. They became the North East Trades after a while, flying fish landed in the cockpit, one hit the back of Barney's head to his fury, dolphins and turtles swam by, and we reached Porto Grande on Sâo Vicente in 6½ days of hard, fast sailing to cover 915 miles.

We were not too impressed with the Cape Verdes and especially as it proved difficult to find fresh water and suitable stores for the boat. We mainly succeeded in the end, sadly said farewell to our friends on *Falconer* for the last time, and left on 27 October, taking 27½ days to reach Rio de Janeiro, 2836 miles away. I suppose that was not too bad considering we were looking for wind for the first three days out of the Cape Verdes, spent four days getting through the dreaded Doldrums (I am afraid we did use the engine), and were hard on the wind for six days against the South East Trades in order to weather the north-east corner of Brazil. The mast zig-zagged alarmingly when the aft lower chain plate burst — it had withstood 40,000 miles

L to r: Ian Savage, Simon Atkinson, Stephen Moon, Barnaby Athay and the Rev Bob

of abuse by schoolboys until then — but a brilliant (?) repair at sea with U-bolts and shackles, and a veritable cat's cradle of spare line tensioned by a handybilly as extra support, allowed us to support the aft lower and mast again, and sail on.

Rio was hot, friendly, very hard on the legs, and we had difficultly finding gas and stores, but we liked both the city and the people. That statue looking down on the city really is very impressive. The next leg was something of a nightmare: light, variable winds, interspersed with long periods of calms, and then a Force 8 gale! Further periods of calm, for Force 8 winds, rain and thunder (once with no pause between flash and crash — not nice), beating against a heavy sea, tacking across our course and making little progress, followed by perfect sailing weather, sunshine and breeze, with petrels and magnificent wandering albatrosses gliding majestically round the boat. It continued in this sort of way down to Port Stanley, with the wind going right round the compass in twenty-four hours on two occasions, and five separate gales contrasting with $54\frac{1}{2}$ hours of motoring in calms. We saw our first penguins swimming off Volunteer Point, and then a strong beat at dead of night brought *Dodo* into Port William and through the narrows to arrive at Port Stanley at 0200 on 18 December. We had made it by Christmas.

And the Falklands are home from home — if you happen to come from Scotland. It will be difficult to leave, but ... now for Antarctica. A long way to round the Horn perhaps? We shall see.

THEY DID NOT WANT TO BE ORGANISED

by Heather Watson

Before Dodo's Delight *sailed south, a few clandestine preparations were carried out.*

My daughter once asked me if I enjoyed a challenge — this certainly was one! Having battled for three years to help form the **Enterprise Sailing Trust** and raise the money to make the project viable, the departure date in September was drawing closer. Whilst helping (they might say 'hindering') with the preparations in those frantic last weeks I quietly did a 'kit muster' — of, I must emphasise, *domestic* equipment only! For starters there were no vegetable knives on board at all, tins only had been the order of the day on previous voyages. And the stove had splendid 'fiddles'; unfortunately the pans would not fit between them and balanced precariously on the top! So when no one was looking I whipped out a tape measure and made a *large* shopping list.

The next problem was how to get it all on board *Dodo* and stowed away when the Skipper was not looking! My luck was in — I managed to 'acquire' the key for two whole days in his absence. That was wonderful, I even got a friendly carpenter on board to put up tin-openers on the wall, tea-towel holders, hooks for oilskins, towels etc. All the new gear was installed — bread-making bowls, loaf tins, graters, choppers and plastic containers to keep the weevils at bay! The biggest challenge was yet to come — to teach them how to use it all. They were being very tolerant and included me in the crew to sail down to Falmouth for departure — what fun we had (or rather I had — I am not sure about them)! We made bread, chopped onions and vegetables — the Skipper was heard to say, 'did he really have to cook the onion first, couldn't he just chuck them raw into the tinned stew?' I took the lads through the cookbook I had written and a book of 'do's and don'ts'. They were very patient and, I am sure, thankful when I transferred to *Saecwen* off the Royal Cornwall Yacht Club, but I did eventually get a warm thank you from the Canaries. They had caught some fish but the crew did not like it as it was not out of a tin!

CLUB MATTERS

THE 1993 AWARDS

Judge's Commentary by Kit Power

This year there were twenty-seven logs for competition — three up on each of the last two years. As usual, there is a tremendous diversity with cruises varying in length between two days and a year, in latitudes between 59° South and 68° North and, believe it or not, at altitudes between sea level and 12,500 feet (though admittedly most were at the lower end of the range).

With so much, such diverse, material to choose from the judge has the difficult — perhaps impossible — task of comparing the incomparable and his problem is compounded by the changing pattern of member's cruises. Those whose cruising is constrained within a four week holiday can compete for the Founder's and Claymore cups on a more or less level field. At the other end of the scale, there are those who can cruise for six months and more clocking up dazzling achievements reaching, to borrow a phrase, the parts that other cruises cannot reach. For them, the RCC Challenge cup and the Romola cup are the main prizes. The difficulty comes in between where more and more members are making magnificent cruises of two or three months but whose achievements in terms of sheer distance covered and remoteness of area visited cannot possibly compare with those of the world girdlers. Perhaps we need a specific means of rewarding this 'marzipan layer' of achievement.

In writing a log for the *Journal*, it seems to me that the key objective must be to maximise its usefulness to others contemplating the same voyage. We should be left knowing what it was really like, what was important and what was not, which were the high points and which the low. We like a good read but we really want accurate information. I have tried to bear this in mind in making the awards.

Most of the logs fall into five clearly defined categories: Long complete cruises; Parts of long cruises; 'Midi' cruises — over four weeks but under about four months; Cruises of four weeks or less; Cadet cruises.

In the first category — long complete cruises — there are five logs and all show so clearly the weight of experience and careful planning which is necessary to cover great distances to remote places in safety and without unnecessary hardship.

Willy Ker, with two RCC Challenge Cups, the Tilman medal and the Goldsmith Exploration Award already under his belt, has produced a beautifully written account of his voyage from the Falklands to the Russian far east and western Canada by way of Chile, Hawaii, Alaska and the Aleutians. As usual, he makes it all sound so easy — rather as if he had done it all in some elaborately equipped vessel purpose-built for exploration in high latitudes where every conceivable difficulty can be efficiently handled by some marvellous piece of high-tech wizardry. Instead, he sailed his well prepared Contessa 32 and the difficulties are overcome — or more often simply pre-empted — by consummate seamanship and forethought.

Hugh Clay discovered that working in England made Tasmania a rather inconvenient berth for *Aratapu* so he brought her home by way of Tierra del Fuego (which he circumnavigated for good measure, making light of exploring new channels in swirling tides using charts bereft of soundings), Chile, the Galapagos, Panama, Labrador and home, just in time for the Beaulieu meet.

In thirty-eight weeks he covered 20,250 miles and has given us a log which makes utterly absorbing reading especially because of the fascinating historical detail which he provided. One's enjoyment in reading a log — and the writer's enjoyment of the cruise itself — is greatly increased by the knowledge that, for example, this was the place where Slocum saw off the natives with tin tacks. We see what he saw and can put ourselves in his place. Typical of Hugh's thorough research is his practice of marking such places on the chart in advance, something I shall do myself in future.

Pete and Annie Hill's voyage took them in the other direction, from England to the Falklands, and is remarkable for the meticulous pilotage information they prepared, virtually amounting to a complete pilot book in its own right. They visited, and wrote up, no less than eighty-three different ports and anchorages on the coasts of Brazil, Uruguay and Argentina and they did all this with no fuss, and obviously a great deal of enjoyment, in a boat whose only engine is a Seagull outboard.

Tim and Ginny Le Couteur found a window in their children's education and seized the opportunity to leave their New Zealand home, buy a boat in Gibraltar and have a tremendous family cruise making a good circuit of the Mediterranean before crossing to the West Indies by way of the Cape Verde islands and Barbados. This is a lovely account of the pleasures of long distance family cruising, extremely well planned, competently conducted and uncomplicated by the constraints of crew changes and the need to keep the necessary rendezvous. In the course of this cruise the Le Couteurs have contributed a tremendous amount of carefully recorded pilotage information.

Finally, and perhaps most unusual of all, is the cruise by Miles Clark in *Wild Goose*. Using Miles' log and notes, his father Wallace has put together a fascinating account of an extraordinary voyage from Ireland to North Cape and the White Sea Canal to Lake Onega and thence by lakes, canals and the rivers Volga and Don far to the east of Moscow to the Sea of Azov and so into the Black Sea. As an example of seamanship and enterprise this journey is outstanding but perhaps its most remarkable achievement was the courage and perseverance which brought victory over a hostile bureaucracy bringing problems which most of us only contemplate in our worst nightmares.

The next category, parts of longer cruises, all come from members on circumnavigations. There is almost no way of writing a short log of a very long cruise (although one member did describe a circumnavigation in a single page of text in the 1990 *Journal*!) and a detailed log of an interesting part of it is one way round the problem. Each of the four logs in this category convey something of the wonderful timelessness of circumnavigations — there is always tomorrow if today is unsuitable. I particularly liked Hugh Merewether's log. He sails, 90 percent of the time singlehanded, from Tasmania to Singapore by way of Papua New Guinea, the Solomons and Indonesia. These are not the easiest of waters and the unexpected can be dangerous, especially when it must be dealt with singlehanded. Hugh's easy account hints at the difficulties but doesn't make a drama of them and is full of the sort of picturesque detail that leaves one feeling one has been there with him.

Next we have six 'midi' cruises, over four weeks and under four months. Ewen and Hamish Southby-Tailyour sailed round Britain in their brand new boat but whilst this was a race they confirmed their cruising credentials by conducting it as a cruise but still finishing well up in the field. Charles and Elizabeth Nodder took a 'maternity cruise', also round Britain, with Suzanna (aged thirty-three days at the start!). I particularly like Ann Thomas' evocative drawings made on their cruise through the Western Isles to Norway and back. David and Judy Lomax describe a well organised six week cruise in Norway with a log full of the sort of detail which makes me want to go there — and I will next year! Christopher Lawrence-Jones celebrated his retirement with a three month two-handed circumnavigation of Ireland with his wife Gail and has given a meticulous and well-observed account of their experiences on the west coast of Ireland. I liked, and hope others will copy, his inclusion of a reading list to help one do one's homework.

In the under-four-weeks category there are eight logs, all of them covering various combinations of Ireland, Norway and the islands around Scotland. Not so long ago, France or the Low Countries were the most frequent destinations for these shorter cruises and the fact that we are now going further afield has less to do with faster, more modern boats (none were new and five were nearly twenty years old) than with a greater determination to get away from the crowds and break the newest grounds available in the time allowed. Nobody demonstrated this more clearly that Winkie Nixon who, in only two weeks, sailed with a strong crew from Howth to the Faeroes and back, still finding time to cruise in the Western Isles on the way home. 1,200 miles in two weeks (they averaged 6.3 knots under way) means keeping moving and with that sort of schedule they did well to keep engine time down to 22 percent. John and Sue Sharp went rather less far in twice the time, but their four week cruise with their three children on the west coast of Norway and in the Shetlands and Orkneys illustrates another way of getting away from the beaten track — lay up your boat away from base and start off again next year. The Sharps clearly know that cruises with children are happiest when there is lots of shore time. They went equipped with climbing boots to make the most of the mountains ashore and their log is full of helpful details about their explorations on land.

In the final category, Cadet cruises, there were three logs — all very different. Gillie Watson and four friends had a laugh a minute cruising in the Channel Islands. Pete Ingram, on his roundabout way home after crewing for Hugh Clay in *Aratapu*, found himself on the shores of Lake Titicaca and got the altitude record, sailing for two days in a bright yellow Mirror dinghy. Perhaps not quite a 'cruise', but an adventurous and rare exploit, successfully conducted and recorded in a highly enjoyable account full of interesting detail which shows that he made the very most of a marvellous opportunity. James Burdett bought his Vertue *Mary* back across the Bay of Biscay at the time of the September Meet and I can well remember our anxiety then when we heard the forecasts for storm force winds at that time. Now that he and his crew, Tom Hasler, are safely home we can read his account of what happened and I can only say I was scared out of my wits. His description of a vast wave breaking astern of them and at such an altitude that it was momentarily mistaken for a cloud will live with me for a long time. This was a storm in which two yachts were lost and James' account is an extraordinary story of skill, endurance and courage.

Very occasionally, a member makes a cruise which does not qualify under the rules for any of our awards but is such an exceptional achievement that one feels justice demands proper recognition. Miles Clark's journey through Russia is just such an achievement but the fact that the account is not written by Miles makes it ineligible for our existing prime awards. It is true that the Vase and the Decanter can be used to cover such situations but their award is inevitably seen as secondary to the Club's main cups. I was therefore very glad when the Flag Officers approved my suggestion that we should revive The Cruising Club Prize to be awarded on these very rare occasions where a really extraordinary achievement would not otherwise be properly recognised. Why the Cruising Club Prize was discontinued in 1888, eight years before the Challenge Cup was first awarded and before the Club received its Royal status is a mystery which the archives, and the memories of very senior members, cannot explain but I hope that in future it will occasionally be awarded in recognition of any truly astonishing feats ineligible or inappropriate for our existing awards.

RCC Challenge Cup	Hugh Clay
Romola Cup	Pete Hill
Founder's Cup	Winkie Nixon
Claymore Cup	John and Sue Sharp
Irish Cruising Club Jubilee Bowl	Sir Christopher Lawrence-Jones
Irish Cruising Club Ship's Decanter	Hugh Merewether
Royal Cork Yacht Club Vase	Tim Le Couteur
Sea Laughter Trophy	James Burdett
Cruising Club Prize	Miles Clark

Ladies' Cup

The Commodore has awarded the Ladies' Cup to Elizabeth Nodder:
In *The Maternity Cruise* Elizabeth and Charles Nodder set off from Christchurch with their thirty-three day old baby in a 27ft Pintail sloop.

The timing of the whole operation, including the arrival of the baby, maternity leave, and leave of absence from both their employers, was immaculate. The stores they mention make unusual reading — a forecastle full of nappies and two sets of ear plugs.

This is a delightful account of a family cruise with a tiny baby and I can think of no more deserving recipient of the Club's Ladies' Cup than Elizabeth.

Medal for Services to Cruising

The Medal for Services to Cruising has been awarded to Oz Robinson, Director of the R.C.C. Pilotage Foundation. Since taking up this post, Oz has made an already thriving organisation thrive further. The number, range, and sales of RCC Pilotage publications have all increased impressively, and there are several others imminent or planned. The Club and the cruising fraternity at large have benefitted enormously from his efforts.

RCC Seamanship Medal

The Seamanship Medal is awarded to James Burdett with Tom Hasler for reasons that are only too obvious from James' account of weathering a storm while on passage across the Bay of Biscay in the pages of this year's *Journal*.

Tilman Medal

The Vice Commodore has awarded the Tilman Medal to Paddy Barry:
The Tilman Medal is awarded to Paddy Barry for a remarkable voyage in his Galway Bay Hooker, *St Patrick*, far up the west coast of Greenland, direct from Ireland. Meticulous planning and impressive seamanship meant that Paddy and his crew were able to combine cruising with treks and climbs ashore in the best traditions to Tilman.

Dulcibella Prize

Well, it certainly makes a change in these pages to come across a story about canoeing. Add to that an eye for nature and a great deal of charm in the telling and Tim Trafford's *Rule 2* was an easy choice for 'Maldwin's Lamp'.

MEETS

The Beaulieu River Meet

The threat of bad weather did not prevent a good attendance. The Harbour Master had laid the now customary heavy duty moorings below Needs Oar point and early on Friday evening both *Juno* and *Hirta* arrived to form the centre piece of the raft. The majority of the fleet was comfortably anchored by mid-day on Saturday.

Late on Saturday morning the Hon Mrs Pleydell Bouverie arrived as a guest of the Commodore, gallantly keeping up a long-standing tradition having first attended this meet as far back as the early '30s. The afternoon's fun and games were arranged by Colin de Mowbray and the usual evening party took place on the main raft to be adjourned only for sustenance before many returned for some fine singing which went on well into the night. The bad weather started to arrive from the south-east early on Sunday morning and by lunchtime the fleet had dispersed. The Commodore was last seen heading up the Beaulieu River to a quieter anchorage and a well earned rest.

The following boats attended: *Aratapu, Astros, Avocet of Ryme, Border Rival, Bow Bells, Callisto Mio, Capricho of Sark, Chinita, Dash, Decibel, Dyola III, Enki III, Felicia Fisher, Fidget, Firedancer, Foggy Dew, Freedom Freyja, Fubbs, Galliard of Lymington, Gang Warily, Gaviotta, Hirta, Kataree, Konistra, La Snook, Lalji, Lectron, Mahjong of Taipei, Matawa, Mary Briant, Moletta, Moon Magic, Naiad, Nicodemus, Oboe V, One and All, Palamedes, Pastime of Innisfree, Patriot, Q2, Quiver, Reeve, St Radegund, Saria Marais, Sea Scoter, Sea Tonic, Senecta, Stren, Stroller, Tehari II, Warrior Shamaal, Wayfarer of Emsworth, Windflower.*

AVF

RCC Sailing For the Blind

The weather was kind to what amounted to the first RCC meet of the season, from 30 April — 2 May. The fleet of seven yachts assembled at Lymington Yacht Haven and each embarked two blind or partially sighted crew, all experienced from courses run by the RYA Seamanship Foundation. Saturday was a day of gentle sea breezes. Some anchored off Hurst Castle for lunch; all rafted to the fueling pontoons at Beaulieu for the night. Sunday gave us splendid sailing in a northerly Force 3–4. We secured for the night at Cowes on the pontoons of the Powers and their neighbours, and the crews were entertained to supper by John and Caroline. The next day in very little wind some anchored for lunch in Newton Creek before the fleet dispersed at Lymington. It had been a very happy occasion.

Taking part were *Buran, Enki III, Kattaree, St Radegund, Tallulah, Tehari II, Vigilant* and *Wandering Moon*.

AP

East Coast Meet

Mid May proved as popular a time as ever and those on passage northbound were in luck, blessed as they were with a fair wind for the River Orwell. Others intending to sail from the north were less fortunate as a strong contrary wind against the tide in these waters proved a daunting prospect, though these conditions did not deter *The Bandicoot* from sailing out of the River Ore to endure a very bumpy passage.

Once again *Dorado V* was berthed conveniently close to the lightvessel in the Suffolk Yacht Harbour so Bill and Chris Green dispensed a proper welcome to all who stepped aboard. They were not alone by any means and thereby was set the tone for what became an excellent evening. *Morning Sky* came in good time from the Isle of Wight as seems to happen every year with Oliver Roome wearing his usual happy smile.

The kindness of the Haven Ports Yacht Club in continuing to make us welcome in their lightvessel in hugely appreciated. To have a fine dinner in these surroundings does so much to encourage the high degree of conviviality which prevailed. This was heightened by the presence of The Commodore and Susanna who made a great effort to be with this contented band of East Coasters.

There were there: *The Bandicoot, Bosham Dreamer, Dorado V, Morning Sky, Ready About, Margaret Catchpole II, Kiebitz*.

TH

The After Christmas Newtown Meet

Despite a stormy forecast which promised heavy rain and strong winds, eight boats gathered in Newtown on 28 December to be rewarded with bright sunshine and just enough breeze to keep collars turned up and hot punch circulating at regular intervals (ie — all the time). We were particularly glad to see *Owl* with several Club members among her distinguished crew.

Present: *Born Free, Cymbeline, Kinit, Owl, Reeve, Sarie Marais, Tehari II, Valkari of Guernsey*.

EG

Butley River, 1993, a raft up on Hermione

East Coast Mini-Meet

Following a week of monsoon quality rain, the forecast for Saturday, 2 October still boded ill. But by lunchtime the sun had gone about his business on the lower reaches of the Butley river, five Club burgees flew convivially above the hub-bub on the raft below and this end of the season frolic was enjoyed by all who took the news of an impending gale with a pinch of salt. Tom Miszewski lived up to his reputatiaon for exemplary seamanship by rafting up under sail, only slightly to diminish it *immediately after lunch* by running aground. Thank you, Clem (Lister), for having the idea.

The following boats attended: *Bosham Dancer, Faolag, Hermione, Quern and the Bandicoot.*

TW

OBITUARIES

Captain Henry Denham CMG RN

Henry Denham's life, all ninety-four years of it, like Somerset Maugham's concept of the ideal novel, was divided into three parts. Beginning, Middle and, alas, End.

Henry was a modest man, though exceedingly handsome. From Osbourne and Dartmouth — it's extraordinary to think that he was born before the turn of the century — he had been honed, polished and hardened in the greatest Service our world has known, the Royal Navy. In the fearsome Gallipoli campaign, August 1915, as a midshipman in *Agamemnon*, he commanded a steam picket boat landing allied troops under fire at Suvla Bay. Between the wars he saw much service in the Mediterranean, serving finally in the light cruiser *Penelope* on stand-by patrol off the Spanish coasts during Spain's civil war. One would suppose that it was during those years that he formed his enduring love for the Mediterranean which was later to serve the Royal Cruising Club and other foreign-going yachtsmen so well.

Before the Second World War he already had his mind on sailing because in 1933 he joined the RCC as a naval member. Later, in Naval Intelligence, he created an Information Correlation Centre which indexed details supplied by yachtsmen and the fishing fleet ... Fascinating thought: had Henry been influenced in this by *The Riddle of the Sands*? ... In any event, after the war he was one of the committee that instituted the Club's invaluable Foreign Port Information service.

When, in 1940, the German army invaded Denmark they found Henry with my older brother, James Millar, burning SECRET documents in our Copenhagen legation, where Henry was Naval Attaché. Both, having diplomatic status, were repatriated, and Henry was appointed Naval Attaché in Stockholm where, as he has described in one of his books (*Inside the Nazi Ring*), he was able to shadow the German battle fleet. As his CMG and various foreign decorations indicate, he had an outstanding naval career, individualistic and innovative. During it he met his remarkable wife. In 1920, while serving in *Renown* when she carried Edward, Prince of Wales, to New

Zealand and Australia, Henry first met an exceptionally interesting young woman, Madge Currie. But he was then appointed to the Rhine Flotilla, and for two years commanded an armed motor launch as part of the Occupation forces. In 1924 Madge came to London, and they were married.

I must revert for a moment to Henry as a cadet at Osborne. Not long ago I wrote a foreword to a new edition of Lady Brassey's *Voyage of the Sunbeam*. Henry telephoned from London, "When I was a nipper at Osborne," he said, "there was a Royal Review of the Home Fleet and various visiting ships, among them Sir Thomas Brassey's full-rigged yacht *Sunbeam*." He said, "We youngsters were mad with excitement, rowing about among the fleet. In the evening all the crews went ashore for fireworks, beer and so on. We noticed that *Sunbeam* appeared to be deserted so, unchallenged, we swarmed aboard, she being the loveliest ocean-going yacht imaginable and, furthermore the first genuine auxiliary yacht, since she carried a steam engine aft, with a collapsible funnel."

During the war Henry had acquired the smart Nicholson cutter *Korby*. He retired from the Navy in 1947, turning his energies to the RCC and to annual extended cruising covering the Mediterranean, the Adriatic and the Aegean.

I knew plenty of people who sailed with Henry in *Korby*. To my deep regret I never did because, in those days, I always had my own boat and my wife as crew. Henry, by contrast, had grown up in crewed ships run navy-fashion. He Liked to sail *Korby* with a complement of five; himself, two men friends and two women. He also believed in changing crews at fairly short intervals. So, in the winter months, he and Madge would jointly work on the logistics for the coming summer's cruising. And to maintain his schedule,

Henry and Madge Denham in Herald's *cockpit*

Henry always had to sail to a timetable. I think that suited his temperament, if not Madge's. There were times when she disliked *Korby*'s (forward) galley, and she had a family of three to care for. Quite rightly, she put her children before Henry's sea-restlessness. When any of the children sailed in *Korby* she usually went along.

Henry was an invaluable friend to us. His knowledge of people, places and wangles in the Med were fathomless. In the 1950s no marinas existed — paradise indeed — and the Royal Navy benevolently ran Gibraltar and Malta. Before approaching Gibraltar one wrote a polite note to the Flag Officer, a flag officer whom Henry invariably knew, asking permission to berth and stating ETA. Off the harbour mouth one hove-to, flying the requisite signal. A junior naval officer would emerge in the bows of a pinnace, and would lead the yacht to a berth in the torpedo camber, which was better than any marina, and free. It was there in the torpedo camber that we first met, aboard the last of his yachts, *Diotima*, the fascinating and wonderful 'Goldbags', Admiral Sir M Lennon Goldsmith, then RCC Commodore.

"Midday, Sir," one of the crew would say when *Korby* was on passage. "Make it so," HMD would reply, and the gin, *ouzo* or whatever would be brought on deck. Henry at sea regularly took a siesta after lunch. While he lay in his quarter-berth he had an alarming habit of noticing the ship's behaviour. Sometimes he would call to the helmsman, "Check our course on the compass, would you?" And once he called to Pam Hoare. who was steering, "There are a lot of sea serpents around, Pam." She, mystified and alarmed, exclaimed "Serpents?" 'Just glance astern at your wake" came from the recumbent figure below.

Henry's personal tastes were simple. He was never one for the fleshpots. When *Korby* was in port at one of his planned or weather-enforced stops he liked to walk a lot, and study the history of the place. He kept a straightforward and terse log, but asked his crew to keep a Ship's Diary of all happenings ashore and afloat.

When at last he decided to sell the gallant *Korby*, and built a smaller and more modern yacht, he asked me over to Wivenhoe to see his new *Herald* nearing completion. I think it was while he and I worked together in *Herald* — so named, brilliantly I thought, after the Survey ship of a naval ancestor — that we finally discussed Henry's major opus, the Sea Guides. Together we formed the notion that nobody was better qualified than Henry to write Sea Guides to the Mediterranean, Adriatic and Aegean waters, anchorages and harbours he knew so well. And I think it was that day in *Herald* that I told him John Murray would be the ideal publisher. Henry and Madge put an immense amount of work into his Sea Guides, which, rightly, had an immediate and lasting success.

One key to Henry Denham was his physical strength. He did not care for motor cars, and did not own one. But he was restless in the London winters and, from 1950 on, frequently did canoeing explorations with his cousin, Dr Alex Moulton, the inventor. The doctor could carry a couple of kayaks on the roof of a car, and in that way he and Henry were able to explore, afloat, the lagoons and waterways of Venice on one trip, the Loire, from its shallow headwaters to the mouth, on another. In the late autumn of the '70s I was surprised to hear from Humphrey Massie, then owner of Crinan Boats, "This morning your friend Captain Denham with his cousin, Doctor Moulton, paddled into the yard in two canoes." I imagined the pair paddling all the way round England and Wales to Argyllshire, but learned subsequently that Dr Moulton had acquired an unusual craft called *Ankle Deep*, originally built for Uffa Fox and propelled by two outboards. Dr Moulton had put in a third outboard, a tent and two kayaks and, thus conveyed, the cousins had set off to investigate the lochs and rivers of the West Highlands. On another occasion they were in the inventor's 'steamboat', going down the Beaulieu River.

"Henry was stoking," Dr Moulton told me. "Perfectly clean job, because the coal was in sealed paper bags. But he got rather embarrassed when we met a couple of Cruising Club yachts coming upstream."

Madge Denham became seriously ill in 1977 Her elder daughter, Jane O'Cock, interviewed applicants for the nursing job and made an inspired choice, Margaret Penman, who shared her patient's Australian background. Henry and Margaret devotedly cared for Madge until her death in 1979, by which time Margaret had become part of the Carlyle Square household. They had, all the while a strong support team in Henry's son and two daughters, and his grandchildren.

In July 1993, Henry Denham died peacefully in his sleep.

GM

Group Captain Geoffrey Francis, DSO, DFC

The man in the corner of the railway carriage was wearing the Club tie. I introduced myself. "Geoffrey Francis" he responded, in a quiet engaging voice, as he extended his hand. So this was the Geoffrey Francis who had been my father's second in command in Singapore before the war, and whose name was synomymous with two famous yachts, *Madcap* and *Ma On Shan*.

Not only did Geoffrey Francis bear a passing resemblance to Bobby Somerset but, like him, he has a penchant for old pilot cutters. *Madcap* (22 tons) was built in 1875. Geoffrey bought her directly from the pilot service and she must have looked splendid moored off RAF Calshot among the flying boats which were Geoffrey's other concern. He and his first wife, Patience, took *Madcap* on channel cruises with their bull terrier Phyllis.

However, in 1936 Geoffrey was posted to Singapore, so the time came to part with *Madcap*. Phyllis disgraced herself by eating the first course of the dinner at which the price was to be discussed. His new posting turned Geoffrey's mind from the very old to the very new. He determined to replace *Madcap* with a yacht built to his own specification in Hong Kong and then sail here from there to Singapore. *Ma On Shan* was to be similar to *Tai Mo Shan*, the ketch whose voyage from Hong Kong to Dartmouth with a crew of young naval officers has caused such a stir in the early 1930s. Geoffrey knew her well, because his brother Philip (RCC) had been on the voyage. He commissioned her architect, H S Rouse to build a slightly larger vessel of 34 tons, 57ft 7in overall. Further, rather than being a conventional ketch, she was to be rigged with a wishbone.

Ma On Shan was built by Messrs Wing On Sing and, in the nature of things, was launched much later than planned. Patience and Geoffrey finally set sail on 29 April with a couple of Hong Kong Chinese for crew. On 2 May they found themselves in the midst of a typhoon. Patience wrote 'the chief impression gained of the wind was its noise, and the fact that it held the ship over about 15°-20° when only a point or so on the quarter, by virtue of mere mast, rigging and hull windage. The wind speed was impossible to gauge as it was so far in excess of anything we had experienced before; it was also impossible to reckon speed through the water owing to the fact that the surface was being blown bodily to leeward and the log had had to be taken in as warps were streamed astern to check her speed. The seas were enormous but for fear of provoking an argument we will not attempt to estimate their height'.

They later learned that the P&O liner *Rawalpindy*, estimated to be within twenty or thirty miles of the storm centre, had calculated the wind force at 11 to 12 with speed at about 100 mph. *Ma On Shan* was at the typhoon's centre. After the wind had steadied at about west for a couple of hours, one of the Chinese crew observed cheerfully "typhoon come again very strong", and so it did. Somewhat battered, they put into Saigon to repair damage. Finally, they dropped anchor off the Royal Singapore Yacht Club, just two hours before Geoffrey's leave was due to expire.

Ma On Shan became their floating home. Phyllis, the bull terrier, who had had the good sense not to come on the maiden voyage, took up residence, as she had done on *Madcap* in those home waters so far away. They had planned to sail home to England after Geoffrey's Singapore posting. However, very soon other considerations intervened, Geoffrey was to serve first in Ceylon and then the Mediterranean, but he had to leave *Ma On Shan* behind in Singapore, to the less than tender mercies of the Japanese.

In those years, sailing was not uppermost in his mind. Having succeeded my father as commander of 230 Squadron, he contributed magnificently to the rescue of 700 British personnel and a number of Greek and Yugoslav leaders in the evacuation of Greece. Subsequently, with the evacuation of Crete he attempted to establish contact with some British forces thought to be holding out there. Although flying at night, often along an unfamiliar coast, he skilfully landed his Sunderland in rough seas five miles offshore. When a small craft was launched from the flying boat, the enemy opened fire with machine guns at short range. The Sunderland was hit, but he managed to take off and drop messages to the British troops on the island. This was the type of exploit which well justified his DSO and DFC.

With peace restored, Geoffrey turned his mind again to sailing but with his new wife, Joan, by his side. Ahead lay many years of cruising marked not so much by ambition as by dedication to introducing a growing number of children to the sea. The first of his post-war boats was *Spica* (22 tons) a de Voegt sloop build in The Netherlands in 1915. She was replaced, when he retired in 1951, by the 23 ton *Ben More*, a ketch built at Burnham-on-Crouch in 1929. Then came three motor yachts better suited as floating homes for a growing young family, the most distinguished of which was *Centaurus* of 31 tons, built by Silver in 1935. In 1971 he turned again to sail, purchasing *Valiant Maid* (10 tons) built by Rodney Warrington-Smyth for 'Bir' Robertshaw (RCC) in 1962. It was good, following Bir's untimely death, that she thus remained in the Club.

In 1975, Geoffrey bought the Sadler designed *Binkie 11* (10 tons) from another club member, the late Mike McMullen, who had sailed her in the singlehanded trans-Atlantic race. Then, in 1979, he bought what was to be his last boat, a twin-keeled Westerly. Just as he had shared the ownership of *Ma On Shan* with Patience, so this new *Spica* was shared with Joan and together they were to sail in her far further afield than Geoffrey had in any other boat, from Sweden to Turkey, taking in most places in between. This was despite the fact that she was by far the smallest of his boats. In one of only two brief contributions to the *Journal* he disparaged her twin keels, but he kept her, nonetheless, longer than any other.

Geoffrey was diagnosed as having cancer a week before he and Joan set off on their 1991 summer cruise to France in his 85th year. *Spica* was sold just before he died. By coincidence, his first yacht, *Madcap*, was on the market at the same time, but for rather more than the £120 he had paid for her. Though *Ma On Shan* never came to British waters, *Madcap* is still with us, something of a memorial to a very full life under sail.

RB

Jim Bate

Jim Bate was a caring, competent and enthusiastic man. On qualifying as a chartered accountant he set up his own practice, retiring as a partner in Grant Thornton. He cared for his clients, most of whom became good friends. His enthusiasms ranged from sailing and fly fishing to vintage cars. He taught Liz to drive in his first 'modern' car, a $4\frac{1}{2}$ litre Rolls Bentley.

TB at the age of twenty-three put paid to a naval career started at the RN Engineering College, Keysham, but only temporarily to the sea. He had started sailing while still at Blundell's in an open boat in the Bristol Channel. A succession of boats, owned, borrowed or chartered, included an engineless

Plymouth Hooker, *Fat Anne*, a 25ft fishing boat, *Zadig*, an 8 metre and a converted lifeboat in which his three children started to cruise.

In 1954 he bought *Freedom of Poole*, an 8 ton sloop designed by John Tew, which only three years later was tragically rammed and sunk by a French tug. The circumstances are reported at the end of the 1958 Journal. She was succeeded by *Viking O* and for ten years Jim, Liz and the family sailed to France and Spain.

Jim circumnavigated Spain in his last boat, *Petritis*, a 40ft Salar, sailing to Gibraltar in eight days and home with Liz via Paris in three months. Keen as he was there was 'No Sailing in the Mayfly Season'.

With Liz he enjoyed a full and happy family life. His many friends will sorely miss him, his entertaining company and constant kindness.

JG

Miles Clark

Miles Clark, who died last year aged thirty-two, was already winning himself a place in the long tradition of British literary adventurers and sailers. He was, in a sense, raised for it: his father, Wallace, is a distinguished member of the Club, and his godfather was Miles Smeeton whose 130,000 miles of deep-sea voyages produced such classics of the sea as *Once is Enough*. Miles' adventures began early: he joined Operation Drake at seventeen in the Panamanian rain-forest, and as a geography student at Downing College, Cambridge, he organised an expedition to climb volcanoes and undertake scientific research in Atka, a rarely visited island in the Aleutian archipelago. In 1984, as a young soldier, he was one of the oarsmen who rowed Tim Severin's replica Greek galley through the Black Sea to Georgia; he is remembered as a particularly robust and even-tempered member of the crew on that tough journey. Later on, writing his biography of Miles and Beryl Smeeton, Miles was to quote Nevil Shute's words about 'the great cloak of competence that wrapped them round'. The same garment distinguished him, too, both in his travels and his army life.

By his mid-twenties he became aware that action and travel were not enough. It was as important for him to communicate the wonders of the earth as to see them first-hand, and he determined to be a full time writer. With considerable professional courage he gave up his military career for the uncertainties of freelance writing and photography in the crowded and competitive field of travel. He worked as Features Editor of *Yachting Monthly* to acquire professional craft, and travelled independently, contributing to many magazines and writing a short book on sky-diving. But it was the publication in 1991 of *High Endeavours*, his biography of the Smeetons, which established him as a serious and forceful writer. He won widespread critical acclaim both for his deft and stylish handling of a mass of material, and more importantly for the unexpected depths of sensitivity and psychological insight which he brought to the task. The achievement fuelled further his determination to make distinguished voyages, and write distinguished books about them.

He achieved the first goal last summer sailing *Wild Goose* to the White Sea and through the canals and rivers to the Black Sea (see *The Swan's Road* elsewhere in the *Journal*). It was a hard journey, made in hard times, and he had harrowing encounters with despair, pollution and war. He was writing the book at the time of his death.

Miles Clark was an enthusiast: a stimulating companion and a sweet-natured friend, with an endearing willingness to ask advice from other writers and a passion for learning. He set relentlessly high standards for himself, but in the midst of an active life remained a young man of profound kindness, who would remember to send amusing notes or computer-drawn pictures to friends' children, following up conversations with them. He is survived by his wife Sarah and their three-year old son Finn.

LH

Jolyon Savill

The following is taken from an address given by Tim Trafford at St. Nicholas Church, Brockenhurst.

Jolyon's love of the sea formed a common thread throughout his cruelly foreshortened life. He was a fine shipmate and an instinctive seaman, and as a skipper he was thoughtful, modest and thorough. He would insist that he stood the coldest and darkest nightwatch, and religiously kept up the ship's log, always including a comment on the glass and weather. As crew it was always Jolyon who volunteered to go forward to change down the headsail. Returning from Cherbourg one blustery night it was Jolyon who came aft from the foredeck after a hasty sail change wearing only his Canterburys and donkey jacket. He looked like a drowned rat but he had a sparkle in his eyes and was grinning from ear to ear.

I first met Jolyon outside the Royal Cornwall at the beginning of the RCC cruise-in-company in Spain in 1985. During the ensuing four day passage we talked twice a day on the radio and Jolyon kept us amused with tales of his daily foray to *St Radegund's* focsle to obtain fresh strawberries from the vegetable patch. During this cruise Jolyon developed firm friendships with myself and many other cadet members of the RCC, and over the following years we spent many sailing holidays together. In the winter months the same team would gather to plan the next season's activities.

In the mid 80's Jolyon flirted with the antiques trade and the Life Insurance Business. He must have been a good salesman for I took out one of his policies. Whenever I mentioned this to him a wry smile spread across his face. City life came to an abrupt end when, after a May Ball in Cambridge,

Jolyon turned up late (unusual for him) to a morning meeting with his boss in London ... still wearing his white tie. It was time for him to return to ships and the sea. He enroled as a Shipwright's apprentice and it was his finely honed skills that made the *Saint* (as she is fondly referred to) one of the most carefully maintained boats on the Solent.

Jolyon toyed with the idea of acquiring a larger floating/sailing home but he concluded that bricks and mortar were more practical. In February 1990 he bought a cottage in Middle Road and shortly afterwards met Victoria. In early January this year they went on holiday to the Canaries – Jolyon's first non-sailing holiday for five years – where they became engaged. He was very close to his mother, Betty, and before she died last December he told her of his intention to marry Victoria. In March, 1993, Jolyon and Victoria were married.

Jolyon never complained of his illness which he fought with indomitable courage, talking of the future, and of the Spring maintenance programme for the *Saint*. I shall remember him at his happiest, standing at the wheel of *Saint Radegund* with her wake widening astern and his father on one side; his face cracked with a cheeky grin, he always made sure that everybody was enjoying themselves.

THT

Margaret Leonard

Margaret's membership of the R.C.C. stretched from 1949 to 1988, when she reluctantly resigned because of ill health. Her love of the sea and competence as a sailor were combined with an acute sense of humour, a great love of animals, great knowledge of the theatre and an exceptionally wide range of interests. Margaret, who died in August aged 94, was the first lady member of the Ranelagh Sailing Club, and it was there that she met Peter Edwards, already a member of the R.C.C.

In 1948 she flew to Famagusta to join *Selamat*, Peter's 30 ft Harrison Butler cutter, which had been built in Malaya and shipped from Penang to Port Said. With Geoffrey Knocker as the third member of the crew they sailed the then engineless yacht westward through the Mediterranean. From Gibraltar Peter and Margaret set out again, but gales and torn sails forced them into South Portugal where they left *Selamat* for the winter, returning the following spring to complete the voyage to England. In subsequent years, with Margaret as First Mate, the yacht cruised extensively in home and Irish waters, on the Brittany coast and in the Mediterranean.

Margaret will be remembered by those fortunate enough to have known her as a warmhearted, discerning and generous person who was always ready to share her knowledge and to give encouragement, whether to her students at the Guildhall School of Drama and Music or to less experienced or would-be sailors.

MB

BOOK REVIEWS

Turkish Waters and Cyprus Pilot, Rod Heikell
(Imray, Laurie, Norie and Wilson Ltd — £25.00)

This new edition — the first since 1989 — of *Heikell's Turkish Waters Pilot*, which Aegean sailors have long regarded as essential reading, is, like its predecessors, beautifully produced. The text and harbour plans have been brought up to date and, as previously, the same consistent treatment throughout has been given to the main harbours — with headings for Approach, Mooring, Facilities (always very detailed) and General. A further continuing feature of the book, which adds to its completeness, is the coverage devoted to the many Greek, Roman and other archaeological sites to be found along the Turkish coasts.

In the late summer of 1977, cruising with Colin and Glenys Hunter in the Dodecanese islands from Kos to Patmos and round Samos and the adjacent Turkish coast, we saw just six yachts at sea in three weeks. Not so today. It is quite a different scene, particularly in the more popular parts round Bodrum and along the Southern Turkish coast. However, Turkey, fortunately, has a very long coastline and much remains which is totally unspoilt and idyllic, and it is for these lesser-known parts that this new edition is especially useful.

In fact, the book has been much enlarged generally — from 239 pages in the First Edition to 332 pages now. Also the book now has a longer chapter on both Greek and Turkish Cyprus.

In addition, there is an entirely new chapter on the Black Sea, covering the 700 miles or so of Turkish coast from the Bulgarian border in the west to the border with Georgia in the east — one long lee shore, it is pointed out, which few boats visit and is little touched by tourism, although it is a coast which has many artificial harbours, with mostly only a few miles between them, where a yacht can apparently easily find shelter when coast-hopping.

RB

Voyaging on a Small Income, Annie Hill (RCC)
(Waterline Books — £12.95)

The title of Annie Hill's book implies that *Voyaging on a Small Income* is only relevant to those who do just that. This is simply not the case.

The book deserves a place on the bookshelf of cruising classics. Within its pages lie some of the most wonderful descriptions of what ocean voyaging should really be about. Turn to page 135 and read Annie's account of Landfall. This is more reminiscent of Peter Pye than the words of a mere cruising guide.

In a practical sense, *Voyaging on a Small Income* provides some of the best advice yet written on preparing for ocean cruising. The appendices on provisioning and storing meat, fruit and vegetables are essential reading for any ocean voyager, whatever their income.

However, what this book really describes are not mundane practicalities; it is an account of a cruising philosophy which shines out from its pages — and which pushes the world of electronic gadgets, ARC rallies and crowded marinas back into their proper unadventurous and unromantic context.

When looking back into the history of our Club, there is no need to feel nostalgic about bygone days of those great adventurers in their gallant little ships: the Pyes, Hiscocks, Smeetons. With Annie and Pete Hill their spirit is still alive and afloat — crossing oceans and flying our burgee.

CW

Northwest Passage Solo, David Scott Cowper (RCC)
(Seafarer Books — £14.95)

This is an account of David's heroic struggle to achieve the first singlehanded voyage through the Northwest Passage and his subsequent circumnavigation, returning to Newcastle after four and a half years and 29,000 miles. At 200 pages the book is mercifully longer than his discription of the same voyage in only two pages of the 1990 *Journal*. Here is the full account of this strenuous voyage and a remarkable tale it is too; David Pelly helped assemble the material, making sense of David Scott Cowper's notes and scribbles.

The book begins with an historical summary of the many attempts to penetrate the maze of channels, bays and sounds which lured explorers — many to their death — into discovering a passage to the Pacific, initially in search of the inevitable spices and latterly 'because it was there'. The details of David's own voyage, the logistical support and preparation, make absorbing reading, and there are dozens of excellent colour photographs — including some charming ones of his encounter with a polar bear.

TW

The Lord of the Isles Voyage, Wallace Clark (RCC)
(Leinster Leader Ltd — £8.50)

The Lord of the Isles Voyage tells the full story of the research, building, sailing and voyaging of *Aileach*, a replica 16th century West Highland Galley (featured in *Roving Commissions* 32) in 1991 and 1992. Wallace Clark first dreamed about galleys while dozing in the heather above Loch Aline. To turn such a dream into reality was a considerable achievement, thanks in part to his making the acquaintance of Ranald MacDonald, the 24th hereditary Captain of Clanranald and a direct descendant of the great Somerled.

If Wallace's earlier book *Sailing Round Ireland* is a 'must' for the shelves of a boat cruising in Irish waters, then the *Lord of the Isles* is another 'must', but this time for the Western Isles. The slim volume is packed with historical anecdotes and would be an excellent companion on a voyage up the West Coast, bringing to life the struggles of the past and the deeds and misdeeds of its renowned heroes.

TW

Officers of the Club

1993/94

Commodore
G W NOCKOLDS

Vice Commodore
DR M GILL

Rear Commodore
K A POOL

Trustees
HIS HONOUR JUDGE A PHELAN
MAJ GEN O M ROOME, CBE, DL
J H TRAFFORD

Hon Secretary
PETER PRICE, MBE

Hon Treasury
R P BURDETT

Hon Steward
MRS S GLEADELL

Hon Editor
T WILKINSON

Hon Solicitor
J GUILLAUME

Hon Secretary
Foreign Port Information
CDR A J R WATSON, RN

Crewing and Cadet Members' Secretary
MAJ M C LEWIN-HARRIS

Hon Librarian
M V WALFORD

Committee
R W BOURNE, J T BURDETT, A V FRENCH, MRS E GORER
C J DE MOWBRAY MBE, M BURNFORD, P M KENNERLEY
SIR CHRISTOPHER LAWRENCE-JONES BT, G M PULVER
CBL WATSON

288